THE WORLD OF WORDS

THE WORLD OF WORDS

AN INTRODUCTION TO LANGUAGE IN GENERAL AND TO ENGLISH AND AMERICAN IN PARTICULAR

BY
ERIC PARTRIDGE

THIRD EDITION

 BOOKS FOR LIBRARIES PRESS
FREEPORT, NEW YORK

First Published 1938

Second Edition (Revised) 1939

Third Edition (Revised) 1948

Reprinted 1970 by arrangement with Eric Partridge

STANDARD BOOK NUMBER:
8369-5366-5

LIBRARY OF CONGRESS CATALOG CARD NUMBER:
73-117913

PRINTED IN THE UNITED STATES OF AMERICA

TO THE MEMORY OF
OTTO JESPERSEN
MOST HUMAN OF PHILOLOGISTS
MOST ILLUMINATING OF GRAMMARIANS

CONTENTS

	PAGE
PREFACE	ix

PART ONE

CHAP.
- I. FAMILIES OF LANGUAGES ... 1
- II. THE ENGLISH LANGUAGE ... 7
  - A. *A PRELIMINARY SKETCH*
  - B. *THE ELEMENTS OF THE LANGUAGE*
  - C. *A FEW GENERAL FEATURES*
  - D. *AMERICAN INFLUENCE*
- III. THE AMERICAN LANGUAGE ... 46

PART TWO

- IV. HOW WORDS BEGIN ... 59
- V. WHY WORDS GET NEW MEANINGS AND WHY LANGUAGES CHANGE ... 76
- VI. WHY SOME WORDS LIVE, SOME DIE; FASHIONS IN WORDS ... 89

PART THREE

- VII. ENGLISH: GOOD; BAD; AND WORSE ... 101

PART FOUR

- VIII. WHAT GRAMMAR IS—AND WHY ... 119

CONTENTS

PART FIVE

CHAP.   PAGE

IX. THE FUN OF WORD HISTORY   145

    A. *GENERAL: SYMBOLISM; ETYMOLOGY; FOLK ETYMOLOGY; SEMANTICS*

    B. *PARTICULAR: ENGLISH HISTORY IN ENGLISH WORDS; AN ASPECT OF OCCIDENTAL CIVILIZATION; AMERICAN HISTORY IN AMERICAN AND ENGLISH WORDS; WORD HISTORY RATHER THAN HISTORY IN WORDS*

APPENDIX: PHONETIC SYMBOLS   190

INDEX   191

    I. *AUTHORS, AUTHORITIES AND SUBJECTS*
    II. *WORDS AND PHRASES*

FOLDERS

Diagram I. THE FAMILIES OF LANGUAGES *facing p.* 6

Diagram II. THE INDO-EUROPEAN FAMILY OF LANGUAGES   „ 10

PREFACE

THIS book is intended both for younger people (of pre-University standard) and for such other persons as desire to have a brief yet tolerably comprehensive view of language in general and the English and American language in particular. The latter group may be extended to include University students.

There have, on words, been several books written for beginners: they are splendid books, I doubt not. But they do not cover the same ground as this of mine covers, nor is their treatment the same as my treatment of the subject: to me, though not perhaps to others, these are adequate reasons. Moreover, I like to think that *The World of Words* is in some ways better suited to serve as an introduction to the study of language in general and of English in particular. I am acquainted with the difficulties of beginners (was I not once a beginner myself?); with those of parents—being one of that despised class; and with those of teachers—having formerly been one of that selfless band, so seldom praised, so rarely even thanked.

My debt—for in such work there is always debt—is, in the main, to those three learned, entertaining, vitally interesting scholars who have always avoided pedantry: Professor Otto Jespersen (especially), Professor Ernest Weekley and Professor G. H. McKnight; a Dane, an Englishman, an American. And in the course of the book, I make other acknowledgements. Wherever I felt that I could not put the matter so well and wherever I wished to alter the argument in no way, I have quoted verbatim; and now and again I have quoted at considerable length. On several occasions I have, within a chapter, followed the admirable ordonnance of a predecessor. I like to acknowledge every debt, but in fairness to myself I must add that I have planned the book most carefully; that I have aimed at a clear picture of general linguistics and at a spacious and many-vista'd panorama of the English (and American) language; that even where I owe most, I have usually simplified a tricksy argument or clarified a difficult theory, or enriched the text with more or, so I think, better examples; and that half a hundred times I have been almost original, quite independent rather more than once.

PREFACE

In the third edition I have made such changes as the intervention of the war of 1939–45 and the completion of *A Dictionary of American English* (1936–44) have rendered necessary in a book that appears to fill the gap between the formal text-books and the over-simplified 'books for the general public': the latter have too seldom been written by scholars, the former too often by scholars (and others) that have forgotten they once were either young or beginners.

ERIC PARTRIDGE

London
February 6, 1948

THE WORLD OF WORDS

PART ONE

CHAPTER ONE

FAMILIES OF LANGUAGES

So long ago as 1822, that great German thinker and linguist, Wilhelm von Humboldt, stated, and exactly a century later Otto Jespersen, the famous Danish writer on language, repeated, that languages are so different in form that it is impossible to classify them both accurately and comprehensively, or to divide the languages of the world into groups or families in such a way as to account satisfactorily for absolutely all of them.

That is true. But we can, after all, account satisfactorily for most of them; and this 'most' includes all the important languages. So why despair? No method of grouping, no 'system of classification' (as the learned prefer to call it) is, because no method can, for certain, be perfect or complete: but the fact that we cannot get £1,000 is a poor reason for refusing £900: we must make the best of what is available, in languages as in life.

Originally there may well have been only three or four languages in all; it is barely possible, though extremely improbable, that there may have been one language and one only. But we have no proof that there were ever so few as even three or four languages. It is easy to theorize—to build up all sorts of wild ideas—when there are no facts to contradict us. If, however, we keep to the facts and hold fast to what is known, we see that there are either thirteen or fourteen linguistic groups, thirteen or fourteen families of languages. It is not to be assumed that the various members of any one family do not, as it were, stand on their own feet: do not possess certain perhaps very important qualities and defects that are theirs alone: are not as individual as the persons forming an ordinary family. We do not deny but emphasize the strength and the reality of a human family when we point out how individual is each member of that family. In the same way, we do not lessen the reality and the usefulness of a linguistic family if we admit that there is a great deal of truth in Humboldt's opinion that each separate language and even the lowliest dialect[1] should be looked

---

[1] A dialect is such a variety of a language as arises from—is caused by—local conditions and peculiarities; a provincial manner of speaking. It is then, a kind of language *within* a language.

upon as a whole with a life of its own; that each language, each dialect, is different from all other languages or dialects; that it expresses the character of the people speaking it; that it is the outward expression of that nation's soul; and that it points to the particular way in which that nation tries to reach its 'ideal of speech'—a speech that, to the nation concerned, seems to be the best it can have. But some (often many) words in a language are thrust upon that language from outside or inherited from a people once related to it or connected with it: and these words form one of the means by which we are enabled to divide languages into groups and discover which are the members of a family.

To relate precisely how these groups have been arrived at, how these families have been gathered together, lies beyond our scope: for the excellent reason that such a relation can be readily understood only by those who have an advanced knowledge of philology (or linguistics), as the science of language—that body of knowledge which concerns the speech of human beings—is generally called. It is best for the younger, as for the less erudite, among us to take for granted the various reasons for the grouping of the world's languages into groups or families: but that there are families of speech is certain. The older we are or the more deeply we think, the more clearly do we see that it is both a convenience and a necessity to assume that, so far as has been discovered, certain things are facts—certain things are true: it is neither bluff to assert nor folly to believe that there are facts: in language generally and in languages particularly.

It is, on the other hand, well to note that variation in speech, differences in language, are a result of the movements of population and the migrations of peoples. There may originally have been one race upon earth; more probably there were several or many races or primitive nations. They, like the later racial divisions and communities, have, 'from point to point through the whole life of man on the earth', not only 'spread and separated' but jostled against or interfered with one another; have 'conquered and exterminated',[1] or conquered and absorbed, or mingled with one another and thus formed new units: and these spreadings and separations, jostlings and interferences, conquests and peaceable minglings have had a tremendous influence upon the various languages of the races affected. So long as evidence of original unity is discoverable, we speak of the languages concerned as being 'related' and combine them into a family. A family of

---

[1] Here I owe much to Whitney's article in the *Encyclopaedia Britannica*. That some of Whitney's opinions have been proved wrong, I know: that some are right, no one has denied.

languages is simply a group of languages that have descended from 'one original tongue'. Now 'of some families we can follow the history ... a great way back into the past; their structure is so highly developed as to be traced with confidence everywhere; and their territory is well within our reach.... But these are the [comparatively] rare exceptions; in the ... majority of cases we have only the languages as they now exist.' (See the first diagram: facing page 6.)

Yet, to digress for a moment, a classification of languages is not precisely the same thing as a classification of races or nationalities. Languages are, in many ways, as much institutions as a country's religion or its law is an institution. Languages can be, sometimes are, transferred: circumstances force them to be transferred. 'Individuals of widely differing races are often found in one community: yet they all speak the language of that community. The most conspicuous example ... is that of the Romanic countries of southern Europe'—Italy, France, Spain, Portugal— all using variations of a language that, '2,500 years ago, was itself the insignificant dialect of a small district in central Italy'; it is only fair to add that the inhabitants of that district, the Romans, were a people so remarkable that they have changed the whole history of Europe. 'Such are the results of the contact and mixture of races and languages.... Mixture of race and mixture of speech are ... connected processes; the latter never takes place without something of the former; but the one is not [an exact] measure of the other, because circumstances may give to the speech of the one element' or part 'of population' a power and a widespread use quite out of proportion with the size of that element of population—as we have seen it do in Italy. There remains in French only a small trace of Celtic, at one time the language of the most populous and important people in Gaul or France; French as we know it is, in the main, a modern form of the language spoken by 'the Latin conquerors of Gaul'; French was adopted by the Normans, who were originally Norsemen; these Normans conquered England, and their language became mixed in with Old English (or Anglo-Saxon as it is still called not very accurately) —but that mixing is another story, told, as it happens, in the next chapter.

To return to the groups of speech, the families of languages. Such a classification is a classification of languages only, although it may, and often does, also throw light on 'movements of community', movements that, in their turn, 'depend more or less upon movements of races'. And it must be remembered that language families as important as some of those set down here may have disappeared; certainly some families remain in a very incomplete form.

1. By far the most important family is the *Indo-European*[1] or, as it used to be called very inaccurately by over-ambitious German philologists, the Indo-Germanic; some prefer to call it the *Aryan* family. This group includes virtually all the modern European languages, as well as Greek and Latin and Ancient Celtic; and the Asiatic Indian languages (Hindi, Bengali, original Gypsy), themselves related to Persian; Sanskrit (often spelt Sanscrit), the easternmost, and oldest, known member of the Indo-European family; Armenian; Russian and allied languages; Albanian.[2] To this 'family' belong those nations who have, for many centuries, been the leaders in the history of the world; its literatures, especially in modern times, are among the greatest; the records of its achievements are the fullest; its development has been much the most varied, much the richest. These 'advantages[3] have made Indo-European language the training-ground of comparative philology' (the study of various languages in their relation one with another), 'and its study will [probably] always remain the leading branch of that science'.

2. Undoubtedly second in importance is the *Semitic* group, comprising Hebrew[4] (the language of the Bible and the Talmud), Syrian and Assyrian, Arabic, Aramaic, Phoenician. This family may originally have been part of the Indo-European family, but this conjecture has not been incontestably proved. The Semites were that 'race of mankind which includes most of the peoples mentioned in Gen[esis], x, as descended from Shem, Son of Noah' (*The Shorter Oxford Dictionary*).

3. The *Hamitic* family, of which easily the most important member is ancient Egyptian; the Berber (or Libyan) languages of northern Africa; the Ethiopic languages of eastern Africa, including Haussa—a language spoken in the Sudan and even more valuable than Swahili (in group 11) as a means of communication in Africa. This family bears certain resemblances to the Semitic: therefore *Hamitic, Semitic, Indo-European* may all have been, originally, dialects of the one language, or rather some *one* primitive language may have branched off into these three. The name comes from Ham, the second son of Noah.

[1] See the second diagram: facing page 10.
[2] For a fuller list of the Indo-European languages, see the table of that linguistic family.   [3] Whitney.
[4] Note that Yiddish—the lingua franca of the Jews—consists mainly of German, to which have been added many words from the Balto-Slavonic languages (see diagram II) and from Hebrew; it is written in Hebrew characters.

4. The *Monosyllabic* group or *South-eastern Asiatic* family. The leading member is Chinese, spoken by some 400,000,000 people. The other members of the family are Burmese, Siamese, Tibetan (perhaps the oldest language in the whole group). The family is called monosyllabic from the fact that Chinese consists of one-syllable and unchangeable words: it consists of words like *cat* and *dog*, but it has no forms corresponding to *cat's* and *dog's*, *cats* and *dogs*. Ancient Chinese—Chinese before the records—may have been quite different and of the same family as:

5. The *Ural-Altaic* family, sometimes known as the *Scythian* or the *Turanian*, 'China and Tibet are bordered on the north and west by the eastern branches of another immense family, which stretches through central and northern Asia into Europe, overlapping the European border in Turkey, and reaching across it in Russia and Scandinavia to the very shore of the Atlantic' (Whitney). The chief languages are Manchu, Mongol, Turkish (or Tatar[1]), Samoyed ('from the Altai down to the arctic shore of Asia'), and the Finno-Hungarian languages, of which the chief are Finnish and Magyar (or Hungarian); Japanese and Korean probably belong also to this family.

6. The *Dravidian* group—the *South Indian* family, spoken by some 50,000,000 people. This is the language of the descendants of that race which had occupied India before the great invasion from the north-west—an invasion taking place somewhere about 1500 B.C.

7. The *Malay-Polynesian* family. Principally Malayan (in Malay, Sumatra, Java, Borneo, Madagascar) and Polynesian (in Polynesia), whence springs the Maori language; and probably Melanesian.

8 is at least two other families, both in the Pacific: *Australian Aborigine* and *Papuan* (or *Negrito*).

9. The *Caucasian* family, including the Circassian and Georgian languages.

10. Remnants of families in Europe: the *Basque* family; the *Etruscan* family. (The Etruscan language has long been extinct.)

11. The *Bantu* (or *South African*) family, which (except for the Hottentot and Bushman territories) occupies the whole of southern Africa from some degrees north of the Equator. To it belongs Swahili, spoken in Zanzibar. This group is remarkable for the fact that, to an extent unparalleled in any other group, it employs prefixes instead of suffixes: the cases in the declension of nouns, like the persons and tenses of verbs, are shown by prefixes: the obscure system of genders is indicated by prefixes; these prefixes

---

[1] Less correctly, Tartar.

recur, in exact agreement, in the other members of the sentence and thus produce an alliteration somewhat like, but much more monotonous than, that in Old English poetry.

12. The *Central African* group is hardly to be called a family, for it consists of a great mass of what are rather dialects than languages, and the interrelations of these dialects are very obscure. The same remark applies to:

13. The *Amerindian* family; that is, the Red Indian dialects of North America: their number is astonishingly large, their structure astonishingly varied. If there is any connexion between the Amerindian family and any of the Asiatic, African or European families, it has not been proved: but it is not impossible that Mongols should have crossed the narrow sea that separates easternmost Asia from Alaska; there is a certain facial resemblance between the Mongol and the Red Indian.

14. The South American Indian languages and dialects, more probably still the Central American ones, are rather to be related to the North American Indian languages and dialects than to be considered as a separate family.

Note. The best general-reader book dealing with this intricate subject is *The Tongues of Men*, by Professor J. R. Firth.

I. THE FAMILIES OF LANGUAGES
AND THEIR CHIEF MEMBERS

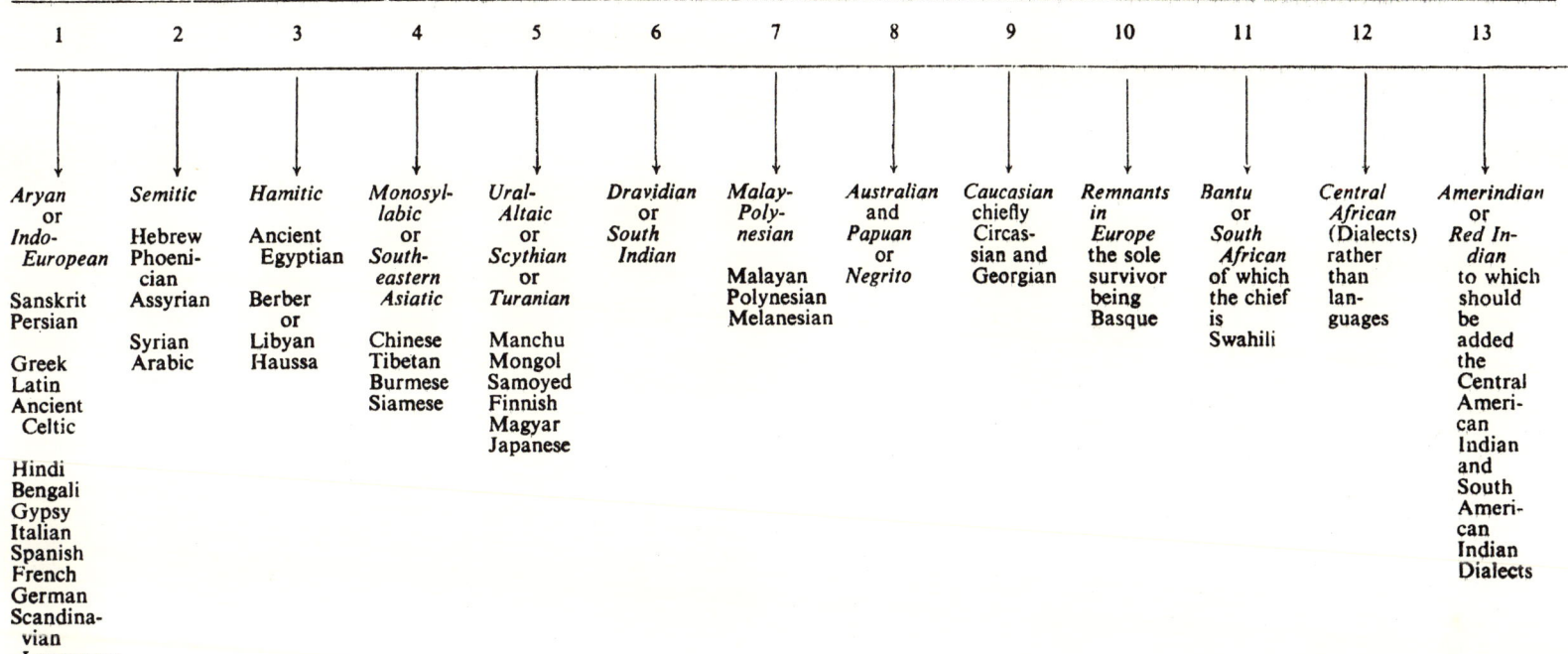

1	2	3	4	5	6	7	8	9	10	11	12	13
Aryan or *Indo-European*	*Semitic*	*Hamitic*	*Monosyllabic* or *South-eastern Asiatic*	*Ural-Altaic* or *Scythian* or *Turanian*	*Dravidian* or *South Indian*	*Malay-Polynesian*	*Australian* and *Papuan* or *Negrito*	*Caucasian* chiefly Circassian and Georgian	*Remnants in Europe* the sole survivor being Basque	*Bantu* or *South African* of which the chief is Swahili	*Central African* (Dialects) rather than languages	*Amerindian* or *Red Indian* to which should be added the Central American Indian and South American Indian Dialects
Sanskrit Persian	Hebrew Phoenician Assyrian	Ancient Egyptian				Malayan Polynesian Melanesian						
Greek Latin Ancient Celtic	Syrian Arabic	Berber or Libyan Haussa	Chinese Tibetan Burmese Siamese	Manchu Mongol Samoyed Finnish Magyar Japanese								
Hindi Bengali Gypsy Italian Spanish French German Scandinavian Languages English Russian Welsh Irish Breton												

CHAPTER TWO

THE ENGLISH LANGUAGE [1]

PERHAPS the most illuminating method of treating this subject which also forms the inescapable basis of any consideration of the American language, is to give first a brief preliminary sketch, then a shortish account of the elements of the language, then a few general comments (General Features) on the language as a whole and throughout its history, and finally an extremely brief sketch of the American influence on English.

A. A PRELIMINARY SKETCH [2]
(THE NATURE OF ENGLISH)

A person cannot be characterized in a word or a phrase; no language can be summed up in one word, one phrase, or even in a sentence of normal length: but, in comparison with other languages, English can perhaps be classified, not unfairly, as masculine: 'it is,' says Jespersen, 'the language of a grown-up man and has very little [that is] childish or feminine about it'.

Take the sounds of English. The English consonants are clearly separated, one from another, in sound; and they are clearly pronounced. A consonant is seldom changed by the vowels on either side of it; and the vowels are, for the most part, independent of the consonants flanking them. English has, all in all, become clear-cut in its sounds, though this impression is blurred by those English vowels which are really diphthongs (i.e., combinations of two originally distinct vowel sounds), as for example $\bar{\imath}$, where the vowel is not single but double—Continental *a* (in 'father') and English long $\bar{e}$ (in 'complete') pronounced in rapid succession, *ah-ee* becoming *ai* (the long English $\bar{\imath}$), as a little practice will show you.

A language with a great number of its words ending in a vowel (Italian, Spanish, Portuguese) or a language with all its words

---

[1] Except in section *D*, this chapter owes a tremendous amount to Professor Jespersen's *Growth and Structure of the English Language*, 1912; edition used, that of 1935.

[2] Throughout, 'Old English' is English before ca. 1100; 'Middle English', 1100–1450; then 'Modern'. In general, 'Old English' is preferred to 'Anglo-Saxon'.

ending thus (Hawaian) is more musical but less manly and vigorous than English, which abounds in words ending in two or more consonant *sounds*, as in *wealth, tent, tempt, helped, hence*: these words require an effort, actual muscular work. But there are not so many such words in English as to render the language harsh or ugly. English, considered on the basis of its sounds (or, more learnedly, of its phonetic system), may be said to possess 'male energy, but not brutal force'.

'If briefness, conciseness and terseness are characteristic of the style of men, while women as a rule are not such economizers of speech, English is more masculine than most languages. . . . In grammar it has got rid of a great many superfluities found in earlier English as well as in most cognate' or related 'languages, reducing endings, etc., to the shortest forms possible and often doing away with endings altogether'. With the English *all the wild animals that live there*, where only *animals* and *live* show a change caused by the plural number, compare the German *alle diejenigen wilden Tiere, die dort leben*, where the only word not affected by the number is the adverb *dort* (there), and the French *toutes les bêtes sauvages qui y habitent*, where five words show the change and where, in addition, one word (*toutes*) has to record the feminine gender. One result of this shortening of forms and hence of words has been that many words consisting formerly of two syllables, consist now of one: by this change, English has perhaps lost something in melodic elegance—and certainly gained in force. If it had not been for those very numerous long foreign (especially Latin and Greek) words which have constantly been admitted, English would now be almost as monosyllabic (i.e., composed of words of one syllable) as Chinese. This tendency to monosyllabism appears in such proverbs as *live and learn* and *haste makes waste, and waste makes want* and in such a passage as this from Macaulay, 'Then none were for the party; Then all were for the State; Then the great man help'd the poor, And the poor man loved the great'.

A business-like brevity appears in that convenient omission of the verb (and often its noun or pronoun) which is so common in English: 'To be left until called for'; 'Did they go? Rather! I *made* them.' These shortenings and short-circuitings are in syntax what morphological[1] shortenings are in words; 'I should like to [do it], but I can't [do it]' is in syntax what, in words, *cab* is to

---

[1] Relating to form. Morphology is the science of the change of form or shape, and the term is used in both philology and medicine. The morphological shortening of a word, therefore, is simply a shortening in the spoken form of that word.

cabriolet, or *bus* to *omnibus*, or *landau* to *Landau carriage*, or *rifle* to *rifle gun*.

This result is inseparable from sobriety in expression. 'As an Englishman,' Jespersen shrewdly remarks, 'does not like to use more words than are strictly necessary, so he does not like to say more than he can stand to. He dislikes strong or hyperbolical expressions of approval or admiration; "that isn't half bad" or "she is rather good-looking" are often the highest praises you can draw out of him . . . German *kolossal* or *pyramidal* can often be correctly rendered in English *great* or *biggish*; and where a Frenchman uses his adverbs *extrêmement* or *infiniment*, an Englishman says only *very* or *rather* or *pretty*'; *pretty good* is highly eulogistic. 'An Englishman does not like to commit himself by being too enthusiastic or too distressed, and his language accordingly grows sober, too sober, perhaps, and even barren when the object is to express emotions': another masculine trait of the language.

This masculinity appears further in the fewness of the diminutives and in the rarity with which even those are employed. Of these diminutives (nouns with endings denoting affection; 'hypocoristic forms' is the term beloved of the philologists, who, however, tend to restrict it to *Pat* for *Patrick*, *Kit* for *Christopher*, *Meg* for *Margaret*, and so on), *-let* is the commonest, save one. This *-let* is seldom seen before the late eighteenth century and its frequent use in the twentieth arises largely from its popularity among scientists (*budlet*, *fruitlet*). The suffixes (or endings) *-kin* and *-ling* are mostly derisive (*princeling*) or jocular (*princekin*), though *-kins* is a true endearment (*babykins*, *hubbykins*). The truest English fondling-suffix is *-ie* or *-y* (*auntie* or *aunty*; *Rabbie*), but even this is more or less confined to use in the nursery or in speaking to children: and is rather more Scotch than English.

'The business-like, virile qualities of the English language also manifest themselves in such things as word-order. Words in English do not play at hide-and-seek, as they often do in Latin . . . or in German, where ideas that by right belong together are widely sundered in obedience to caprice or, more often, to a rigorous grammatical rule. In English an auxiliary verb does not stand far from its main verb', in fact it is very rarely further away than in 'He has almost never done such a thing'; 'and a negative will be found in the immediate neighbourhood of the word it negatives, generally the verb (auxiliary). An adjective nearly always stands [immediately] before its noun', the only notable exception being in such a phrase as 'an interruption too brief and isolated to attract more notice'. In nine sentences out of ten, the subject precedes the verb, and that verb precedes its object or its complement: this order, in short, is abandoned only for the specific purpose of emphasis, as in '*Him* I don't like; *her* I do'; and even then, inversion is used only for very great emphasis or in oratory. 'Order and consistency,' Jespersen declares, 'signalize the modern stage of the English language'; it has not always been so orderly, nor quite so consistent.

Although no language is wholly consistent, wholly logical, yet it is true to say that, with the exception of cultured Chinese, English is the most logical of the modern languages. 'Look at the tenses,' exclaims the admiringly critical Jespersen; 'the difference between the past *he saw* and the [present] perfect *he has seen*', which is a composite tense, 'is maintained with great consistency as compared with the similarly formed tenses in Danish, not to speak of German. . . . And then the comparatively recent development of the expanded (or "progressive") tenses has furnished the language with the wonderfully precise and logically valuable distinction between "I write" and "I am writing", "I wrote" and "I was writing"': even French, long supposed to have been the most logical European language, can show nothing so logical, nothing so convenient, for in the one 'time' (the past) in which there is a similar distinction (*j'écrivis* and *j'écrivais*), the distinction is rapidly breaking down; the distinction exists in Slavic (or Slavonic) languages, but there, instead of the constant -*ing* devices these languages employ an intricately changing system.

In English, the logic of facts often—indeed, generally—overcomes the logic of grammar where the two are at variance. This appears most clearly in number: *Cabinet, clergy, committee, family* and their like are, grammatically, singular in number, but, as a matter of hard fact, they connote more than one person. Now, in most languages these nouns must take a singular verb, but in English they will take either a singular or a plural verb as the particular case demands: thus, they take a singular verb when the idea of unity predominates, as in 'This committee is more capable than that one'; and a plural verb when the idea of plurality is essential, as in 'The committee were not unanimous in their rejection of this plan'. This liberty of choice is a great advantage, for it conduces to clarity. As a counterpart, we have the liberty of expressing as a singular what is, grammatically, a plural, as in 'I do not think I ever spent a more delightful three weeks' (Charles Darwin) or 'Ten minutes is heaps of time' (E. F. Benson).[1]

'A great many other phenomena in English show the same freedom from pedantry': for instance, in such uses of the passive

---

[1] These two examples are from Jespersen, but many of the examples in this chapter are my own.

voice as 'He was well taken care of'; in prepositional combinations and adverbs employed as adjectives, as 'his then residence' or 'his outside-the-pale companions', a tendency carried even further in 'He glanced sharply at me with his don't-bother-me-now look' and 'the pretty diamond-cut-diamond scene between Pallas and Ulysses' (Ruskin). Such liberties, which might easily be multiplied, could not be taken in French, where condemnation is unfailingly applied to everything that breaks a rule laid down by the grammarians. The reason lies partly in the inherent elasticity of the English language itself; partly—and probably more—in the fact that 'the English language would not have been what it is if the English had not been for centuries great respecters of the liberties of each individual and if everybody had not been free to strike out new paths for himself'. The tendency is to be resisted only when it leads to ambiguity.

This tendency appears also in the vocabulary. In Great Britain, in the Dominions, and also in the United States, writers have always been at liberty to choose those words which have seemed best to suit their purpose: in brief, the purpose has determined the choice of words, instead of words circumscribing the display of the purpose. No academy, as in France and Italy, has been allowed to set up a corpus of words and phrases suitable for 'proper' or literary use. The result of this freedom from straitness and conscription is that the English language consists of a vastly greater number of words than is possessed by any other language; or, regarded in another way, the British comity of nations has at its disposal such a multiplicity and such a variety of words as render it easy for a writer to excel in any field whatsoever. (The same freedom holds for American writers.)

In summing up, we cannot do better than to quote Jespersen: 'The English language is a methodical [but not rigidly methodical], energetic, business-like and sober language, that does not care much for finery and elegance [though it can be delightfully elegant when the need arises], but does care for logical consistency [in such large issues as syntax] and is opposed to any attempt to narrow-in life by police regulations and strict rules either of grammar or of lexicon. As the language is, so also is the nation.'

With this summary, compare the following passage quoted in William Camden's *Remains of Britain*:[1]

[1] First edition, 1586; the last ed. revised by its author was the 5th, appearing in 1607. The quotation is taken from that reprint of the 7th edition (1674) which was published by Messrs John Russell Smith in 1870. But note that 'The Excellency of the English Tongue' (whence this passage) is a communication to Camden from Richard Carew (1555–1620), the author of the well-known *Survey of Cornwall*.

'The Italian is pleasant, but without sinews, as a still fleeting water. The French, delicate, but even nice as a woman, scarce daring to open her lips for fear of marring her countenance. The Spanish, majestical but fulsome, running too much on the O, and terrible like the Devil in a play. The Dutch,[1] manlike, but withal very harsh, as one ready at every word to pick a quarrel. Now we, in borrowing from them, give the strength of consonants to the Italian, the full sound of words to the French, the variety of terminations to the Spanish, and the mollifying[2] of more vowels to the Dutch,[1] and so (like Bees) gather the honey of their good properties and leave the dregs to themselves. And thus when substantialness combineth with delightfulness, fulness with fineness, seemliness with portliness, and currantness[3] with[3] stayedness,[3] how can the language which consisteth of all these sound other than most full of sweetness.—Again, the long words that we borrow, being intermingled with the short of our own store, make up a perfect harmony; by culling from out which mixture (with judgment) you may frame your speech according to the matter you must work on, majestical, pleasant,[4] delicate,[5] or manly, more or less in what sort you please. Add hereunto, that whatsoever grace any other language carrieth in verse or prose, in Tropes[6] or Metaphors, in Ecchoes[7] and Agnominations,[8] they may all be lively and exactly represented in ours.'

With these two laudatory opinions it is amusing to contrast that expressed in the following passage from Samuel Putnam's *Marguerite of Navarre*, 1936, the lady in question having in 1527 married Henry of Navarre and, at the age of some fifty-six years, died in 1549: 'She seems to have held the opinion which Charles V [1500-1558] was to voice, to the effect that Latin was the language of prayer, Italian the language of music, Spanish the language of love [a position that later was accorded to Italian], French the language of courts, German the language in which one addressed one's servants, and English the language in which one spoke to one's horses.'

B. THE ELEMENTS OF THE LANGUAGE
OLD ENGLISH

English came to England within thirty or forty years of the departure of the Roman legionaries in the year A.D. 407 or 410; the earliest texts of which we have records did not exist until

[1] Not what we now call Dutch, but the German language.
[2] Softening effect.
[3] Fluency with sobriety; or possibly, present idiom with linguistic stability. [4] Humorous or facetious; amusing or funny. [5] Elegant.
[6] Uses of words or phrases in senses other than those proper to them.
[7] Echoic words or echo-words: either term is infinitely preferable to 'onomatopoeia'. [8] Alliterations.

ca. 700. The latter date is comparatively unimportant, for there may have been writings long before that; but the former and earlier date marks the approximate point at which the main Germanic invasions began. By some date before the end of the sixth century,[1] those Germanic tribes which had settled on all the British lowlands were cut off from intercourse with their Continental relations: but already had they made their Anglo-Saxon tongue the tongue of Britain; and in the process of settling, they ousted British, which, with its speakers the Britons, found refuge in Wales; therefore Welsh is a descendant of the language spoken in England before the Anglo-Saxons arrived, and English was unknown in England until somewhere about A.D. 440.

These Germanic settlers spoke dialects belonging to the Gothonic (less happily, the Germanic or Teutonic) branch of that most important of all linguistic families, the Aryan (less happily, the Indo-European): a family that includes also Sanskrit and Prakrit (and the modern languages of northern India), Persian, Greek, Latin, French, Italian, Spanish, Celtic, Russian, and many other languages mentioned in Chapter I. Of the Gothonic branch of languages, Gothic has been extinct for nearly four hundred years; the chief living ones are German (High and Low), Dutch, the Scandinavian group, and English; and Modern English seems —along with Frisian—to stand midway between German and Dutch, on the one side, and Danish, Swedish, Norwegian and Icelandic, on the other side.

But before English became a separate idiom—a self-supporting and independent language—certain words had, in the pagan or pre-Christian period, been adopted by the barbaric inhabitants of Britain (chiefly of what we now call England) from their Roman conquerors, whose help was enlisted not in words expressive of Roman logic and philosophy and culture, but in words representing everyday objects, trades and processes: words that were 'easy to pronounce and to remember, being of the same general type as the indigenous words, and therefore ... very soon ... regarded as part and parcel of the native language, indispensable as the things ... they symbolized'. Among these adoptions from Rome were *wine* from Latin *vinum*; *cheap* (through Old English *ceapian*, to barter, to buy) from L. *caupo*, a wine-dealer; *monger* (as in *fishmonger* and *costermonger*), a vendor or merchant, from L. *mango*, a retailer; *mint* (coin: L. *moneta*); *pound* from L. *ponda*; *mile* from L. *mille*, a thousand (paces); *chest* (or box) from L. *cista*; *cook* from L. *coquus* (a cook), itself from the verb, *coquere*,

---

[1] English history from the departure of the Roman legionaries to the coming of Christianity (A.D. 597) is extremely obscure.

and the related *kitchen* from L. *coquina*; *mill* from L. *molina*; many names of plants and their produce; and a number of words now extinct. All these words[1]—as you might guess—were learnt orally.

But the Roman soldiers and governors' staffs did not greatly influence the English language, for the simple reason that they departed from Britain before English was brought to England by certain Germanic tribes: indeed the five greatest forces operating on English have been those exercised by (1) the series of Germanic invasions and settlements, although these constitute the main *origin* and not an influence properly so called, (2) the Scandinavian invasion, (3) the Norman Conquest, (4) the Renaissance (or Revival of Learning and Art), and, considerably less important, (5) the interacting influence of American English and (though as yet difficult to assess) the various kinds of Colonial English in the late nineteenth and twentieth centuries. But number 1—the first conquest and settlement of England by the English—is easily the most important, for this event not only brought the English language to Britain but also 'was, perhaps, fraught with greater consequences for the future of the world in general than anything else in history' (Jespersen).

The invasions covered a long period, but Britain was—for the most part, at least—settled by the Germanic tribes before the end of the fifth century A.D. And who, precisely, were these invaders? Angles, Saxons, and Jutes, according to Bede: a statement open to doubt. Two things, however, we do know for certain. First, the dialects comprising Anglo-Saxon or Old English are three in number: in the North of England, the Anglian dialects, consisting (in the main) of Mercian and Northumbrian; in Kent, the Kentish dialect; in the rest of the South, the Saxon dialects, predominant among them being the Wessex (i.e., the West-Saxon) dialect. Second, that Continental language which bears the closest resemblance to English is Frisian, from which we are probably justified in deducing that the Frisians were not only the neighbours but the relatives of the English before the emigration of the latter to England.

But what language or languages did the English find spoken in Britain when they arrived? The population was Celtic; the influence of the Roman conquerors (Claudius, don't forget, had arrived in A.D. 43) has to be taken into account—a much disputed account. The probability is that, when the English came, saw, and conquered, the position was that Celtic was still being spoken by

---

[1] Many of them had also been adopted by the Anglo-Saxons before *they* came to England.

the people in the country districts (comprising far the greater proportion of the population), whereas in the towns some of the people spoke Latin. One naturally inquires, what was the effect of the native population's language on the English invaders and settlers? 'The net result of modern investigation seems to be that (apart from numerous place-names) only about a dozen words did pass over into English from the British aborigines,' among them being *ass, bannock, binn, brock,* but not *gown* (adopted from medieval French), *curd, cart* (introduced by the English themselves), nor *pony* (from medieval French, via Lowland Scotch)—four words chosen and laboured by historian Gardiner (swept along in the wake of historian Freeman) to illustrate, almost to prove, survival of Celtic and its female and farm-labouring users. But there is no need to rush into wild statements about massacre: 'The Britons were not exterminated, but absorbed by their Saxon conquerors. Their civilization and language vanished, but the race remained.' After all, 'it is not the foreign language a nation learns that it turns into a mixed language'; it is its own native language which becomes mixed. In other words, a victorious people does not adopt the language it finds in the conquered country and then retain certain words of its own language; it retains its own language, but intermixes with it and adapts certain words—as a rule extremely few—belonging to the language of the defeated people. 'There was nothing to induce the ruling classes' (the invasive English or Saxons) 'to learn the language of the inferior natives; it could never be fashionable for them to show an acquaintance with that despised tongue by using now and then a Keltic word. On the other hand the Kelt would have to learn the language of his masters, and learn it well; . . . and if the first generation did not learn good English, the second or third would, while the influence they themselves exercised on English would be infinitesimal.'

At the end of the sixth century or at the beginning of the seventh century, England was converted to Christianity, with considerable linguistic consequences. In *Beowulf,* a great epic poem that makes excellent reading, there is an odd element of Christianity in the mainly pagan setting and attitude. But it must not be supposed that the English, whether as Saxons on the Continent or as Anglo-Saxons in England, did not possess an acquaintance with at least the outward aspects of Christianity long before conversion to Christianity: they had names for Christian objects and phenomena in the pre-Christian period. The Old English *cirice* (or *cyrice*), a church, is a very early loan-word, from Greek *kuriaka,* which is literally '(houses) of the Lord'. As *The Oxford English Dictionary* has remarked, 'from 313 onwards, Christian churches with their sacred vessels and ornaments were well-known objects of pillage to the German invaders of the [Roman] Empire'. *Minster*, from Latin *monasterium*; *devil* from *diabolus*; and *angel* from *angelus* were other very early adoptions.

'The number of new ideas and things introduced with Christianity was very considerable.' The English, in adopting the ideas and practices, adopted also many Christian terms—mainly Greek, but in the Latin form; for example, *apostle* and *disciple*; *pope*, *bishop*, *priest*; *monk* and *nun* and *abbot*; *shrine*, *cowl*, *pall*, *mass*. 'It is worth noting that most of these loans were short words that tallied perfectly well with the native words and were easily inflected' (changed, to indicate number and case) 'and treated in every respect like these.'

More notable, however, is the extent to which the English used the resources of their own language, chiefly in three ways: from the foreign words, new terms were created by means of native prefixes[1] and suffixes[1]; existing English words were invested with new senses; new words were formed from native roots or stems. At that period, the English freely set native endings (suffixes) to foreign roots: *had* (modern -*hood*) is frequent, as in *preosthad*, Modern English *priesthood*. In the second group (native words new-sensed), we find *God*, *Easter*, *tithe*, and *sin*. *Easter* is, in Old English, *Eastron*, the name of an ancient festival named after *Austro*, a Spring goddess. In the third, some of the new terms were a mere translation of the separate elements or parts of the Greek or Latin original, as in *god-spell*, Modern English *gospel*, whereas *heathen* derives from the Old English *haeth*, a heath. For *discipul* (modern *disciple*) there were no fewer than ten synonyms of English manufacture—e.g., *folgere*, literally a follower, and *leorning-man*; and the number of excellent compounds from *God* is astounding. In this old system of naming, everything was native and therefore accessible to even the most illiterate. 'Nor was it only religious terms that were devised in this way; for Christianity brought ... also some acquaintance with the higher intellectual achievements in other domains': witness *laececraeft*, 'leechcraft' or medicine, and *tld*, 'tide' in the sense of time, for tense in grammar. 'In short, a number of scientific expressions of native origin, such as is equalled among the Germanic languages in Icelandic only.'

One of the reasons was probably that few people knew Latin,

---

[1] The adverbs or prepositions placed respectively before and after an original root to form a new word; suffixes and prefixes are together called 'affixes'.

and therefore words of native formation were advisable. Nevertheless, it is very natural that a language should tap its own resources before borrowing from others. 'The Anglo-Saxon principle of adopting only such words as were easily assimilated with the native vocabulary ... and of turning to the greatest possible account native words and roots ...,—that principle may be taken as a symptom of a healthful condition,' for a nation as for its language.

In fact, Old English was potentially a wonderful instrument, for it could be made to express, never too laboriously and often neatly and felicitously, all that a language is called upon to express. Had Old English been left to itself—had there been no Scandinavian, no Norman invasions, or even no Revival of Learning—it would, of itself, have remedied such defects as it is seen to have possessed before the Norman Conquest: its proved ability to cope with the new earth-and-heaven that is Christianity indicates its powers and potentialities.

Old English prose, it is true, was often clumsy, unwieldy, long-winded, but then 'a good prose style is everywhere a late development', whether in a nation or in an individual; even as it is, there are in Old English prose a few passages of considerable strength and literary merit, as Alfred's account of the voyages of those great, those daring Scandinavian explorers, Ohthere and his companion, in lucid, simple yet moving narrative, or parts of Wulfstan's homilies, in powerful, rhythmic, impassioned prose.

But if, on the whole, Old English prose was callow and clumsy, Old English poetry—revealed in a comparatively small but very rich and various literature—was mature and adroit, ranging from picturesque accounts of battle and of single-handed fights with such mythical monsters as Grendel (in *Beowulf*) to idyllic utopias and lovely recitals of mood or of distilled experience. The language employed in this poetry was different from that used in the prose: not only in sentence-structure and choice of words, but also in word-forms. These differences have been common to the prose and poetry of most nations, and are more marked in old, or primitive, languages than in modern languages: especially, however, is this true of England, where even to-day, when there exists a very widely held belief that there is no—or should be no—such thing as poetic diction, we find the (in their own opinion) most emancipated poets backsliding into the use of words that would ring false or at the least very oddly in prose. 'The language of poetry seems to have been to a certain extent identical all over England, a kind of more or less artificial dialect, absorbing forms and words from the different parts of the country where poetry was composed at all, in much the same way as Homer's language had originated in Greece.'

This poetry was highly alliterative, and alliteration had remained a constantly recurring feature, both of poetry and of the most earthy prose: *bold as brass, busy as a bee, cool as a cucumber*, (*play*) *ducks and drakes, manners makyth man, might and main, rack and ruin*, (*from*) *top to toe*.

THE SCANDINAVIANS

Old English was self-sufficing, but there impinged on, and then penetrated and pervaded it, three forces; as it were, three superstructures on the Anglo-Saxon foundation: a Scandinavian, the Norman variety of French, and a Latin element much greater than that introduced with Christianity.

The English had lived in England, without suffering invasion from abroad, for some three centuries—during which their relations with the Danes had been friendly—when, about A.D. 790, there began that long series of incursions by which the Danes rendered their name synonymous with that of pirates. At first, these Danish invaders plundered what they could (mostly on or near the coast) and sailed away, but from ca. 850 the attack changed in character: 'the petty squadrons which had till now harassed the coast of Britain made way for larger hosts . . .; [and] raid and foray' became a 'regular campaign of armies who marched to conquer, and whose aim was to settle on the land they won' (J. R. Green). In the Peace of Wedmore (878), King Alfred was obliged to cede to the Danes about two-thirds of England—the district that came to be known as the Danelaw. In the poem celebrating the Battle of Maldon (993) we find the earliest record of a Scandinavian loan-word, (*to*) *call*.

Names of places ending in *-beck, -by, -dale, -thorpe* and *-thwaite*, as well as many names of persons, testify to the preponderance of the Scandinavian invaders in large tracts of the country. Yet 'England still remained England; the conquerors sank quietly into the mass of those around them; and Woden yielded without a struggle to Christ' (J. R. Green). But whereas to the Celts the English (or Saxons) had been foreigners, to the English the Scandinavians were not foreigners. The life of the Scandinavians was not strange. 'Their customs, their religion, their social order were the same' as those of the earlier Englishmen; 'they were in fact kinsmen bringing back to an England that had forgotten its origins the barbaric England of its pirate forefathers' (J. R. Green).

Not all the Scandinavian invaders and settlers were Danes;

Norsemen (Norwegians) came too. Attempts have been made to distinguish Norse from Danish origins in the Scandinavian loan-words: but 'in the great majority of cases . . . the Danish and Norwegian forms were at that time either completely or nearly identical, so that no decision . . . is warranted' (Jespersen). Moreover, Old English and Old Norse were so much alike that 'an enormous number of words were then identical in the two languages'. The result was the existence, side by side and sometimes for centuries, 'of two slightly differing forms for the same word, one of the original English form and the other Scandinavian. . . . In some cases both forms survive in standard speech, though, as a rule, they have developed slightly different meanings', as in *whole* (English) and *hale* (Norse), *no* (English) and *nay* (Norse), *from* (English) and *fro*, *shriek* (English) and *screech*, *-less* (as in *nameless*) and Norse *loose*. Where only one of the two forms survives, it is rather more frequently the native English than the imported Scandinavian; in *hence, thence, whence*, however, the form seems to have been determined by that of the Scandinavian originals. Occasionally the old native form has come down to us with the sense of the corresponding Scandinavian word: thus, Old English *dream* meant 'joy', Old Norse *draumr* meant 'dream'; Old English *eorl* meant 'a nobleman of any degree' or loosely 'a man' or specifically 'a brave soldier', but later it took on the sense of the Old Norse *jarl*, 'an under-king'.

Sometimes the Scandinavians were able to provide the English with such words as agreed so well with English words as to be associated with them and ultimately to survive them. 'The most important importation of this kind was that of the pronominal' (pronoun) 'forms *they, them*, and *their*, which entered readily into the system of English pronouns beginning with [*th*] and were felt to be more distinct than the old native forms which they supplanted.'

The Scandinavians introduced certain military and naval terms —these were the first to be lost from English; many law terms, of which the best known is *law* itself—but all except four (*law, by-law, crave, thrall*) disappeared when the Normans took over the law courts; a few domestic terms—e.g., *window*[1] from Scandinavian *vindauga*, 'wind-eye', and *steak*, and probably *knife*; 'such everyday nouns as *husband, fellow, sky, skull, skin, wing, haven, root, skill, anger*'; commonplace adjectives like *happy* and *seemly, low* and *meek, scant, loose, odd, ill, wrong, ugly* and *rotten*; commonplace verbs—e.g., *die* and *thrive, cast* and *hit, skulk* and *scowl, drown* and *ransack, call* and *scream, gape* and *scrape, want* and

[1] Cf. *daisy*, 'day's eye'.

take. 'It is precisely the most indispensable elements of the language that have undergone the strongest Scandinavian influence, and . . . a certain number of those grammatical words, the small coin of language, which Chinese grammarians call "empty words" . . ., have been taken over from Danish into English: pronouns like *they, them, their, the same* and probably *both*; a modal verb'—a verb of mood—'like the Scotch *maun, mun*'; the originals of *hence, thence, whence*; several conjunctions (especially *though*); several prepositions—e.g., *fro* and *till*.

In summing up, Jespersen writes thus: 'The bulk of Scandinavian [importations into English] are of a purely democratic character. . . . They are homely expressions for things and actions of everyday importance. . . . In many statistical calculations of the proportion of native to imported words in English, Scandinavian words have been more or less inadvertently included in the native elements.' Passing to syntax and accidence, he says: 'As the Scandinavians and the English could understand one another without much difficulty, it was natural that many niceties of grammar should be sacrificed, the intelligibility of either tongue coming to depend mainly on its mere vocabulary. So when we find that the wearing away and levelling of grammatical forms in the regions where the Danes chiefly settled was a couple of centuries in advance of the same process in the more southern parts of the country, the conclusion' seems to be that this speeding-up of the simplifying process was caused by the Danish and Norwegian settlers, 'who did not care to learn English correctly in every minute particular and who certainly needed no such accuracy in order to make themselves understood'.

THE FRENCH

A.D. 1066, the Battle of Senlac (or Hastings), is a date even more famous than 55 B.C.: the Norman Conquest of England changed, profoundly and permanently, the character of the English language.

'The Normans, much more than the Danes,' writes the Danish scholar so often quoted in this book, 'were felt as an alien race; their occupation of the country attracted much more notice and lasted much longer; they became the ruling class and as such were much more spoken of in contemporary literature and in historical records than the comparatively obscure Scandinavian element; and finally, they represented a higher culture than the natives and had a literature of their own.' Their influence was as dominant in language as in political and social life.

As another Scandinavian scholar that has done much good work in English remarks:[1]

'With the Norman kingship there followed an influx of Norman nobles and clerics, and feudalism was introduced. . . . Foremost of all changes: the native language lost its social value. English came to be regarded as "churlish"; the upper ruling classes spoke French. French, in its peculiar Northern form, became the language of the Court, of the estate owners . . . and of the Church, where . . . Latin was also tolerated. In all fields of human activity, French was the necessary means for ascending the social ladder. French had come like an avalanche, breaking all barriers, and settled on the population for at least two centuries. Under its ice there were certainly brooks of pure Old English, but they flowed in the lowest social strata. Gaining in power the brooks became rivers, and finally melted the French avalanche. But on that very day, what was left of English presented a most bewildering aspect. Everybody wrote according to his taste, or to his dialect. The English which turns up on the surface was indeed then a churlish language, much more so than in 1070, when the Norman nobles and clerics said it was so. . . . The character of Middle English as it emerges out of the hubbub of linguistic confusion is essentially a language of the lower classes of society, although later on ennobled and adapted to literary purposes. But the uncertainty in handling the language after' —in accordance with the demands of—'foreign metres betrays the humble origin of the idiom. There is another important sequel: the syntax is generally not to be explained by literature . . . ; but by a quite new language spoken originally'—i.e., during the Norman occupation of England—'only among socially unimportant people.'

But though the conquerors were both powerful and numerous, their influence would have been much less if they had not, for centuries, kept in touch with 'the French of France, of whom many were induced by later kings to settle in England' (Jespersen). The Normans, who, as soon as they had 'settled in', formed the upper classes, left intact the two words *king* and *queen*, but gave to English 'nearly all words relating to government and to the highest administration': witness *sovereign* and *crown* and *reign*, *realm* and *country*, *state* and *government* (and *to govern*), *council* and *counsel*, *parliament* and *exchequer*, *chancellor* and *minister*; the Old English *theod* had soon to give way to *people* and *nation*, both of French origin. With Feudalism, there came such feudal terms as *feudal* itself, *fief* and *vassal* and *liege*; *prince* and *peer*, *duke* and *duchess*, *marquis* and *viscount* and *baron*, *count* and *countess*, though *earl* and *lord* (and *lady*) were retained from Old English. *Court* and the courtly adjectives, *courteous*, *fine*, *refined*,

[1] *Select Studies in Colloquial English of the Late Middle Ages*, by Gösta Langenfelt (1933: Lund).

and *noble*, came from France, which sent us also *honour* and *glory*, and *heraldry* with its vast number of terms, these last being often distorted in their English form.

The English armies were henceforth officered by Normans; military affairs were controlled and directed by the Norman upper class, from whom the English (although for French-derived *army* they retained both *here*, originally a harrying force, and *fird* or *fyrd* until the fifteenth century) learned a host of French military terms, as for instance *war*, which in Middle English was *werre*, taken unchanged from Old Northern French; *peace*; *battle*, *assault* and *siege*; *arms* and *armour*; *banner* and *ensign*; *soldier* and *officer*; *sergeant* and *lieutenant*; such now general, originally military words as *enemy*, *force* and *company* and *guard*, *prison* and *escape*, *hardy* (bold) and *gallant* (brave), *challenge* and *march*. Even the navy adopted three notable words: *navy* itself, its leader or *admiral*, and its *vessels*.

Even more far-reaching was the Norman influence on the law of England: for naturally the law fell into the hands of the invaders. Indeed, most law terms are of Norman French origin: as in the *justice* of the *judge*, whether *just* or not so just; the *court* and the *jury*; *plaintiff* and *defendant*; a *cause*, a *plea* (with the verb, *plead*), and a *suit*; to *accuse*, to *sue* and to *summon* (by the way, *to summons* is not good English); an *assize* and a *session*; *felony* and *crime*; *damage* and *injury*, *demesne* and *property*, *real estate* and *tenure*. Of the same origin are many words that, now in general use, began their career in the law courts at a period when the entire legal procedure was conducted in French—for although English was made the official language of the courts as early as 1362, Law French (an extraordinary and ludicrous mixture of French and Frenchified English) continued to be used there until 1731, when it was abolished by Parliament, even Cromwell having been unable to get rid of it:—Such words, then, as *case*; to *oust*, *defend* and *prove*; *marry* and *marriage* and *heir*; *male* and *female*; *petty* and *puny* with its still legal doublet *puisne*, which, meaning 'younger', is merely the French *puis né*, 'later born'. But the general *theft* (English) has resisted the particular *larceny* (French); likewise *to steal* has easily survived the competition of *purloin*. In the combination of an adjective following a noun, however, the influence is French—French of the law courts—as in *heir male* and *issue male*, *proof demonstrative*, *letters patent*, and *attorney general*. With those French-derived terms which have not penetrated into general use, we need not concern ourselves.

Religion, like the law and the naval and military forces, was, especially in its higher offices, controlled by the ruling classes; that is, by the Normans. The following religious and ecclesiastical terms come from Norman French: *religion* itself ('a being bound' to God); *Saviour* and *Trinity*, with their common-name forms (*saviour, trinity*) and senses; *angel*, whereas the Old English *engel* derived straight from Latin; *clergy* (literally, the body of learned men) and *parish*; *abbey* and *cloister* and *friar*; *saint* and *relic*; *feast* (originally applied to a religious festival held on an anniversary) and *sacrifice* and *altar*; *prayer* (with *to pray*) and its now merely literary synonym, *orison*; to *preach* a *sermon* or a *homily*, the latter being a practical sermon or discourse intended to improve the congregation spiritually or morally, and not to set forth a point of doctrine. Among religious words now general, we notice *rule* and *lesson*, *save* and *tempt*, *order* and *nature*; with these may be linked the following terms derived from the clergy's preoccupation with moral ideas—*virtue* and *vice*, *charity* and *mercy*, *conscience* and *duty*, *cruel* and *jealous*, *to covet* and *to desire*.

From other domains, but most significant of the relations between English subordinate and Norman superior, are *sir* and *madam* (the form *madame* being French—and pronounced as such); *master*, *mistress*, *servant*; *obey* and *command*; *rich* and *riches*, with *poor* and *poverty*; *money* and *cash*; *rent* and *interest*.

First remarked on by a mid-seventeenth-century grammarian and popularized by Scott in *Ivanhoe* is the fact that animals alive bear English, animals dead and served as food bear French names: thus the English *bull*, *cow*, *ox*, *steer*, *heifer* become *beef* (French *bœuf*); *calf* becomes *veal* (French *veau*); *sheep* duly changes to *mutton*; *swine* and *boar* turn to *pork* or, at another stage, *bacon*; *deer* is eaten as *venison*: the explanation being, not (as used to be said) that the Normans left the animals to the care, though not the meat to the teeth, of the lower classes (the English), but that the French *cuisine* was vastly superior to the English *cooking*. This point is supported by the fact that such words as *boil* and *fry*, *roast* and *toast*, *pasty* and *jelly*, *soup* and *sausage*, *sauce* and *dainty* come from French, as do *supper* and *dinner* and *feasts*, whereas 'the humbler *breakfast* is English'.

The Norman masters were adepts at getting what they wanted and at enjoying what they got: *flowers* and *fruits* were theirs; theirs too were *ease* and *comfort*, *pleasure* and *delight* and *joy*,[1]

---

[1] In fairness, however, it must be added, as Jespersen did not add, that *pain* and *despair* and *horror* were French in origin. But then, almost less in language than in life is it possible to generalize without being, at the same time, conscious of many exceptions.

the English being condescendingly permitted to retain *hope*. In the world of *leisure* and *sport*,[1] the number of French words is very large, for though *chase* never drove out *hunt(ing)*, yet *track* and *scent*, *warren* and *quarry*, *leash* and *falcon*, *brace* and *couple* are French. Of the indoor sports and games, *cards* and *dice*, along with *partner*, *suit*, *trump*, *ace*, are likewise French.

In the Middle Ages, the French led the fashion—as they still do for women's clothes, though London has displaced Paris as the home of male fashion. *Apparel*, *costume*, *dress*, *garment*, like most of the clothing-terms in the Prologue to Chaucer's *Canterbury Tales*, are of French origin. So too are most art-terms: *art* itself; *image* and *figure*, *design* and *colour*, *ornament* and *beauty*, as well as many terms too technical to deserve mention in this place. In architecture we owe to the French such generalities as *chapel* and *cloister*, *castle* and *palace*, *manor* and *mansion*, and such particularities as *arch* and *tower*, *column* and *pillar*, *aisle* and *porch*, *choir* and *transept*. It is noticeable that whereas 'the more homely or more elementary' craftsmen and artisans have retained their native or English names, 'such as *baker*, *miller*, *smith*, *weaver*, *saddler*, *shoemaker*, *wheelwright*, *fisherman*, *shepherd* and others', those occupations which 'brought their practitioners into more immediate contact with the upper classes, or in which fashion perhaps played a greater part' have French names, the practitioners being *tailor* and *butcher*, *mason* and *painter*, *carpenter* and *joiner*, which names are, like *choir*, *table*, *furniture*, taken with very little change from French; note, too, that whereas *baker* is English, *confectioner* and *pastry* are French—though here it must be demurred that both *confectioner* and *pastry* are unrecorded before the sixteenth century.

As early as the twelfth century, John of Salisbury remarked that, French words being thought fashionable, to sprinkle one's speech with them was the modish thing to do: a fact that accounts, either wholly or in great part, for the adoption of many non-technical French words, as, for instance, *age*, *air* and *to arrive*; *to change*, *to turn* and *to use*; *manner* and *matter*; *point* and *reason*; the doublets *to nurse* and *to nourish*; *large* and *feeble*. It was natural enough that the English, the lower classes, should ape the language of their social superiors, who, in addition to having political mastery and the monetary power, were the better educated, the more cultured and refined. There were, however, a few medieval writers that 'went all Anglo-Saxon' and employed

---

[1] *Sport* is an aphetic form (i.e., deprived of its first syllable) of *desport* (or *disport*) which comes direct from Old French: it is amusing to see the French use of *sport* as an essentially English word.

almost no Gallicisms and very few French-derived words, but they were fighting a hopeless battle, for French, the language of the upper classes, 'also made inroads on the spoken everyday Early Middle English language, through those many skilled workmen, foreign (mostly French) mercenaries, and, above all, the monks and friars who mixed with the lower classes, thus exposed to pressure from two quarters' (Langenfelt).

Statistics concerning the grafting of French words on the English stock show that this 'linguistic influence did not begin immediately after the Conquest, and that it was strongest in the years 1251–1400, to which nearly half [43%] of the borrowings belong'; and if we proceed to the Age of Dryden (say 1670–1700), we find that at this period far fewer French words came into English than philologists used to suppose.

But what do we know of the relation of English to French in England, during the Middle Ages? One of the most valuable testimonies is this of Robert of Gloucester, writing ca. 1300: 'The Normans at that time could speak only their own language, and spoke French just as they did at home, and had their children taught in the same manner, so that people of rank in this country who came of their blood all stick to the same language that they received of them, for if a man knows no French, people will think little of him. But the lower classes still stick to English and to their own language.'

How, then, was it that the English learnt so many of these foreign words? And to what extent did they assimilate and absorb them? In a few instances it was easy to assimilate French words: when they happened to resemble native (English) words, and especially when these foreign words had themselves been borrowed, mostly at a much earlier period, from some Germanic language or even from some Germanic dialect. It is impossible to tell what the modern English *rich* owes to Old English *rice*, 'rich', originally 'powerful'; what to the French *riche*. 'When French *isle* (now île) was adopted, it could not fail to remind the English of their old *iegland, iland* and eventually it corrupted the spelling of the latter into *island*.' Greater help may have been received from the habit of using a French word alongside its native synonym, the latter explaining the former to those still ignorant of the more cultured, the French, word: thus, in the *Ancrene Riwle* written[3] ca. 1225, we find 'Cherité that is luve', 'Ignoraunce, that is unwisdom & unwiteness' (lack of knowledge); and there are many other examples from this and from poems. In all these pairings, it is now (and long has been) the native words which would need explaining. Indeed, nearly all the French words adopted before 1350, and many of those imported later, 'have become part and parcel of the English language, so that they appear . . . just as English as the pre-Conquest stock of native words'.

It is noteworthy that, in the surviving pairs of synonyms, the native or English synonym has the stronger associations with the primitive, the basic, and with those popular things, actions, feelings which are near the heart of the nation, whereas the French one is, usually, the more formal, more polite, more cultured, but further removed from the nation's heart. Thus a *hut* is simpler than a *cottage*, a *bill* unfit to name a hawk's *beak*, *friendship* more friendly than *amity*, *help* more sympathetic than *aid*, *hearty* much warmer and more widely used than *cordial*. In some pairs, the native term is more colloquial than the French: *begin* than *commence*, *end* than *terminate*, *feed* than *nourish*, *hinder* than *prevent*. On the other hand, though this happens much less frequently, the native word is the more dignified or literary: *deed* than *action*, *dale* than *valley*.

The grammar of French differed considerably from that of English. French nouns and adjectives were usually adopted in the accusative or objective case, which, in most words, differed from the nominative in having no *s*. In the course of two or three centuries, 'those words which had for a long time, in French as in English, formed their plural without any ending', remained the same, as in *cas*, and 'were made to conform with the general rule' (singular *case*, plural *cases*). French adjectives were, with very few exceptions, treated precisely as though they were English. In verbs, 'the rule is that the stem of the French present plural served as basis for the English form': *survive* comes, not from *survivre* but from *nous survivons* (or *vous survivez* or *ils survivent*); *resolve*, not from *résoudre* but from *résolvons, résolvez, résolvent*.

Moreover, all French words have, as a matter of course, shared in and been controlled by all those changes which have affected English since they were adopted: as in *fine* ('feen' is the French pronunciation), *price* (French *prix*, pronounced 'pree'), *advice* (French *avis*, pronounced 'avee'), in which instances the long Continental *i* (pronounced 'ee') has been turned into the long English *i*, properly a diphthong; as also in French *tour* ('toor'), English *tower*, where the phonetic long *u* has become the diphthongal *au* (ow); as again in French *grâce* ('grahss'), English *grace*, where the Continental long *a* has become the English long *a*. The accent took three or four centuries to change from the last syllable, the French position, to the English position on the first syllable.

Soon after the Norman Conquest, there arose hybridism—a very general feature of the English language from the twelfth century onwards. The earliest and simplest form of hybrid or 'mongrel'—a word formed of elements from different languages, e.g., *amoral*, which has a Latin radical (or root or stem) and a Greek prefix—is that which occurs when an English inflexional ending (an ending showing a change in number or person or case) is attached to a foreign word, as in 'the *Duke's* children' for 'the children of the Duke' (French *duc*) or in 'the *noblest* of them all' for 'the most noble . . .'; but hybridism so simple is inevitable and was perhaps hardly noticed. Much more noticeable but, coming later as it did, hardly more surprising, is the forming of verbal nouns in *-ing* and *-ung*[1] from French verbs, as in *prechinge* from French *prêcher*, and *riwlunge*; *-ness* began to be added to French adjectives as soon as the fourteenth century, *faintness*, *secretness* (now obsolete) and *closeness* being early examples; among English suffixes attached to French common nouns to form English abstract nouns are *-dom* (as in *dukedom*) and *-ship* (as in *companionship*); *-ful* and *-less* were added to French nouns to form English adjectives, as in *beautiful*; *-ly* was appended to French adjectives to form English adverbs, as in *easily* and *nobly*, as also to nouns to form adjectives, as in *princely*. But whereas such hybrids as these may be found in large numbers in most Indo-European languages, the less obvious hybrids composed of a native root or stem and a foreign ending or suffix are much more frequent in English than elsewhere. 'Before such hybrids could be formed, there must have been already in the language so great a number of foreign words with the same ending that the formation'—this foreign ending (a suffix) tacked on to an English root —'would be felt to be perfectly transparent.' Noun hybrids are usually in *-ess* (*shepherdess*) or *-ment* (*endearment*) or *-age* (*mileage*) or *-ance* (*hindrance*) or *-ry* (*bakery*) or *-ty* (*oddity*) or *-fication* (*uglification*); a common verb hybrid is that in *-fy* (*fishify* in Shakespeare); adjective hybrids are those, for example, in *-ous* (*murderous*) and, especially,[2] *-able*, which is addable to a few nouns, and, above all, to verbs, as in *eatable* and *drinkable* and *unutterable* and hundreds of others—whence come the nouns in *-ability*, as in *suitability*: in fact, if one wishes to form a new adjective of this kind, one can now do so without being punishable or finable.

[1] The suffix *-ung*, which did not survive Middle English, gave way to *-ing*.
[2] Properly, it is appendable only to words of Latin (or Latin-derived French) origin, but this too strict rule began to be broken centuries ago; *eatable* arose in the fifteenth century.

French influence has been spread over a long period, and, to quote a longish passage from the already much-quoted Jespersen, 'it is interesting to compare the forms of old loan-words with those of recent ones, in which we can recognize traces of the changes the French language has undergone since medieval times. Where a *ch* in an original French word is pronounced as in *change*, *chaunt*, etc. . . . , the loan is an old one; where it is sounded as in *champagne* . . . , we have a recent loan. *Chief* is thus shown to belong to the first period, while its doublet *chef* . . . is much more modern. . . . Similarly, *g* as in *age*, *siege*, *judge* . . . is indicative of old loans', whereas the pronunciation of *g* as in *rouge* indicates a modern adoption. Initially, however, *g* is, in English, pronounced *j*: 'thus *gentle*, *genteel* and *jaunty* represent three layers of borrowing from the same word [*gentil*], but they have, all of them, the same initial sound'. Other examples of a French word in two borrowings are *suit* and *suite*, *liquor* and *liqueur*, *rout* and *route* (pronounced 'root'). But, 'in some cases, we witness a curious re-shaping of an early French loan-word, [a re-shaping] by which it is made more like the form into which the French has meanwhile developed. This, of course, can be explained only by the uninterrupted contact between the two nations. Chaucer had *viage* just as Old French, but now the word is *voyage*; *leal* has given way to *loyal*', except in archaistic writing; '*marchis* to *marquis*. . . . Similarly the signification of Middle English *douten* like that of Old French *douter* was "to fear" . . . , but now in both languages this signification has disappeared. *Danger* was at first adopted in the Old French sense of "dominion, power", but the present meaning was developed in France before it came to England.' The French influence, in short, has continued ever since its beginning in 1066, whereas the Scandinavian influence was 'broken off somewhat abruptly after the Norman Conquest'.

LATIN AND GREEK

We have already seen that in the pre-Christian and the early Christian period in the England of the English, a considerable number of Latin words were adopted and adapted. Indeed there has been a continuous possibility of Latin influence; but after the two early sets of importations, there was no great influx until the Revival of Learning. The latest stratum (or layer) of loans is composed mainly of either abstract terms (philosophical[1] and theological) or scientific terms, both groups having come to us almost exclusively through the channel of medieval manuscripts and modern books. Very few of them have become as popular—as

[1] Comprising metaphysical, ethical, logical and psychological.

generally serviceable—as the words belonging to the two older strata. Not all the more modern loans are from Latin: if we took the whole of the vast English vocabulary, we should perhaps find as many Greek as Latin elements (or radicals or stems); nevertheless, 'the more important words are Latin, and most of the Greek words have entered into English through Latin, or have, at any rate, been Latinized in spelling and endings before being used in English, so that we have no occasion here to deal separately with the two stocks'. It was the Revival of Learning which gave to Greek and Latin a renewed vitality of influence. England began to be affected by the Renaissance in the fourteenth century, thanks largely to France and Italy: ever since then Classical words have sought entry into the English language, which shows a greater number of importations in the fourteenth, sixteenth and nineteenth–twentieth centuries than in the intervening ones. This influence has been stronger in English than in any language except French. 'The natural power of resistance possessed by a Germanic tongue against these alien intruders had already been broken' in English 'by the wholesale importation of French words', themselves of Latin origin and therefore tending to prepare the English people for words derived straight from Latin.

It is, therefore, natural that the Latin cannot rigidly be separated from the French loans: many English words would have assumed the same form, whether they derived from Latin or from French, 'and their first users would probably know both languages': such words as *consolation*, *grave* (adjective), *position*, *infidel* and *infernal* might have come as naturally from the one as from the other language. The Greek and Latin words in English increase with every new scientific discovery and ensuing treatise. In Greenough and Kittredge's *Words and their Ways in English Speech*, it is stated that, by 1902, the English vocabulary had enlisted 'one in four or five' of all the Latin words in a well-known Latin dictionary, either directly or, more frequently, through French; the proportion would now be one in four.

Not all the loans retain the senses and the pronunciations of the Greek and Latin originals; the latter soon were changed (and they need not detain us here), the former changed only over a long period. Compare the English *enormous* with Latin *enormis*, 'irregular'; *item* in English with *item* in Latin; English *premises* with the Latin sense ('things already mentioned or statements already made'); *climax*, 'a culminating point', with Greek *klimax*, 'a ladder'. But we, who are not pedants, will remember 'that when once a certain pronunciation or signification has been firmly established in a language, the word fulfils its purpose in spite of ever so many might-have-beens, and that, at any rate, correctness in one language should not be measured by the' standard of correctness 'of another language'.

When, in the Revival of Learning, Greek and Latin literature arrived in England, they were as a revelation: not as one flash of forked lightning nor even with the less momentary illumination of sheet lightning, but with the steady brilliance of noontide in high summer. These literatures brought old ideas so long forgotten as to be new; as the ideas were eagerly adopted, so were those fascinating words which indicated—which clothed—the ideas. And when those ideas were outgrown, and new, non-Classical ideas gained ground and, in fact, became general, the educated classes in England as in the rest of Europe still 'drew upon the Latin and Greek vocabulary in preference to their own native stock of words'—for the simple reason that they had been so trained and nourished on Greek and Latin, that it did not occur to them, now that they had stepped far beyond the boundaries of the Classical world, that they might seek elsewhere. This appears the most obviously in the nomenclature (name-system) of modern science with its thousands of terms, mostly compounds, formed from either Greek or Latin roots—or from both. Many words supposed to have come direct from the Classics are modern, coined on the analogy of Classical words: such are *eventual* and *eventuality*, *climatic*, *fragmentary*, and *annexation*; coinings in *-ism*, as in *favouritism* and *realism*, *colloquialism* and *mannerism*; or in *-ist*, as in *dentist* and *florist* and *oculist*, *tourist* and *socialist* and *scientist*. It is worth noting that the Greek endings *-ism* and *-ist* (actually these are shortenings of the Greek suffixes) are attached indifferently to stems of Latin or Greek or French origin. It is not much use, at this date, to object to such words as *scientist*, *suicide*, *telegram*, *facsimile*, *tractarian*, and *vegetarian*, on the grounds that they are incorrect Latin or Greek formations: the fact that they would have been the most shocking of solecisms in Greek or in Latin does not make them shocking in English.

There are also hybrids in which a Greek or Latin element is added to an English one—that some of the former elements have been 'imported through French' does not vitally affect the issue —as, for instance, *-ation* in *starvation*; *-ite* in *Ruskinite*; *-ism* in *heathenism*; *-ize* in *Londonize*; *-ology* in *weatherology*; *-ative* in *talkative*. The addition may be a prefix, consisting of a preposition, as *ex* (from, out of) in *ex-king*; *anti* (against) in 'the *anti-taxation* movement'; *co* (along with) in *co-godfather*; *de* (down from) especially in verbs ending in *-ize*,[1] as in *denationalize*; *inter* (among, between) as in *intermingle*; *pre* (before) in '*pre-railroad days*'; *pro* (for, siding with) in 'the *pro-Boers*'; or the adverb *re* (again or backwards), in *re-leather* and *resound*.

But it is also in style and syntax—not only in the vocabulary, which we have hitherto been considering—that Latin and, to a much smaller extent in these two matters, Greek have influenced English. The absolute participle is the English equivalent of the Latin ablative absolute: such a Latin phrase as *re infecta*, literally 'with the matter undone', Anglicè 'nothing having been done', is almost exactly represented in such an English phrase as *everything considered*, punned-on by G. K. Chesterton in his title *All Things Considered*, to which he might have added, 'This is what I think'. This construction rarely occurs in Old English, and then only in translations of the Latin; it is frequently seen in the more Latinized Elizabethan writers, though seldom elsewhere. 'But after 1660, when English prose style developed a new phase, which was saturated with classical[2] elements, the construction rapidly gained ground and was finally fixed and naturalized in the language.' Certain other Latin idioms have been tried, found wanting, and, except occasionally in poetry, abandoned.

It was natural that Latin syntax should be imitated, for, as late as the seventeenth century and even on into the eighteenth, Latin grammar was the only grammar taught in schools—where education, by the way, was predominantly Classical. In the matter of the influence exercised by the Classics on English writings in general and on English style in particular, it is refreshing to find Jespersen aligned with Darwin, T. H. Huxley, and Herbert Spencer against the vast majority of schoolmasters and grammarians. Darwin 'had the strongest disbelief in the idea that a classical scholar must write good English; indeed he thought that the contrary was the case'. (This is not the same thing as denying that an intelligent study of the Classics is an excellent training of mind and taste.) In 1890, Huxley wrote: 'My impression has been that the Genius of the English language is widely different from that of Latin; and that the worst and the most debased kinds of English style are those which ape Latinity. I know of no purer English prose than that of John Bunyan and Daniel Defoe; I doubt if the music of Keats's verse has ever been surpassed; it has not been my fortune to hear any orator who approached the

---

[1] These verbs are often spelt in *-ise*: *-ize* is preferable, for the suffix originally is Greek; *-ise* is a French verbal ending (as, for example, in *civiliser*). The present tendency is to adopt *-ize* thoroughgoingly. See especially my *Usage and Abusage*. [2] Better, 'Classical'.

powerful simplicity, the limpid sincerity, of the speech of John Bright. Yet Latin literature and these masters of English[1] had little to do with one another.' And Spencer, in his last book (*Facts and Comments*, 1902), spoke very strongly on the same side. To these authorities cited by Jespersen, let us add several comments: Goldsmith wrote a much better prose than Dr Johnson. Johnson himself, writing simply, was superior to Johnson indulging in Johnsonese; Edgar Allan Poe, simple, was preferable to Poe ambitious; and, to take a more recent example, James Joyce in his early novels and short stories wrote much better English than in his later cerebrations.

And, returning to the vocabulary, we may ask whether the Classical (especially the Latin) element is, on the whole, a benefit to the English language. The answer has been judicially given by Jespersen, who writes: 'The first advantage that strikes the observer is the enormous addition to the English vocabulary. If the English boast that their language is richer than any other, . . . the chief reason is . . . the greater number of foreign and especially of French and Latin [and Greek] words adopted.' But, as Selden pointed out in his *Table Talk*, 'we have more words than notions, [often] half a dozen words for the same thing'. It is insufficient to know many words and their meanings: one must also know their quality and their value, both in themselves and in association with other words; one must discover their adequacy to those ideas which are indicated by them. The resources of English were such as to make it probable that its words, whether singly or compounded with others or in phrases, could have dealt with nearly every need—possibly with literally every need, as we have mentioned in the section on Old English: for Old English was astonishingly versatile in overcoming linguistic difficulties. But gradually the English people forgot the resources of their native language and looked abroad for new terms. Learned writers not only cared little whether their readers knew the Classics or not, but also disregarded the 'unborn generations, whom they forced . . . to carry on the burden of committing to memory words and expressions that were really foreign to their idiom'.

Adjectives were comparatively few in Old English; so that, in Middle and Modern English, resort has been had to hundreds of Classical formations. This tendency appears very strikingly in the surprisingly large number of English nouns with Classical adjectives: as in *eye—ocular*; *mouth—oral*; *nose—nasal*; *mind—mental*; *son—filial*; *house—domestic*; *town—urban*; *moon—lunar*; *star—*

---

[1] This is the belief underlying, and exemplified in, my anthology, *English Prose: 1700–1914* (Edward Arnold, London; 2s. 6d.).

stellar; *the Middle Ages—medieval*. Yet it would have been quite easy to form native adjectives for these nouns, as we see in those groups of adjectives in which a native adjective exists alongside a learned one: to take a few examples, witness *fatherly* and *paternal*, *motherly* and *maternal*, *truthful* and *veracious*, *timely* and *temporal*, *heavenly* and *celestial*, *earthy* (or *earthly*) and *terrestrial*. In these groups, the two adjectives have grown apart and come to express shades or even differences of meaning; yet the native adjectives might advantageously have been allowed to retain those abstract nuances which have been usurped by the Classical synonyms.

In many instances there was so little need to coin a foreign adjective that there was no need to coin any adjective at all! Look what can be done with compounds: *birthday* is superior to *natal day*, *eyeball* to *ocular ball*; and so are the virtual compounds *taste nerve* to *gustatory nerve*, *chin nerve* to *mental*[1] *nerve*. 'Mere position before another noun is really the most English way of turning a noun into an adjective': thus, 'the *London* streets', 'a *Yorkshire* pudding', still better 'a *Yorkshire*man', 'the *Shakespeare* Society'; 'a *feast* day', '*family* affairs', 'an *adjective* clause', 'the *summer* season' not 'the *estival* season', 'an *autumn* day' not an *autumnal* one, 'a *winter* (or *winter's*) night' not an *hibernal* one, 'a *spring* shower' not 'a *vernal* shower', '*to-day's* post' not 'the *hodiernal* post', 'a *five-year* plan' not 'a *lustral* plan', a '*ten-year* (or *ten years'*) lease' not 'a *decadal* lease'. And when one needs a word that is an adjective in form as well as sense, why prefer superfluities—*lachrymatory* to *tearful*, *avuncular* to *uncle's*, *postprandial* (speech) to *after-dinner*? At times, doubt concerning the correct form to be given to a Classical adjective leads to unnecessary duplications: *festive* and *festal* were formed and have been used without a strict observance of the distinctions of the Latin; instead of *winding* or *maze-like*, we find *labyrinthine* and five other forms.

Very rich, then, is the English language in synonyms, whether exact synonyms (of which there are few) or approximate synonyms. It is this latter class which is the more useful: by it, speakers and especially writers are enabled to express subtle distinctions and delicate shades[2] of meaning[2]—or, more basically, nice discriminations of thought. There is a considerable difference between *juvenile* and *youthful*, as there is also between *youthful* and *young*; *portion* is not the same as *share*, nor is *same* exactly equivalent to *identical*; *edify*, literally to *build*, is now used only in a spiritual or

---

[1] This adjective, from Latin *mentum*, a chin, is an example of linguistic lunacy, for we already have *mental*, of the mind, from Latin *mens*, mind.
[2] Or nuances.

a moral sense, although *edifice* is, except in tone, an exact synonym of *building*; *science* is more restricted than *knowledge*, *sentence* than *saying*, *magnitude* than *size* (or *greatness*); *masculine* and *feminine* are more abstract than *manly* and *womanly*. Sometimes the difference between the synonyms is only stylistic, as in *building* and *edifice*, in *hand over* and *deliver*. But these sets of synonyms—whether pairs, or triplets (*kingly, royal, regal*), or quadruplets (*female, feminine, womanly, womanish*), or quintuplets (*male, masculine, manly, mannish, virile*)—are useful only to the person who thinks clearly and precisely; to careless thinkers and half-wits and nit-wits they are a snare, a stumbling-block, a delusion, and often a nuisance. To the stylist they are a blessing, for even where two or more terms are exact synonyms in sense, they are not exact equivalents aesthetically (that is, in beauty and suitability) or emotionally (in length and stress): Jespersen supplies two excellent examples in Shakespeare's 'blind *forgetfulness* and dark *oblivion*' (where nowadays we would say *obliviousness*— if we used the word at all) and Swinburne's '*manifold multiform flower*'.

A further point, applying not merely to synonyms but to all speech, is that words formed from Classical elements, whether radicals or affixes, are more intelligible internationally than are native English words, whether simple (e.g., *horse*) or compound (e.g., *horseman*). True; but with important reservations. A thing, relation, act or process that is used, performed, undergone (or controlled) every day should receive a native in preference to a Classical name, for 'national convenience should . . . be considered before international ease'; English *to*, for instance, is preferable to Latin *ad*; so, though to a lesser extent, is a *wire* to a *telegram*. Scientific names are, for the most part, international: and heaven knows we don't particularly lack—nor wish for—separate national names for, say, the *dinosaurus* or the *foraminifera*, though the French often have separate terms. Yet, in so far as science becomes general knowledge, its technical names should, as a rule, be discarded for native words: *insomnia* for *sleeplessness* affords a good example. That, to become international currency, a word need not be of Classical origin, is seen from the fact that, from ca. 1820, many English words have been adopted on the Continent: *sport, handicap, jockey, football, tennis* (lawn tennis); *cheque* and *trust*; *sulky* and *gig*; *dock* and *tender*; *waterproof*; *coke*.

A drawback of another kind is felt in such pairs as *affect* and *effect*, *emit* and *inmit*, *emerge* and *immerge*, *elude* and *illude*, *elicit* and *illicit*· the drawback of confusion in rapid speech and careless writing. But borrowings do not lead necessarily either to confusion or to lack of harmony. Many 'foreign elements have been so assimilated in sound and inflexion as to be recognisable as foreign only to the eye of a philologist'; a fact that holds for 'the pre-Conquest borrowing from Latin into English, of the Scandinavian and of the most important among the French loans, nay even of a great many recent loans from exotic languages'. But one need hardly be a philologist to perceive that *phenomenon* (Greek) or *latitudinarian* (Latin) are 'out of harmony with the real core or central part of the language'; and the same remark applies to such plurals[1] as *phenomena, nuclei, chrysalides, stigmata*. Many words of Classical origin are mere eye-words: we recognize them in print, we ourselves may even use them occasionally when we rush into print (or try to do so); yet we very rarely use them in speech: with the result that not only we but the learned are doubtful concerning their pronunciation, and indeed the pronunciation of some of these terms has not been determined—not, at any rate, fixed in one mould only, as it ought to be: *gaseous* is pronounced in six different ways, *hegemony* and *phthisis* in nine!

A more commonplace, yet more weighty objection against many words of Classical origin is that their meaning (unless, of course, one happens to know their meaning already) is deducible only by those who have had a Classical education, whereas a term formed from a native word or compounded of native words is clear to everyone that possesses a tolerable knowledge of English.

The abuse of Classical (especially Latin) terms reached its height in the more ponderous and ambitious of Dr Johnson's essays and articles. In the nineteenth century there was a strong and healthy reaction against Johnsonese in particular and a too frequent use of learned, and polysyllabic Classical, words in general: a reaction aided and exemplified by Tennyson in his *Idylls* and dramas. It is chiefly the half-educated who think it cultured and genteel to use big words; and even newspapermen that should know better are often seen wallowing in such words and phrases as *eventuate* or *transpire* for 'to happen', *vast concourse* for 'great (or, very large) crowd', *conflagration* for 'fire', *call into requisition the services of* for 'send for', *decease* and *expire* for 'to die', *indigent* for 'poor', *peripatetic mendicant* for 'a tramp', *rejoinder* for 'answer', *interrogate* for 'to ask', *beverage* for 'a drink', *edibles* for 'food', *mentality* for 'mind'. Some of these examples are taken from Jespersen, whose admirable *The Growth and Structure of the English Language* was written ca. 1911; but

---

[1] What are the plurals of *octopus* and *rhinoceros*? Seek and ye shall find —some odd plurals. See *English: A Course for Human Beings*.

since 1911, this ambitious manner and this pompous style—'stylistic inflation and turgidity', as Johnson might have said—have become less general in the Press.

It must not, from the last six or seven paragraphs, be inferred that all words of Greek and Latin origin are either bad or unnecessary: we would find ourselves in an impossible position if we tried to exclude Classical terms wholly from our language.

VARIOUS SOURCES

Only Scandinavian, French (at first through the Normans), Latin and, later, Greek have changed the character of the English vocabulary; only French and Latin and, to a smaller extent, Scandinavian have modified English syntax and style. Loans from Italian, Spanish Dutch and German have, in the aggregate, been numerous: but in no important way have these words changed the structure of the English language or modified English style.

Nevertheless an examination of the borrowings from Italy, Spain, Holland, Germany, and such less fertile sources as Portugal, Russia, Hungary, Turkey, Persia, India, and Red Indian America, throws a very interesting light on the political, social and commercial exchanges and relations between those countries and the English-speaking ones. Italy has furnished us with such musical terms as *piano*, *opera*, *libretto*, *alto* and *soprano*, *tempo* and *adagio*; such art and architectural terms as *corridor* and *colonnade*, *cornice* and *grotto*, *fresco* and *miniature* and *profile*; such more general terms as *lava* and, to differentiate for convenience between the meanings of the one word, *maccaroni* (dandies) and *macaroni* (food), the latter sense being the original. Spain has contributed *sherry* and other wines and *negro*. To Holland we owe *easel* and *landscape* and *sketch*, and many nautical terms. Germany has, *at the psychological moment* for *plunder*, invaded England with *uhlans*, *kindergartens*; invaded America with *to loaf*, *dumb* (stupid), and *fresh* (impudent), and many other terms, especially of food and drink (for example, *pretzel* and *lager*). Russia, with *knout* and *ukase*, has, from the almost countless *versts* of her *steppes* and *tundras*, tried to make us *Bolshevik*. Imports from Hungary include the *hussar* and the *shako* and *paprika*. Turkish imports are *bey*, *bosh*, *burgoo* and *caftan*. Persia has sent us *caravan* and *dervish*. India has furnished us with so many terms that it were perhaps fatuous to mention *calico* and *pagoda* and *jungle*. Arabia is responsible for *mufti* (very useful) and *harem* (less useful). From Malaya come *bamboo* and *paddy* field; from Polynesia *taboo*. Mexico provides us with *tomato* and *chocolate*, both eaten by the *gaucho*. The Red Indians let us have *tomahawks* and *moccasins*.

Most of the terms in this paragraph are to be found in the various Continental languages.

English, nevertheless, is more apt than the Continental languages to swallow foreign words unchewed and to leave them undigested; more apt to be satisfied with them in an undigested state. Or, put it another way, English is less likely to find a native equivalent for those foreign words which appeal to it as striking or useful. English, in short, is omnivorous.

The reason lies not in the national gift for learning languages; indeed, English people tend to pride themselves on *not* learning foreign languages. The Englishman 'is content to pick up a few scattered fragments of [foreign] speech—just enough to impart a certain local colouring to his narratives and political discussions'. This laziness is increased by the tendency to prefer words from Greek and Latin. Certainly the frequent loans are not made necessary by any deficiency in English itself: new terms are formed from native elements whenever their need is peremptory, especially by the uneducated. Witness the terms coined by the settlers in Australia: for instance, *whip* (or *coach*) *bird*, *lyre bird* and *friar bird*; *frog's mouth* and *honey-eater*; *trumpeter* (a fish); *sugar grass* and *iron heart*. Such coinings of compounds and senses reveal the right sort of speech talent: and how much happier they are than *telegram* and *microphone*!

But then, the English language has been best enriched by precisely such words as have been formed by natural processes, hence by processes that have been regularized: processes inherent in the very shape and in the very growth of the language: processes that, to the words coined thereby, have given a form and a character so English, so familiar, that the resultant terms seem to be natives. 'The whole history of English word-formation may be summed up as follows—that some formative elements' (affixes, formulas of construction, etc.) 'have been gradually discarded, especially those that presented some difficulty of application' (i.e., were clumsy, inconvenient, or unnatural in actual practice), 'while others have been continually gaining ground, because they have admitted of being added to nearly all words without occasioning any change in the kernel of the word.' Whereas *-en*, denoting female sex, has been abandoned except in *vixen*, a she-fox, that other Old English suffix, *-isc* (applied at first only to nation-names), has, as *-ish*, become capable of being added to many sorts of nouns, as in *childish*, and hence, with a different shade of meaning, to adjectives, as in *biggish*, or even to phrases, as in *five o'clockish*. But *-en* as a verb-ending has become a frequent addition to adjectives (*harden*, *soften*, *weaken*, *lessen*). Still more frequent are the agential nouns ('agents') in that *-er* which has developed from the *-a* and *-ere* agential endings in Old English and has taken the place of the ending in *-end* (as in *Scieppend*, the Creator); in fact, *-er* can now be added to any verb, in order to form an agent—or, for that matter, an instrument (as in *rubber* and *typewriter*). A frequent noun suffix is *ness*; adjective suffix, *-y* (*fiery*); adverb, *-ly* (*fierily*). Prefixes often used are *dis-* and *mis-*, *be-* and *un-*: *distasteful*, *misbehaviour*, *becalmed*, *unhappy* and *unfasten*. 'By means of these formatives' and others like them, 'the English vocabulary has been and is being constantly enriched with thousands . . . of useful new words.'

There is a specifically English and extremely valuable way of forming nouns from verbs and verbs from nouns: an easy way yet an effective: that of rendering them identical (*love* and *to love*) or virtually identical (*practice* and *to practise*). Take *lufian*, the Old English verb for 'love', and its noun, *lufu*: over a long period they approximated steadily towards the one form *love*. Very many other nouns and verbs, throughout the same period (Middle English), came to have but the one form: hence it was not merely natural but almost (? wholly) inevitable that the English people concluded that, whenever a verb was needed, this verb might be formed from the corresponding noun: as in *cook* and *drink*, *care* and *deal*, *charm* and *comfort*, *fire* and *fight*, and many, many others. And verbs have, unchanged, become nouns with perhaps even greater frequency, although the process was impossible until the final *-e*, present in most verb forms, had disappeared; 'and accordingly we see an ever-increasing number of these formations from about 1500'. Among the earliest are *bend* and *cut*, *fetch* and *reach*, *frown* and *fawn*, *dislike* and *dissent*, *gather* and *gaze*, *burn* and *lend*, *dip* and *drain*. Sometimes a noun of the same form as the verb has been created in addition to another noun already made from the same verb: *to move* has given us *movement* and *motion*, and also *a move*; from *to remove* come both *removal* and *a remove*. Note, too, the difference between *a meet* and *(a) meeting*, *a read* and *(a) reading*, *a smoke* and *smoking*, *a shoot* and *(a) shooting*, *dress* and *dressing*. Apparently slight, yet actually important differences in meaning are conveyed by small differences in sound; the words are formed with delightful ease and memory-aiding regularity: such word-building and such a system of differentiation are superior to those indicated in such pairs as *youthful* and *juvenile*, *occult* and *hidden*. There is often an amusing game of musical chairs played by verbs and nouns, nouns and verbs: we *sit* on a *seat*, and the good *sit* of a coat may help to *seat* us better on our horse.

In these mergings of the parts of speech (especially of nouns and verbs; nouns and adjectives), some pedants and last-ditchers profess to see a danger, or at the least a likelihood, of ambiguity: but the danger is imaginary, the likelihood null, for the context provides the answer simultaneously with the words' being read—provided always that the style is clear. Jespersen gives an excellent example, 'Her eyes like angels watch them still', where, theoretically, *still* might be either adjective or adverb; *watch*, noun or verb; *like*, verb or adverb (or quasi-preposition), or conjunction, or adjective; *eyes*, noun or verb; *her*, possessive adjective or accusative pronoun: and yet there is not a single ambiguous word in the whole, theoretically super-ambiguous sentence.

Words formed by addition—of prefix or suffix (or, very rarely, infix); words formed by no change at all—that is, by a noun's becoming a verb, a verb's becoming a noun, a noun's an adjective, and so forth; and now, words formed by subtraction—or, as philologists phrase it, by back-formation. For instance, the adverb *sideling* (sideways) was formed from the noun *side* and the adverbial suffix *-ling*; but in 'The crab walks *sideling*', *sideling* looks like a present participle, for in 'He goes *singing*', *singing* is actually a participle ('He sings as he goes'): hence, a new verb is formed—that it is spelt *sidle* and not *sidel* is due to the fact that *sideling* is pronounced as two, not as three, syllables. Other examples are *greed* from *greedy*, *to laze* from *lazy*, *difficult* from *difficulty*.

In the preceding paragraph and often in the course of the earlier parts of this chapter, we have glanced at the tendency of English to increase its large original stock of monosyllables. Some of the new monosyllables—new as compared with the monosyllables existing already in Old English—are simply shortenings ('by regular phonetic development', the general trend of sound-changes) of longer words: Old English *eahta* becomes *eight*, Old English *hlaford* becomes *lord*. Some are clippings of long foreign words, especially among the less educated; and of these originally illiterate short-cuts, a few have been admitted into Standard English, as in (tele)*phone* and (omni)*bus*; some were rather slang than solecism, as *cab*(riolet), *navvy* (navigator), *mob*(ile vulgus: the fickle crowd), three words so firmly established that the originals have been forgotten by everyone except the scholar and the word-lover.

C. A FEW GENERAL FEATURES[1]

From the preceding section we have caught glimpses of, but

[1] Compare this section, based on and closely following Jespersen, with the middle portion of Chapter VI, which deals with the literary-linguistic trends and fashions of English.

have not examined, certain general features and trends that nevertheless deserve to be considered, however briefly.

Continentals have often remarked that English is the only language in which the pronoun of the first person singular (*I*) is written with a capital letter, whereas in certain other languages it is the second person (especially the pronoun of courtesy) which is thus honoured, as in the German *Sie*, the Danish *De*, the Italian *Ella* and *Lei*, and the Spanish *Usted*; but in the Middle Ages *i* was written *I* whenever the letter came at the end of a word or of a group of figures and whenever the letter was isolated, whether as a pronoun or as numeral.

'On the other hand, the habit of addressing a single person by means of a plural pronoun was ... an outcome of an aristocratic tendency towards class-distinction. ... In England as elsewhere this plural pronoun (*you*, *ye*) was long confined to respectful address. Superior persons were addressed as *you*', *thou* being applied to all others. 'English is the only language that has got rid of this useless distinction', *thou* (and *thee*) having long been discarded. 'When all the artificialities of the modes of address in different nations are taken into account—[for example] the *Lei*, *Ella*, *voi* and *tu* of the Italians ... —the English may be justly proud of having avoided all such mannerisms' and confusing distinctions.

One of the most profound influences on the English language has been that of religion, mainly through the Bible and the Prayer Book. Numerous phrases and allusions bear witness to this influence: for instance, *strain at a gnat, spoil the Egyptians, a still, small voice, howling wilderness, many inventions, whited sepulchres, kill the fatted calf, of the earth, earthy*, and many others. Such scriptural phrases as the *holy of holies* and *the King of kings, and Lord of lords*, which illustrate a Hebrew variation of the usual superlative (*the most* ...) have, in English, originated *in my heart of hearts* (Shakespeare), *the evil of evils* (Lecky), *horror of horrors* (Henry James), and many others. Some proper names—*Jehu, Jezebel,* doubting *Thomas*, and others—have become generic names.

The Puritans influenced the language by causing a diminution both of swearing as a habit and of the number of oaths: whence *Law* (or *Lawks*) for *Lord, drat it*, and *goodness gracious*. 'The English swear less than other European nations and ... when they do swear the expressions are more innocent than elsewhere.' Thus it is to the Puritans, or rather to their lingering influence, that we owe a certain number of English euphemisms—mild words for strong words. Why, it is even customary to speak of oaths as *expletives* or *profane language*! 'Where a French or German or

Scandinavian lady will express surprise or a little fright by exclaiming (*My*) *God!*, an Englishwoman will say *Dear me!* or *Oh my!* or *Good gracious!*' Euphemism reached its height of prudery and ludicrousness in the period 1840–70, when, in England, trousers were called by many comic names of the *unmentionables* kind and, in America, the ladies spoke of the *limbs* of a piano. 'Prudery is an exaggeration, but purity is a virtue, and there can be no doubt that the speech of the average Englishman is less tainted with indecencies ... than that of the average Continental.'

Logically, we should, as Jespersen recognized, treat here and now of such questions as the origin and nature of Standard English, dialects, colloquialisms, slang, cant or the language of the underworld, vulgarisms, and jargon or the words peculiar to a trade or a profession: but it is more convenient (and not too dreadfully illogical) to postpone them to a later chapter, *English: Good; Bad; and Worse*.

At this point, however, we certainly may consider the expansion of English: and on this subject Jespersen has said what must, for very many years, be the last words—which we adopt and adapt. Several centuries ago, he remarks, English was spoken by so few that no one, not even the English, dreamt of its becoming a world language; nowadays, no one in his senses would dream of denying that, in its two branches (English and American English), it has, in the twentieth century and, indeed, from ca. 1860, been *the* world language. In 1582, Richard Mulcaster—not a foreigner, you will have noticed—could say, without fear of contradiction by his countrymen: 'The English language is of small reach, stretching no further than this island of ours, nay not there over all' (everywhere). In an Anglo-Italian dialogue written by John Florio, one of the characters (an Italian), when asked to express his opinion of the English language, declared it worthless beyond Dover; Ancillon deplored the fact that as English writers used English, Continentals could not read them; even so late as 1718, the learned Le Clerc regretfully commented on the paucity of Continental scholars able to read English. Shakespeare's opinion on the subject is to be found in *The Merchant of Venice*, where Portia, in reply to Nerissa's question about the young English baron (Fauconbridge), says, gently yet firmly: 'You know I say nothing to him, for he understands not me, nor I him: he hath neither Latin, French, nor Italian, and you will come into the court and swear that I have a poor pennyworth in the English. He is a proper man's picture'—i.e., a fine fellow—'but alas, who can converse with a dumb show?' And some four years before Le Clerc's wholly justified complaint, one Veneroni issued *The*

Imperial Dictionary, which contained the four most important languages of Europe: Latin, French, German and Italian—though it is to be noted that at this date (1714), as many persons spoke English as spoke Italian. 'Nowadays, no one would overlook English in making even the shortest possible list of the chief languages, because in political, social and literary importance it is second to none and because it is the mother-tongue of a greater number of human beings than any of its competitors' among the Aryan family of languages. Far more people speak Chinese, it is true; but then, very few persons that are not Chinese can speak Chinese, which, therefore, is very far from being a *passe-partout*.

That English is so widespread is due less to its intrinsic merits (Chinese has the advantage here) than to the character of the English and the Americans, the latter great traders and business men, the former great colonizers as well as excellent business men and enterprising traders. Many questions are involved in an examination of rivalry among languages. In the victory of English over other languages, the predominant factor has almost certainly been the political ascendancy of the English and, increasingly, the Americans during the period from about 1850.

The following table, in which English includes American English, shows the advance of English.

Year	English	German	Russian
1500	4,000,000	10,000,000	3,000,000
1600	6,000,000	10,000,000	3,000,000
1700	8,500,000	10,000,000	3–10,000,000
1800	25–30,000,000	30,000,000	25–30,000,000
1900	120,000,000	75,000,000	70–75,000,000
1926	170,000,000	80,000,000	80,000,000

Year	French	Spanish	Italian
1500	10,000,000	8,500,000	9,500,000
1600	14,000,000	8,500,000	9,500,000
1700	20,000,000	8,500,000	9,500,000
1800	27–30,000,000	26,000,000	14,000,000
1900	45,000,000	44–50,000,000	34,000,000
1926	45,000,000	65,000,000	41,000,000

'Whatever a remote future may have in store,' writes Jespersen, 'one need not be a great prophet to predict that in the near future the number of English-speaking people will increase considerably', especially as the British Dominions (and other dependencies) and the United States expand in population. 'It must be a source of gratification to mankind that the tongue spoken by two of the greatest powers in the world is so noble, so rich, so pliant [and adaptable], so expressive, and so interesting' as English: a tribute that, coming from a Dane and one of the greatest philologists of the twentieth century, carries the double weight of unquestionable authority and complete impartiality.

D. AMERICAN INFLUENCE

Finally, we may consider, very briefly indeed, the American influence on English. 'The earliest traces of the American influence ... are to be found about 1800, in connection with rather censorious English protests against supposed ... American coinages such as *belittle, progress* (as a verb), *lengthy*, etc. Such protests were often begotten of ignorance and pedantry. *Belittle* is a very useful word ..., *progress* is ... an American survival from Stuart times, *lengthy* expresses what cannot well be expressed otherwise.'[1]

'The general attitude of the old country, as reflected in its writers and tourists, towards the States was one of unfriendly criticism, or of still more irritating condescension': there was some reason for the former, no excuse for the latter. 'But the use of a common language, commercial intercourse ..., and a blood-relationship which was still a reality' (and is so, even now), 'inevitably resulted in some importation of American words and expressions. The Red Indian vocabulary, with its characteristic metaphor, such as "burying the hatchet", "going on the warpath", etc., was made familiar to the English reading public by the very popular novels of Fenimore Cooper (1789–1851).'

But 'the real flood of Americanisms began with the humorists', for whereas Washington Irving and Nathaniel Hawthorne wrote what was virtually Standard English (and very good English too), Artemus Ward (actually C. F. Browne), who died untimely in 1865, gave his English readers and hearers something absolutely new. 'American humour, with the entrancing oddity of its vocabulary, idiom, and mental processes, conquered England almost at a blow. Bret Harte familiarized us with the vocabulary and metaphor ... of the miners' camp, and Mark Twain ... expressed in droll and unexpected terms the homespun outlook of the cute and humorous American observer.' Two writers of dialect also became popular in England: Lowell with his *Biglow Papers* (New England) and Joel Chandler Harris with the *Brer Rabbit* legends of Uncel Remus.

'Apart from the influence of the professional humorists' and,

[1] Ernest Weekley's essay, 'Americanisms', in *Adjectives and Other Words*, 1930; so, too, until other notice.

to a lesser extent, that of the dialect writers, 'the American element in English has arrived in successive waves': the Fenimore Cooper or backwoods contribution; the contribution of the explorer and the prospector; from almost immediately after, and partly as a result of the American Civil War, the new political vocabulary; 'the era of frenzied finance', with its *wild-cat bills* and *banks* and *bucket-shops*, its 'alternations of *booms* and *slumps*'; the publicity given to the gangster as a result of the activities of the *boot-legger*; the influence of the American 'talkie', reinforcing that of the captions of the American silent film; and, from about 1890, the continuous influence of *big business*, with its *big noises*, and, latterly, *big shots* making *big money*.

'Of late years'—especially since World War I (1914–18)—'English has been inundated with American slang.... The language of the American comic stage and of the cinema ... is rapidly adopted into colloquial English.' Having mentioned the American *vamp* (for *vampire*), *mutt* (for *muttonhead*), and *fan* (for *fanatic*), this writer remarks that 'it is here that American slang has made a real and useful contribution to colloquial English. There is about these American tabloids a terseness and a finality which leave nothing to be said ... It is difficult now to imagine how we got on so long without ... *stunt*, how we expressed the characteristics so conveniently summed up in *dope-fiend* or *highbrow*, or any other possible way of describing that mixture of the cheap pathetic and the ludicrous which is now universally labelled *sob-stuff*.'

The main channels for the irrigation of the English language by the American are American books, magazines and plays; American travellers, sailors, whether English or American; English visitors to America; American films. 'So many Americanisms ... have got into English of late,' Mencken observed in 1923, 'that the English have begun to lose sight of [their] transoceanic origin', a fact confirmed by Professor W. E. Collinson three years later.

It is a long cry from the days when two noted scholars[1] asserted, 'Americanisms are foreign words, and should be so treated.... The English and the American language are both good things; but they are better apart than mixed'; but in view of the fact that, in 1928, Weekley could, in *The English Language*, say, 'The foreign language which has most affected English in our own time is contemporary American', we must recognize American English. We recognize it all the more readily that the plain truth resides in a statement made by John Brophy[2] in 1932: 'English is one

[1] The Fowler brothers, *The King's English*, 1906. [2] *English Prose.*

language[1] wherever it is spoken'. A year later, apropos of slang but with perfect applicability to English and American speech in general, I expressed the opinion[2] that 'perhaps this constant infiltration of Americanisms into English slang is a means whereby, through the enduring best from among these newcomers, the English language shall retain its youth. By all means let us discriminate, select those Americanisms which seem best suited to the genius of English, and adapt them to our linguistic ends: by careful selection and no less careful adaptation, we shall be enabled, if the need arises, to displace an effete or antiquated Anglicism by a vigorous, picturesque Americanism or to welcome a true neologism.' To accept either the inferior or the superfluous would be folly: to refuse either the superior or the necessary would be madness.

---

[1] On November the 5th, 1937, an American newspaper, in a short article entitled Are You There? (Hello?), could permit itself to print the remarkable statement, 'A thankless, profitless business, this trying to reconcile the English and American languages. The end is usually defeat and despair.' This was appropriately written by a journalist who had got his basic fact wrong (the word being *breached*, as applied to an agreement; not *reached*, which is very frequent in England), and who, to establish his point, twisted the evidence and, whether deliberately or ignorantly, made several very odd mistakes. 'The Yankee is merely scornful', he adds to the statement made above: well, well, well!

[2] In *Slang To-day and Yesterday*, in the 'Introductory' chapter of the American section.

CHAPTER THREE

THE AMERICAN LANGUAGE

THAT which forms the subject of this chapter is often called *American English*. A name now rare, once fairly common, is *the American dialect* (*of English*). But the name marked out for general use is plain *American*, despite the fact that *American English* is clearly the most accurate of these three terms.

Before we go into the matter of American, it is to be noted that no adequate knowledge and no trustworthy opinion can be had or formed without an intimate knowledge of English; that is, of *English* English, the ordinary brand of English, English pure and simple—though, like most other languages, it is neither pure nor simple. American, like the varieties of English spoken in India and Australia (to take but two examples), is after all only an off-shoot of English. The speech of the educated American differs, except in accent, very little from that of the educated Englishman or, for that matter, the educated South African or Australian; except for a comparatively small proportion of words, the speech of the average state-educated American differs (again apart from accent) little from that of the average state-educated Englishman; the specific language of the underworld differs from the general speech no more widely in the United States than it does in England; that there are certain American dialects difficult of comprehension by an Englishman is undeniable, and it is equally undeniable that certain English dialects would be understood by an American only with difficulty—but it is also true to add that certain American dialects are as obscure to the cultured Bostonian as certain English dialects are to the cultured Englishman, if we presuppose that neither that Bostonian nor that Englishman had mixed with the speakers of the dialect in question; the speech of the American-Irish and of the New York or Chicago Italian (*Wop*, as he is called in slang) is as far removed from normal American as the speech of the Liverpool Irish and the Soho Italian is from normal English. If, then, this chapter on American is only a third as long as that on English, it is for two simple reasons: American, being an offshoot of English, is (in the main) subject to the same linguistic changes as those which have affected

English; and American has a history of not much over three hundred years, whereas English—but why stress the obvious?

The three best-known[1] writers on American are perhaps Mr H. L. Mencken, the fifth edition of whose provocative and entertaining *The American Language* (now twice as big as the original edition, 1919) has recently appeared; Professor George Philip Krapp, who in *The English Language in America*, 1925, paid much attention both to the history of Americanisms and to American pronunciation and came to that conclusion, 'English and American show few important differences', which Mr Mencken so dislikes; and Professor George H. McKnight in several books and learned journals, but particularly in an admirable chapter in *English Words and their Background*, 1923. That I quote the most extensively from the third writer is due to the fact that his essay 'American English' is admirably suited to my purpose: so very admirably that I was sorely tempted to ask his permission to reprint it in full; but in any case I intend to quote large chunks[2]—to which I shall add comments. Perhaps I should mention that many of Professor McKnight's examples come, fully acknowledged, from Mr Mencken's *The American Language* and that, in his turn, Mr Mencken often refers to Professor Krapp's work (seen first in manuscript).

'A German schoolmaster once enquired of the present writer,' says Professor McKnight, ' "Have you always lived in America?" When answered in the affirmative, he continued, "Where then did you learn English?" That is to say, an educated'—but surely not very well educated?—'German was surprised to learn that the natural language of the United States is English. The story is told that when the English actor, Cyril Maude, was playing in New Mexico, a group of cowboys who had been in the gallery, left the theatre saying, "We can't understand a thing the guy says". In England, before [World War I], one saw on store fronts, not only the familiar signs, "Ici on parle français", [etc.,] but an occasional'—surely a very occasional—' "American spoken here". In all this there is evidence that the language of America is not entirely identical with that of England, that there is a difference

---

[1] Best known both in America and elsewhere. My unassertive choice does not imply ignorance of the work of Dr Louise Pound and other able scholars and writers; nor, of course, depreciation of their most valuable contributions. Moreover, I have intentionally confined myself to post-1918 writings.

[2] 'Unacknowledged' quotations, then, are quotations from the 'American English' chapter of Professor McKnight's delightful, lucid, instructive book.

between the "King's English" and what has been called the "President's English".'

English may be said to have travelled to North America with the good ship 'Mayflower' in 1620; the colonists settled in New England. Virginia had been permanently colonized in 1607 after several unsuccessful attempts. English has changed considerably since the early seventeenth century, and one reason why American differs from English is that in the United States there have been retained many features—old senses of words, old words and phrases, old pronunciations—that have disappeared in England. 'Lowell . . . pointed out that most of the distinctive features of the New England dialect . . . are in reality survivals of the seventeenth-century forms of language [since] abandoned by the English of England.' As examples of pronunciation Lowell gives *critter, figger, git, jine, ketch, obleeged, pizen, sartin, varmint*—and others. 'Lowell also shows that many of the dialectal words of New England are survivals from earlier English': for instance, *afeard* (afraid), *bug* (insect), *chore, fall* (autumn), *loan* (to lend), *sick* (ill). And he might have added *brag, burly, deft, clod-hopper, flap-jack, homely* (plain-looking), *hustle, ragamuffin*; of which, however, the second, third, fourth, and last have never disappeared from English usage.

In the formation of American English there were added to the seventeenth-century form of English many words derived from the languages of the different peoples with whom the English-speaking colonists were brought into contact. First in importance . . . come the words derived from the speech of various [Red] Indian tribes. From the Indians were borrowed not only the many geographical names . . . of rivers, mountains, and lakes, but names for objects of the plant and animal world indigenous to the new country and names of implements and food preparations of a new kind.

Such words[1] as *opossum, moose, skunk, raccoon, terrapin; catalpa* (a flowering tree), *hickory, paw-paw, persimmon; pemmican, hominy* (maize hulled and ground, then boiled, with water or milk, for food), *tapioca*, and *pone* (bread made from maize, hence such bread made very fine and enriched with eggs); *canoe, moccasin, tepee* (a wigwam—*wigwam* itself an Amerindian word —formed of bark or mats or skins, stretched over a pole-framework), *toboggan, tomahawk; squaw* and *papoose* (the baby or young child of Red Indians); *pow-wow*, which, from being a council of or a conference with Red Indians, has come to mean any friendly consultation, a 'palaver'. Many of these words, by

[1] In the following lists of Americanisms, I am, for definitions, heavily indebted to the magnificent *Webster's International Dictionary*, ed. of 1944.

the way, were adopted from the dialect of the Algonquins, occupying a region belonging mostly to Canada, partly to the United States; *toboggan*, on the other hand, derives from a wholly Canadian Indian term. But it was not always adoption: certain American terms have been translated from Red Indian, the most familiar being *fire-water*, spirituous liquor (cf. the Spanish *aguardiente*, literally fiery water, hence brandy), *pale-face*, *pipe of peace*, and *war-path*.

'From the French in America'—especially Canada and Louisiana—'were derived a considerable number of words', such as *levee*, *seep*; *picayune* (a 5-cent piece, hence an insignificant thing or even person—cf. the English use of *tuppenny-hapenny*); *shanty*, *crevasse*, *bayou* (a marshy off-shoot from lake or river—cf. the Australian *billabong*), *prairie* and *chute*, *rapids* and *portage*; *caribou* (the North American reindeer) and *chowder*, that appetizing dish made of fresh fish and stewed with onions, biscuit, and slices of bacon.

Spanish words were adopted at two different periods. In the old Colonial days, American received *Creole*[1]; *mulatto*, *quadroon* and *octoroon*, a 'white' person with, respectively, a half, a quarter, an eighth of Negro blood; *picaninny*, a word that is spelt in many ways and is derived from *pequeño*, little or small; *barbecue*, historically a rude framework on which one sleeps, but latterly a social entertainment at which animals are roasted whole, the link between these two apparently disconnected senses being that intermediate sense which arose about 1760, 'an ox, hog or sheep roasted whole' on a framework resembling the original 'couch'; *palmetto*; *calaboose*, a lock-up or common prison; *stampede*. Then, after the Mexican War (1846–48), 'contact with Spanish-speaking inhabitants of Texas and the Spanish West resulted in the acquisition of such words as *adobe*, *broncho*, burro [a donkey], *canyon*, *chapparral*, [more correctly, *chaparral*, brushwood that is dense and tangled], *chile* [usually spelt *chilli* or *chilly*], *cinch* [literally, the Mexican saddle-girth], *corral*, *coyote*, *fandango* [a lively dance or its tune, hence a dancing, a ball], *lariat*, *loco* [a dangerous weed that, if eaten by horses, affects the brain; hence the American slang *loco*, mad], *ranch*, *sombrero*, *vamoose* [to depart, the word having been adopted independently in England]'.

[1] This word has led to many misapprehensions: originally, a person born and naturalized in the United States or in the West Indies, but of either European or African Negro descent; now, usually intended for *Creole white*, the full sense—or, less generally, for *Creole negro*, a negro born in the West Indies or the States, as opposed to one coming freshly from Africa.

The Dutch settlers of New York—it was the Dutch who, in 1626, founded New Amsterdam, which became New York in 1664—invested the town with much that was typically Dutch, and the Dutch members, for over two centuries, set the tone of New York society (perhaps we should write Society); and the Dutch contributed to American the following words: *boss* (cf. the Boer *baas*); *cold-slaw* (a salad of sliced or chopped cabbage); *cookie*; *cruller*, a cake that, cut from dough and containing eggs, butter, sugar, is twisted or curled before being fried, crisp, in either lard or oil, the word deriving ultimately from Dutch *crullen* to curl; *dominie*; *pit* (of peach or cherry); *Santa Claus*; *scow*; *sleigh*; *span* (of horses); *stoop* (the Boer *stoep*, 'a raised, uncovered platform before the entrance of a house'); and *waffle*, a sort of batter-cake, eaten hot with butter or molasses.

Early too was the German influence: to take but one example, Germantown was settled in 1683 by thirteen lucky families from Crefeld; Pennsylvania, with its wealth of coal and its iron-smelting works, has for two centuries been a stronghold of Germans. German in origin are, most probably, *dumb*, 'slow' or stupid; *fresh*, impertinent; *loaf*, to idle, and *loafer*, an idler; *bum*, to beg; *out of sight*, a mistranslation of German *ausgezeichnet*; and *mucker*, a fanatic or a hypocrite, this slang word being, apparently, taken direct from German *Mucker*, a sulky person. 'The nature of' certain other derivations from, or unashamed adoptions of German words 'suggests a possible explanation', to a small degree presumably, 'of the waning of Puritanic ideals in a latter-day America. Blue laws[1] and Scotch Sundays are not in harmony with the spirit suggested by such words as' *pretzel*, a crisp, knot-shaped biscuit flavoured with salt and taken as a relish with beer; *lager*; *pinocle*, a bezique-like game of cards; *wienerwurst*, a Vienna sausage; *leberwurst*, a liver sausage; *blutwurst*, a blood sausage; *frankfurter*, a highly seasoned sausage, generally of reddish hue; *hamburger*, a Hamburg sausage; *schnitzel*, a Vienna steak; *rathskeller*, literally (in Germany) a Council-house drinking-cellar, hence (in U.S.A.) a drinking-place after the style of the German original; *schweizer*, a Gruyère or an Emmentaler cheese; *delicatessen*, prepared foods, such as cooked meats, preserves, pickles; and *katzenjammer*, a bibulous 'hangover'.

Nor were all the English-speaking settlers English. The Scotch and Welsh elements can be ignored; not so the Irish. 'The English of Ireland, like the English of the United States, is a transplanted language, and the time of transplantation was not far apart in the

[1] *Blue laws* is itself an Americanism: see the list of Americanisms on p. 53.

two cases, since the settlement of English in Ireland took place in great part in the sixteenth and seventeenth centuries ... English Irish and American Irish have features in common. But the Irish also brought with them to America a goodly number of elements in their language that are of Irish creation. ... Some of these words and expressions[1] are ... *cadger*, ... *give in*, "yield"; *let on*, "pretend"; *cowlick* (of hair); ... *didoes*, "pranks"; ... *gazebo*, "tall, awkward person" [from *gazebo*, "a turret ... commanding an extensive prospect"]; *grumpy*, "surly"; ... (beat) *hollow*; ... *jaw*, "impudent talk"; *larrup*, "wallup"; *kybosh*;[2] *wipe*, "a blow"; ... *quit*, "cease"; *mad*, "angry"; *logey*, "heavy"; *wad* [bundle of bank or currency notes]; ... *spuds*; ... *smithereens*.'

But 'it is not to be assumed that the American pioneer was lacking in creative power. Removed to a great extent from the influence of book language, and thrown into new surroundings, he was called on to use his powers of invention in providing names for features of life that were new. The physical characteristics of the new country, particularly, in many respects different from those of the old, called for fresh names, and before the Revolution'—the American War of Independence—'there came into use such names as' *run* (a brook[3]), *bluff* (a steep, broad-faced headland), *barrens* ('plains on which grow shrubs and small trees, but no timber'), *bottom-land* or *bottoms* (low land formed by alluvial deposits), *clearing* ('a piece of land cleared for cultivation'), *knob* (a knoll, or hill), *riffle* (a river-rapid), and *rolling country* (undulating country): 'new applications of older English words'. Such English terms as *downs* and *wold*, *heath* and *moor*, *fen* and *bog*, *combe* and *dell* survive in the United States 'only as literary terms'.

American plant and animal life, differing from the flora and fauna of England, required new names. 'Hence the creation of ... *basswood*, or *bee-tree*, for English *linden* or *lime*; *buttonwood* for English *plane tree*; *cottonwood* for certain American varieties of the *poplar*; ... *buckeye* for *horse-chestnut*; *locust* for *pseudo-acacia*; *bayberry* for the *wax myrtle*; *Johhnny-jump-up* for the *wild pansy*; ... *snowball* for *guelder rose*.' Other plant and tree names invented by Americans are *burr-oak*, *live-oak*, and *pin-oak*; *blue grass* (especially associated with Kentucky) and *eel-grass*; *egg-*

---

[1] Several may have been imported from America into Ireland; most are familiar to Englishmen, some having been, indeed, importations into Ireland from England.

[2] This word is more likely to be Yiddish or Anglo-Hebraic (*O.E.D.*).

[3] This term is from Northern English dialect; cf. Standard English *runnel*.

plant, also called the *egg-apple* or the *mad-apple*; *monkey-nut*,[1] with its other names—*earth-nut* and *Manila nut*, *ground-pea*, *goober* and *pindar*. In some instances, 'an older English name was newly applied'. *Cranberry* is in America applied to a shrub (and its fruit) that even Americans might do well to call by the English name, the *large cranberry* or, preferably, *American cranberry*. *Wintergreen* (a typically English word) is in America the name of a plant that, there, is called also *deerberry*, *groundberry*, *hillberry*, *spiceberry*, *teaberry*, and *mountain tea* and *Canada tea*. *Wake-robin*, in England a variant of *cuckoo-pint*, is in America used of several varieties of *trillium*, called also *three-leafed nightshade*, *white bath*, *wood-lily*, and other names; the purple variety of *trillium* is further known as *Indian balm*, *Indian shamrock*, *nose-bleed*.

'Frequently, as in the case of plant names, the English bird or beast name is falsely, or at least newly, applied in America': *robin* is, in America, employed of a species of thrush; *swallow* applied to a swift; *night-hawk* to a bird that isn't a hawk; *oriole* to an American bird quite different from the English one—but very precise persons generally speak of the former as a *Baltimore oriole*; the *blackbird* is in England a species of *thrush*, of starling in America; the American *meadow lark* is very unlike an English lark; in America, a *rabbit* is what English people would call a hare. And so on, and so on.

This resourcefulness appears also in the names 'devised to suit the new conditions of existence into which American colonists were thrown'. These conditions, and the colonists' adaptability thereto, are reflected in such new words or word-uses as '*shingle* (for wooden tile), *clapboard* (for weather-board), *frame house*, *log house*, and later, *log cabin*. These words, along with others of their kind, such as *back-woods*, *landslide*, *cold snap*, *pine knot*, and *snowplow*, vividly suggest the stern realities of pioneer life'.

The spirit of the pioneers was, in part, creative: and this creative spirit, which enabled its possessors to master and to utilize a vast new country, has served them equally well in another sphere—the coining of words and phrases, or, if not of actual words and phrases, then of new senses for them. Professor McKnight, in illustration of Americanisms, gives the following list,[2] culled from Thornton's *An American Glossary*, 1912: *Blaze*

---

[1] A variant of *pea-nut*, which McKnight, reproducing H. L. Mencken's error, says is not an English name: *pea-nut* is the English name.

[2] Selected by the Professor as seeming to him, in 1923, likely to survive, especially since many of them were already old; I, in 1948, know that they have survived long enough to be, most of them, standard American. I omit *bar* (*room*), which was English many years before it became American, and several other terms on which Thornton, Mencken and McKnight have all gone wrong.

a trail, literally to indicate a trail by marking trees with white or by chipping off the bark, hence figuratively to point a course, show the path to be followed; *blizzard*; *backnumber*; *backbone* (courage); *bee-line*; *belittle*, which few persons would suspect of having ever been anything but English; *bleachers*, forms (seats) that are exposed to the open air and therefore lose their colour—originally slang and now colloquial; *blinders* (blinkers); *blue laws*, very severe laws enacted—allegedly enacted—by Puritans at New Haven, Connecticut, in the eighteenth century; *bluff* (to pretend; impose on; succeed by pretence); *bob-sled*; *bogus*; *to boom*; *to boost*; *brainy*; *bread-stuffs*, a most unnecessary word for either grain or flour; *bully* (excellent, 'splendid'); *campus*, grounds (of college or university)—probably at first a piece of pedantry, for *campus* is simply the Latin for 'field' or 'level space'; *cave in*, to yield or submit; *chipped beef*, smoked beef cut in very thin slices; *clear out*, to depart; *cloudburst*; *cocktail*, a drink and a habit introduced into England from the United States; *collateral (security)*; *commuter*, a season-ticket holder on, e.g., a railway line (a *railroad* in the States); *contraband*, a fugitive or captured slave during the Civil War; the slang *cooler*, a jail—where one has time to cool one's heels; *corn-cob*; *cowboy*; a *cowcatcher* at the front of a railway engine; *crawfish* (the English *crayfish*); *cutter*, a light sleigh; *dead-beat*, a sponging, worthless loafer; *dead-head*, a person admitted, or travelling, free; *to derail*; *the Dipper*, the seven bright stars in the Great Bear, *Little Dipper* being the seven bright stars in the Little Bear; *dive*, an illegal drinking-den, a low resort, is mentioned here because, though its use in England (as an underworld term) preceded its use in the United States by a century, it was re-introduced into England in the 1920's; *doughnut*; *dry up*, to cease talking; *fish story*; *fizzle out*, to fail; *freeze to*, to fasten on (a person)—cf. the equally American *freeze out*, to exclude from society by chilly behaviour or from business by mercilessly keen competition; *grit*, courage; *halfbreed*; *hayseed*, a rustic; *joy-ride*; *make good*; *maverick*, a brandless calf or yearling, hence a masterless person, an aimless rover—from the name of a Texan rancher that neglected to brand his calves; *played out*, exhausted; *poppycock*, nonsense, rubbish; *pot pie*, a pie of pigeon, pork, veal, and the like; *scal(l)awag* or *scallywag*; *shyster*, a lawyer either 'shady' or unprofessional, hence a 'shady' businessman; *to snake*, drag, pull or draw, especially to haul (logs) end-on; *splurge*, an ostentatious display, hence to make such a display, to show off, to be extravagant; *snarl*, a tangle; *spry*, lively (probably from English dialect); *whole-souled*; *to wilt* (certainly from English dialect, and reintroduced into England); and *yegg*, a safebreaker, a dangerous burglar—originally an underworld term.

Two spheres will suffice to show the differences between American and English. Politics; travel by rail. 'As early as 1828 Noah Webster in the preface to his dictionary, included *selectmen* [New England town-councillors], *senate, congress, court,* and *assembly*, in a list of words either "not belonging to the language of England" or "applied to things in this country which do not exist in that". *Presidential, congressional,* and *gubernatorial* [governmental; relating to the Governor of a State] also were comparatively early in origin.' It would be difficult 'to create the atmosphere of American political life' without the following terms: *Banner-state*, a State whose flag is a banner; a *bolter* from one's party; a political *boss*; *dark horse* as applied to a candidate; *favorite son*, 'a politician admired in his own State, but little regarded beyond it' (*The Shorter Oxford Dictionary*); *floater*, a voter of no settled abode, no permanent address; *gerrymander*,[1] to manipulate illicitly, with reference to an electoral system; *heeler*, 'the disreputable follower of a political "boss"'; *henchman*, 'a mercenary adherent'; *joker*, a deliberately ambiguous clause inserted in a legislative bill to render it inoperative or defective; *landslide*, a collapse; *lobby*, 'to frequent the lobby of a legislative assembly for the purpose of influencing members' votes', hence, thus to influence members; *log-rolling*; *machine*, 'the controlling organization of a political party'; *mugwump*, an Independent,[2] especially one who 'sits on the fence'; *omnibus bill*, a parliamentary measure covering unconnected matters; *plank* of a political *platform*; *pork-barrel*, a Federal fund or grant, diverted to local patronage instead of to needed improvements; *precinct*, 'a subdivision of a county or ward for election purposes'; *primary*, a caucus,[3] i.e. a party-meeting, to select candidates and to choose measures, the term being short for *primary meeting* or *primary assembly*; *repeater*, one who attempts, successfully or not, to vote twice at an election; *roorback*, a false report, especially a baseless slander, circulated at election time to spoil or lessen a candidate's chances; *slate*, to register (a person) for a political appointment; *split ticket* and *straight ticket*, a divided or a single electional issue; *stalwart*, 'a sturdy, uncompromising partisan'; *stump-speech*, an electioneering speech; and *wire-pulling*, the act or

---

[1] The spelling *jerrymander* is incorrect: the word derives from Elbridge Gerry, who, in 1812, manipulated the electoral districts of Massachusetts.

[2] See Ch. IX, B, iii (American History).

[3] Another derivation from Red Indian; *caucus* is one of the oldest of American political terms.

series of acts of a *wire-puller*, 'a politician or political agent who privately influences and directs others'.

Even if we omit slang terms, the vocabulary of the American railroad differs considerably from that of the English railway: 'in no other set of words is the difference between English and American as thoroughgoing as' here. 'Beginning at the head of the train we find[1] English *pilot* for American *cowcatcher, locomotive* for *engine*', though *engine* is now very common in England; '*locomotive-driver* for *engineer*' [though *engine-driver* is now the most usual term in England], *stoker* for *fireman, buffer* for *bumper, van* for *baggage car, luggage* for *baggage, goods* for *freight, carriage* for *car, saloon carriage*[2] for *parlor car, guard* for *conductor, brakesman* for *brakeman*. Leaving the train, we find *line* for *track, sleeper* for *cross-tie* or *tie, crossing-plate* for *frog, shunt* for *switch, gradient* for *grade, permanent way* for *road-bed*.

Then 'an American woman in an English dry-goods store almost needs an interpreter. In the first place the name of the establishment is not *dry goods store* but *draper's shop*. American *calico* needs to be translated into English *print*, since English *calico* means a white fabric. *Cheese cloth* needs to be translated by *butter muslin, shoe strings* by *boot* [or *shoe*] *laces, ruching* by *frilling, shirt waist* by *blouse, spool of thread* by *reel of cotton* [or *of thread*], *undershirt* by *vest* [or, for men, *singlet*], *wash-rag* by *face-cloth, corsets* by *stays* [though *corset* is now fairly general in England]. At the dining-table the translation of words is again called for. American *napkin* is *serviette*', but *napkin* or *table-napkin* is the term used by upper-class English people; '*rare* (meat) is *underdone, tenderloin* is called *undercut, dessert* is *sweets*', though *dessert* is often loosely used in England for *sweets*. In England, *sauce* is applied chiefly to that which goes with meat and a *pie* is usually of meat; the English *veal-pie, pork-pie, pigeon-pie* are the American *pot-pie*. The American *cracker* is the English *biscuit*. The English say *beetroot* for *beet, porridge* for *oatmeal, iced water* for *ice water*.

At this point, however, we may insert the rider that educated Americans have shown a certain timidity in accepting American usage: great deference has been shown to English usage, especially in the language of culture. Deference is still shown, but, all in all, it would be safe to say that, now, it is only to such English words as have no American equivalent.

In general, the movement has always been away from English:

[1] The English term precedes the American throughout this list.
[2] Now usually just *saloon*, although *saloon car* is also used; *saloon carriage* is obsolete. But English has adopted *pullman*.

yet it is still true, first, that the American vocabulary is in the main the same as the English; secondly, that even where the American language differs from the English, the former is, in the main, readily understandable by English people; thirdly, that specifically American objects, features, ideas are becoming ever more familiar, along with the words denoting them, to the English public. These cautions and demurrers are made, not to depreciate but to give more point to McKnight's statement that 'assertion of the independence of the American language from English authority followed closely the assertion of political independence'. For 'as early as 1778 Benjamin Franklin, when sent as ambassador to France, was instructed to use "the language of the United States". Noah Webster, in 1789, . . . advocated the establishment of a national language. Later in the Preface to his *American Dictionary of the English Language*, published in 1828, he points out the inevitability of divergence in the languages of America and England, since "if the people of one country cannot preserve an identity of ideas, they cannot retain an identity of languages".' Mencken[1] exaggerated when, about 1925, he stated that, ca. 1840–60, 'every day American became almost unintelligible to an Englishman', for it was 'bold and lawless in its vocabulary, careless of grammatical niceties, and further disfigured by a drawling manner of speech'. 'After the Civil War', in the early 1860's, 'there was an increase of national self-consciousness, and efforts were made to police the language', both in the free schools and by professional grammarians. Even Walt Whitman used a surprisingly small proportion of distinctively American words. 'But the spirit of the language, and of the American people no less, was against such reforms . . . They were reduced to vanity by the unconquerable speech habits of the folk . . . The common speech began to run amok. That common speech is to-day almost lawless . . . It seems destined in a few generations to dispose altogether of the few inflections that remain in English. "Me and her woulda went" will never, perhaps, force its way into the grammar-books, but it is used daily, or something like it, by a large part of the people of the United States, and the rest know precisely what it means.' (So does an Englishman.) 'On higher levels the language of the Americans is more decorous, but even there it is a genuinely living speech,[2] taking in loan-words with vast hospitality and incessantly manufacturing neologisms of its own . . . It runs to brilliantly vivid tropes'—turns of expression and figures of speech. 'It is disdainful of grammatical pruderies . . . Exhilarating novel-

[1] The Mencken quotations are from the article on 'Americanism' in *The Encyclopaedia Britannica*.   [2] So, for that matter, is English.

ties . . . come into universal use, and gradually take on literary dignity. They are opposed violently, but they prevail.'

In this matter of comparison, I shall repeat what I wrote in *Slang To-day and Yesterday: A History and a Study*, 1933. 'Standard American is not nearly so correct grammatically as standard English. It is only very formal writers . . . who aim to be correct at all points, and it is only the old-fashioned men of letters and the cultured scholars who consistently endeavour to combine correctness with the graces. There are still, in the United States . . . many authors who write genuinely "literary" English, but they are men that, to a sound education, add both good taste and natural vigour.' The literary American of 'Mr H. L. Mencken, Mr J. Branch Cabell, Mr Christopher Morley, and others . . . differs from the best English only in the use of [*garbage-can*] for *dust-bin*, *suspenders* for *braces*, and so forth; in a rather fresher use of metaphor; in a slightly less logical and somewhat less musical sentence-building; in a certain disregard of the nicety of *shall* and *will*,[1] *can* and *may*, *would* and *should*, *if* and *though*, *each other* and *one another*, and at the same time in a fondness for the subjunctive, often using the present where an English writer would, if employing the [subjunctive] mood at all, prefer the imperfect subjunctive; and in a rather more hospitable attitude towards slang'.

But what will be the result of 'the struggle in American usage between the forces of purism . . . supported by a deference for English usage, and . . . radical forces supported by the recently stimulated spirit of American nationalism? It would be hazardous to make a prediction', says McKnight in 1923; in 1922, Otto Jespersen had written:

There may be periods in which the ordinary restraints on linguistic change make themselves less felt than usual, because the whole community is animated by a strong feeling of independence and wants to break loose from social ties of many kinds, including those of a powerful . . . literary tradition. This probably was the case with North America in the latter half of the eighteenth century, when the new nation wished to manifest its independence of old England and therefore . . . was inclined to throw overboard that respect for linguistic authority which under normal conditions makes for conservatism. If the divergence between American and British English is not greater than it actually is, this is probably due partly to the continual influx of

---

[1] This lack of nicety may be, in part, caused by the Anglo-Irish usage, which is directly opposite to the English usage,—a point exemplified in the anecdote of that Irishman who, having fallen into deep water, cried, 'I will drown and no one shall save me': and nobody did.

immigrants from the old country, and partly to the increased facility of communication between the two countries in recent times which has made mutual linguistic influence possible to an extent formerly undreamt of.

In 1925 or 1926, Mencken noted that 'of late the increase of travel and other inter-communication . . . has tended to halt the differentiation . . . But the American cinema floods England (and the rest of the English-speaking world) with American neologisms'. And in 1930, Ernest Weekley remarked:

At the present time great efforts are being made in the United States to teach correct English to the children of the foreign-born. It is possible that these efforts, combined with recent measures against multitudinous immigration, may have as a result a fairly homogeneous colloquial speech not too remote from educated English. If, as seems more likely, the American temperament, despite its general docility to standardization, persists in its present attitude towards a standardized language, spoken American must eventually become as distinct from English as Yiddish is from classical Hebrew.

—but this last is not a fair comparison, for Yiddish is basically German, not Hebrew, whereas American is basically English, not (say) German. It is, moreover, to be added that the influence of the talking picture and of the wireless (or, in American and much English, *radio*) makes for standardization, precisely as the increase of education makes for standardization; and that a closer political co-operation and a closer social intercourse between the American and the English peoples will bring the languages nearer, the one to the other. Even if the American influence, as a result of that co-operation and that intercourse, should preponderate, the Americanization of English would narrow the at present by no means unleapable gap between the two languages, as also would a preponderating influence in the opposite direction.

Postscript.—Perhaps we ought just to notice that in American English there is an increasing tendency to employ a simplified spelling. The commonest feature of this simplified spelling is the use of *-or* in all words that in English contain, either in the middle or at the end, the syllable *-our*: thus Americans write *honor* and *honorable* for *honour* and *honourable*; since these words derive from Latin (e.g., *honor*, *labor*), the American usage is etymologically justifiable. Also many Americans write *thru* for *through*.

PART TWO

CHAPTER FOUR
HOW WORDS BEGIN[1]

THE ultimate origin of human speech is a fascinating subject. There are those who assert that speech was given to us by God: yet all the evidence tends to show that language is not God's gift to man, but man's offering to God.

So general a subject of discussion has this origin of speech been, that when, in 1866, La Société de Linguistique was formed, it expressly stated that the Society debarred papers, debates, letters on the matter; and in 1873 Whitney, the great American philologist, feelingly wrote:

> No theme in linguistic science is more often and more voluminously treated than this, and by scholars of every grade and tendency; nor any ... with less profitable result in proportion to the labour expended; the greater part of what is said and written on it is mere windy talk, the assertion of ... views which commend themselves to no mind save the one that produces them, and which are apt to be offered with a confidence, and defended with a tenacity, that are in inverse ratio to their acceptableness. This has given the whole question a bad repute among sober-minded philologists;

but the present century takes a more liberal view, for, as Otto Jespersen, entirely human though a philologist, has said, 'linguistic science cannot refrain for ever from asking about the whence ... of linguistic evolution'. At the very outset we must 'realize that man is not the only animal that has a "language", though at present we know very little about the real nature and expressiveness of the language of birds and mammals or of the signalling system of ants, etc. The speech of some animals may be more like our language than most people are willing to admit.'

Human languages, however much they differ in various aspects,

---

[1] All unacknowledged quotations in this chapter are from Jespersen's *Language: its Nature, Development and Origin*, 1922. Most of this chapter is virtually an abridgement of Jespersen. If I have simplified the arguments here and there, it is more for my own sake than for the sake of beginners, who rightly despise those who write down to them: but some terms in philology are very technical, and so, I think, no apology is necessary for my using less technical words in their stead.

are of the same character in essentials. It is equally certain that there are many circumstances which have greatly helped mankind in forming and developing language. 'First of all, man has an upright gait; this gives him two limbs more than a dog has, for instance: he can carry things and yet jabber on; he is not reduced to defending himself by biting, but can use his mouth for other purposes. Feeding . . . takes less time in his case than in that of the cow, who has little time for anything else than chewing and a *moo* now and then.' In marriage, man and wife remain together, 'and thus sociability is promoted; the helplessness of babies works in the same direction through necessitating a more continuous family life, in which there is also time enough for all kinds of sports, including play with the vocal organs. Thus conditions have been generally favourable for the development of singing and talking, but the problem is, *how could sounds and ideas come to be connected as they are in language?*'[1]

Let us glance at the theories of philologists before Jespersen, for those theories will help us to see how very practical and reasonable and natural his theory is in comparison with theirs: how sane and acceptable it is of itself.

The *bow-wow* theory is that primitive words imitated sounds, especially those made by animals: 'man copied the barking of dogs and thereby obtained a natural word with the meaning of "dog" or "bark"'; man, however, would copy 'not only the cries of inferior animals, but also those of his fellow-men'. We see, therefore, that sounds which, when produced by one creature, had no meaning yet were characteristic of that creature, 'could by man be used to designate the creature itself' (or the sound itself). 'In this way an originally unmeaning sound could in the mouth of an imitator and in the mind of someone hearing that imitation acquire a real meaning.' This supposition would account for echoic words, some of which have given rise to many derivatives: but it falls short of being adequate as an explanation of human speech.

A kindred theory is the *pooh-pooh* theory, named also the interjectional. According to this, language descends from unthinking exclamations called forth by pain, surprise, joy, grief, dread. To this theory it may be objected that the usual exclamations (or ejaculations or interjections) are abrupt expressions indicating sudden feelings, whether sensations or emotions: they are, therefore, widely set apart from the other words of a language. Moreover, it can fairly be stated that interjections, being used only when one cannot—or at best, will not—speak, are the opposite

[1] The italics are mine.

of language proper, language as a means of communication. On the other hand, many interjections have become so usual that one employs them deliberately.

Closely related is the *ding-dong*, more learnedly the nativistic theory, according to which there is an inner harmony or agreement between sound and sense: 'There is a law which runs through nearly the whole of nature, that everything that is struck rings. Each substance has its peculiar ring': such is the theory, which is much too far-fetched to be true. Even its inventor soon abandoned it.

Not quite so fantastic is the *yo-he-ho* (or *yo-ho*) theory. 'Under any strong muscular effort it is a relief to the system to let breath come out strongly and repeatedly, and by that process to let the vocal chords vibrate in different ways; when primitive acts were performed in common, they would, therefore, naturally be accompanied with some sounds which would come to be associated with the idea of the act performed and stand as a name for it; the first words would accordingly mean something like "heave" or "haul".'

The trouble with these theories is that they explain only small parts of language: they hardly touch the core, they barely concern the main body of language. But there are three fields of investigation by which one might sanely expect to arrive at an explanation:

1. The language of children.
2. The language of primitive races.
3. The history of language.[1]

It has occurred to many philologists that mankind may have acquired the faculty (or power) of speech in the same way as a child learns to speak. That was not a very bright thought: mankind started from scratch, mankind had no words and no teacher: a child learns an already existing language, hears words all around him, has several teachers. But in the baby talk of a child before it speaks an accepted language, there is a parallel to the talk of mankind before it had an accepted language: 'here, in the child's first purposeless murmuring, crowing and babbling, we have real nature-sounds; here we may expect to find some clue to the infancy of the language of the race. And, again, we must not neglect the way children have of creating new words never heard before, and often of attaching' a meaning to originally meaningless conglomerations (or clusters) of syllables.

Equal caution must be observed with the living languages of savages, for even a backward race has centuries of speech behind

[1] Jespersen's classification.

it and has a language that is much less primitive than its racial or tribal customs; it can, however, be admitted that the most backward languages represent a stage that is nearer to primitive speech than is, say, English, French, German, Chinese.

The third and most profitable field of investigation is the history of language. Instead of arguing from the unknown to the known, as the *bow-wow*, *pooh-pooh*, *ding-dong*, and *yo-ho* theorists did, let us, with Otto Jespersen, the pioneer and the most consistent propounder of the inductive[1] system, 'trace our modern twentieth-century languages as far back in time as history and our materials will allow us. . . . If the change witnessed in the evolution of modern speech out of older forms of speech is . . . projected back into the childhood of mankind, and if by this process we arrive finally at uttered sounds of such a description that they can no longer be called a real language, but something antecedent to language—why, then the problem will have been solved; for transformation'—a change of form, especially when the change is gradual—'is something we can understand, [whereas] a creation out of nothing can never be comprehended by human understanding.'

It is not unreasonable to start with phonetics—the study of sounds. Looking back over the history of all those languages of which we have satisfactory records, we notice a very general, clearly discernible tendency for pronunciation to become easier, so as to lessen the actual physical effort of speech;[2] only those sounds, and only those combinations of sounds, are retained which can be pronounced with ease. The sound-system of the proto-Aryans, i.e. the sound-system of that language which is the original of the whole great Aryan (or Indo-European) family of languages, was much more difficult, intricate, complicated than that of any of the present-day descendants of proto-Aryan: roughly midway stands Primary Prakrit, of which the sound-system, though less intricate and difficult than that of proto-Aryan, is rather more intricate and difficult than that of, say, Bengali. In most languages of to-day, 'only such sounds are used as are produced by expiration' (a breathing out), the in-breathed sounds and clicks[3] being reserved for disconnected speech

---

[1] Induction is the inferring a general law (or principle or trend) from a number of particular instances; deduction, the inferring particular facts from a general law. The former is the method of science, the latter that of philosophy—a workable distinction, to which there are, however, numerous exceptions.

[2] The process is usually unconscious or, at best, subconscious.

[3] We employ a click when, in impatience, we utter the sounds that are very imperfectly spelt *tut!* or *tcha!*

(exclamations and sounds even less precisely expressive); 'in some very primitive South African languages, on the other hand, clicks are found as integral parts of words; and . . . in former stages of these languages they were in more extensive use than now. We may perhaps draw the conclusion that primitive languages in general were rich in all kinds of difficult sounds.'

In certain languages we note the gradual weakening and the final disappearance of what we call either tone-accent or pitch-accent, i.e. the raising and lowering of the voice. Inseparably connected with the tone or pitch of the voice is that pause or interval which inevitably follows a marked raising or lowering of the voice.[1] 'In the works of old Indian, Greek and Latin grammarians we have express statements to the effect that pitch accent played a prominent part in those languages, and that the intervals used must have been comparatively greater than is usual in our modern languages. In modern Greek and in the Romanic languages' (the descendants from Latin), the tone element has been obscured, and now stress—i.e. emphasis—'is heard on the syllable where the ancients noted only a high or a low tone'. Modern research has shown that tone- (or pitch-) accents are frequent in African languages. We are probably justified in believing that tone or pitch had an important role in many primitive languages.

Now for sentence melody, the modulation of words in a phrase or a sentence. 'The sounds of common conversation', Herbert Spencer once remarked, 'have but little resonance; those of strong feeling have much more.' Now, as civilization has advanced, passion—or rather, the expression of passion (strong emotion)—is moderated. We therefore conclude that primitive or uncivilized speech was more agitated, more widely and richly modulated than ours—more like song. This conclusion is in agreement with what we know of many savage languages of to-day. It seems, then, that, many centuries ago, song and speech were much the same thing: that speech was virtually song.

The whole history of language shows, too, that there has been a general tendency to shorten words. The ancient Indo-European languages (e.g., Zend and Sanskrit) have many very long words; the further back in time we go, the greater the number of very long words do we find. To put it learnedly: 'language proceeds from original polysyllabism'—the use of long words—'towards monosyllabism', the use of short, especially of one-syllabled, words. It is therefore logical, and natural, to argue that, in pre-

---

[1] Try this for yourselves. In fact, test for yourselves all the statements made about sound: such practical tests are infinitely more enlightening than my statements; and in any case this book is not a treatise on phonetics.

historic times, language consisted, for the most part, of very long words indeed.

If, then, we summarize the four preceding paragraphs we are entitled to think of primitive language as consisting, in the main, of many-syllabled words; as having numerous difficult sounds; and as being sung or, more accurately, chanted rather than, in the modern sense, spoken.

From phonetics we pass to grammar. 'Ancient languages have more forms'—shapes of words—'than modern ones; forms originally kept distinct are in course of time confused, either[1] phonetically[1] or[1] analogically,[1] alike in substantives' (nouns), 'adjectives and verbs.'

A very important feature of the structure of languages at an early stage is that every form of a word (especially of a noun and, even more, of a verb) has certain modifications; now these modifications are, at later stages and especially at the stage we have now reached, expressed separately—if indeed, they *are* expressed—by means of auxiliary verbs and/or prepositions. Take the Latin *cantavisset*, which, in one indissoluble whole, contains six quite distinct ideas: primarily, the idea of singing; 2, that point or period in time which we call pluperfect; 3, that modification of the verbal idea which we call subjunctive (mood); 4, the active as opposed to the passive (voice); 5, the third person; and 6, the singular (number). 'The tendency of later stages is towards expressing such modifications analytically'; the Italians express Latin *si cantavisset*, 'if he had sung', in the form *se avesse cantato*; the French by *s'il eût chanté*. But there are many gradations of synthesis (oneness, singleness; etymologically, 'a putting together') and analysis (manyness, a splitting-up): in no language is either synthesis or analysis carried out consistently. 'Latin is synthetic in comparison with French, French analytic in comparison with Latin; but if we were able to see the direct ancestor of Latin . . . , we should no doubt find a language so synthetic that in comparison with it Cicero's would have to be termed . . . analytic.'

Moreover, we must not, from the word 'synthesis', infer that synthetic forms (as for instance, the Latin *cantavisset*) consist of originally separate and independent elements welded together and, thence, presuppose an earlier stage of analysis. For 'synthetic' a better term would be 'entangled' or 'complicated': for 'what in

---

[1] That is, either in sounds (pronunciation) or by analogy. *Analogy* is the philological term for 'the similarity of formative or constructive processes. *Form-associations* is the term now used where the *forms* only of words are considered' (*The Shorter Oxford Dictionary*).

the later stages of languages is analysed or dissolved, in the earlier stages was unanalysable or indissoluble'.

Yet many philologists assert that the ancient forms (e.g., *cantavisset*) are quite as dissoluble as the modern forms (e.g., Italian *avrebbe potuto cantare* or *se avesse cantato* and English *he might have sung* or *if he had sung*); that *cantavisset* might actually have been written *cant-av-isset*; that French *j'don* (*je donne*) and English *i-giv* (*I give*) correspond exactly to Greek *dido-mi* (properly or actually *didomi*). But it is doubtful whether *cantavisset* and *didomi* contain pronouns. Likewise French *il a aimé* (he has loved) cannot be one word (*ilaaimé*) because the elements (1, *il*; 2, *a*; 3, *aimé*) are often separated, as in *il n'a pas aimé* (he has not loved) or *il nous a toujours aimés* (he has always loved us). Similarly *I never give*, *you always give*. The crucial point lies in this: the French and English combinations (e.g., *il aime*, *he loves*) are two or (as in *il a aimé*, *he has loved*) three words because the elements are often separated or, as in *aime-t-il?* or *loves he?*, reversed; Latin *amat* (he loves), *amavit* (he has loved), *amavisset* (he might have loved) are each of them only one word because they can never be divided: they are as indissoluble, as inseparable as English *loves*; but *heloves* can be separated into *he loves* or reversed to *loveshe?*, preferably *loves he?* Some philologists assert that in French combinations like *il te le disait* (he was saying—or, used to say—that to you), the words are really welded together in a polysynthetic verbal form, i.e. a verbal form in which the words constitute a synthesis, an indivisible: that such 'incorporations' are far from genuine is seen from the fact that, in the interrogative, the phrase is *te le disait-il?* 'Nor can it be said that such English forms as *he's* = *he is* (or *he has*), *I'd* = *I had* (or *I would*), *he'll* = *he will*, show a tendency towards "entangling" [synthesis], for however closely together these forms are generally pronounced, each of them must be said to consist of two words': witness *Is he ill?*, *I never had*. Compare *I write* with *I do write* and *I don't write*, *he writes* with *he doesn't write*, *I wrote* with *I did write* and *I didn't write*.

In short, 'the movement is towards flexionless[1] languages (such as Chinese, or to a certain extent [French or] Modern English) with freely combinable elements; the starting-point was flexional

---

[1] Uninflected, unchanging. For instance, French *homme* (except for plural *hommes*) remains uninflected, unchanged; English *man* has several flexions (or inflections): *man's, men, men's*; but Latin *homo* has seven flexions: *hominem, hominis, homini, homine, homines, hominum, hominibus*. The term 'flexions' may be applied also to the changes in verb forms, as, e.g., in *amo, amas, amat*, I love, thou lovest, he loves; *amaveram, amaveras, amaverat*, I had—thou hadst—he had loved.

[or indissoluble] languages (such as Latin and Greek); at a still earlier stage we must suppose a language in which a verbal form might indicate not only six things, like *cantavisset*, but a still larger number, in which verbs were perhaps modified according to the gender (or sex) of the subject, as they are in Semitic languages, or according to the object as in some Amerindian languages, or according to whether a man, a woman, or a person commanding respect is spoken to, as in Basque. But that amounts to the same thing as saying that the border-line between word and sentence was not so clearly defined as in more recent times; *cantavisset* is really nothing but a ' clause-word, as *cantaverat* is nothing but a 'sentence-word, and the same holds good to a still greater extent of the sound-conglomerations of Eskimo and some other North American languages. Primitive linguistic units [or words] must have been much more complicated in point of meaning, as well as much longer in point of sound, than with those with which we are most familiar.'

The early languages contain far more irregularities, exceptions, and those unexpectednesses which we term anomalies than are to be found in modern languages. Admittedly, irregular formations do spring up and displace regular ones; but these are few in comparison with the discards. Language tends more and more to make one word fit, in every circumstance, the thing it designates. The variations in *I, me, we, us—he, him, they, them—father, mother—bull, cow—good, better, best—am, is, was, been*—these are characteristic of an older stage in language: the present or modern stage is represented in such groups as *male parent, female parent—he-bear* and *she-bear—happy, happier, happiest—love, loves, loved*. Contrast also the French *aller, je vais, j'irai* with *aimer, j'aime, j'aimerai*. In the older, more irregular forms (and don't forget that *am, is, was, been* and *aller, vais, irai* and their like are survivals of old forms), you see a trait of primitive psychology—a feature or characteristic of the thinking and feeling prevalent among our remote ancestors. These our ancestors were unable to see, and hence to express, what was common to these ideas or what was the idea common to these forms; they did not perceive that the ideas of present, past, and future (as in Greek *horao, eidon, opsomai*: respectively I see, I saw, I shall see) are subsidiary to the idea of seeing. Their minds did not work systematically; in devising words, these our ancestors separated things and actions that are very closely connected and related. 'Much of their grammar', as Jespersen has appositely noticed, 'was . . . of a lexical character': in their grammar, things were invested with a separateness more proper to the arrangement of words in a dictionary than to a logical classification of ideas.

The foregoing conclusions are borne out by a study of the languages of savages and primitive races of to-day. In most of these languages, the grammar has many intricacies and anomalies. Eskimo and many Amerindian languages have a notoriously complex structure. The Andamese have virtually no culture, yet the language is highly complicated; African languages have a bewildering number of plural formations. Basque, which is supposed to have retained many primeval traits, is exceedingly difficult, especially in its verbs. 'At Béarn they have the story that the good God, wishing to punish the devil for the temptation of Eve, sent him to the Pays Basque with the command that he should remain there till he had mastered the language. At the end of seven years God relented, finding the punishment too severe, and called the devil to him. The devil had no sooner crossed the bridge of Castelondo than he found he had forgotten all that he had so hardly learned.'

All the foregoing portion of this chapter leads inevitably to one conclusion, enunciated thus by Jespersen:

The evolution of language shows a progressive tendency from inseparable irregular conglomerations to freely and regularly combinable short elements. Less felicitously but perhaps more simply expressed, this 'law' runs thus:

Language has progressed from a stage of irregularly formed words of many syllables and many flexions to the present stage of regularly formed and very easily grouped words of few syllables and either no or extremely few flexions.

In vocabulary there is a development similar to that which has taken place in grammar. 'The more advanced a language is, the more developed is its power of expressing abstract or general ideas. Everywhere language has first attained to' terms 'for the concrete and special. In accounts of the languages of barbarous races we constantly come across such' statements 'as these: ". . . For each variety of gum-tree and wattle-tree, etc., [the aborigines of Tasmania] had a name; but they had no equivalent for . . . 'a tree' "; "The Mohicans have words for cutting various objects, but none to convey *cutting* simply"; "The Zulus have no word for 'cow', but words for 'red cow', 'white cow', etc."; in Central Brazil, "each parrot has its special name, and the general idea 'parrot' is totally unknown, as well as the general idea 'palm'. But [the natives] know precisely the qualities of each subspecies of parrot and palm, and attach themselves so much to these numerous particular notions that they take no interest in the common characteristics. They are choked in the abundance of the material and cannot manage it economically. They have only small coin, but in that they must be said to be excessively rich rather than poor." ... In old Gothonic poetry we find an astonishing abundance of words translated in our dictionaries by "sea", "battle", "sword", "hero", and the like: these may certainly be considered as relics of an earlier state of things, in which each of these words had its separate shade of meaning, which was subsequently lost. The nomenclature'—naming, or name-system—'of a remote past was undoubtedly constructed upon similar principles to those which are still preserved in a word-group like *horse, mare, stallion, foal, colt,* [*filly,*] instead of [horse,] she-horse, he-horse, young horse, etc.' Compare the distinctions in 'a *flock* of sheep, a *pack* of wolves, a *herd* of cattle, a *bevy* of larks, a *covey* of partridges' (or of partridge), 'a *shoal* of fish'.

Then there was another powerful reason for the rich vocabulary of primitive and comparatively primitive man: that linguistic superstition which 'made him avoid the use of certain words under certain circumstances—during war, when out fishing, during the time of great' religious 'festivals, etc.—because he feared the anger of the gods or demons if he did not religiously observe the rules of the linguistic tabu' or law regulating the use of words.

There is, too, a close and interesting relationship between poetry and primitive words. Although the development of languages has, on the whole, been for the good, yet in one respect the result is less happy: our modern words, apt in abstraction and in precision, are rather colourless; the old words appealed instantly to the senses, for they were pictorial, eloquent and, in themselves, picturesque. These graphic, concrete words had often to be used figuratively; in especial, metaphorically. The original metaphors were fresh and vivid. Primitive man was very often forced to speak figuratively: to speak in the language of poetry. 'Just as in the literature transmitted to us poetry is found in every country to precede prose, so poetic language is on the whole older than prosaic language;[1] lyrics and cult songs come before science, and Oehlenschlager is right when he sings:

> Thus nature drove us; warbling rose
> Man's voice in verse before he spoke in prose.'

Now we can sum up more clearly. By our delving into the past

[1] By 'prosaic language', Jespersen meant, not 'prosy language' but the 'language of prose'.

we have arrived at a speech whose units (words) contained a modicum of thought and much sound (in many syllables). 'No period has seen less taciturn people than the first framers of speech; primitive speakers were not reticent and reserved beings, but youthful men and women babbling merrily on, without being so very particular about the meaning of each word. They did not narrowly weigh every syllable—what were a couple of syllables more or less to them? They chattered away for the mere pleasure of chattering.... Language originated as play, and the organs of speech were first trained in this singing sport of idle hours.'

Primitive speech was concerned but little with ideas; the earliest speech, probably not at all. It was instincts and emotions which clamoured for expression. The emotions most productive of speech were not hunger and the struggle for existence, these evoking mere exclamations and interjections, grunts and howls that are much the same now as they were thousands of years ago. Language, whether expressive of emotion, or later and in due, natural course, indicative of a desire to communicate that emotion, arose in the poetic, not the prosaic side of life; not in gloom and seriousness, but in play and hilarity.[1] Of the emotions causing outbursts of music, bursts of song, the chief is love: not only the love of lad for lass, man for woman, but the love of parents for children, and of children for their brothers and sisters. Any strong emotion—especially a pleasurable excitement—might easily evoke song; singing flows from excess of energy, an excess worked off in liveliness, above all in the vivacity of song; 'out of the full heart the mouth sings!' Savage races sing to express excitement, and excitement is far from rare; most of these songs are composed on the spot and for the occasion. Primitive races did the same.

'Formerly in our Western Europe, people sang much more than they do now. The Swedish peasant Jonas Stolt (about 1820) writes: "I have known a time when young people were singing from morning till eve", whether at work or at play; "this is all over long ago: nowadays there is silence everywhere." ... The first things that were expressed in song were, to be sure, neither deep nor wise; how could you expect it? Note the frequency with which we are told that the songs of savages consist of or contain totally meaningless syllables. ... Even with us the thoughts associated with singing are neither very clear nor very abstruse;[2] like humming or whistling, singing is often nothing more than an almost automatic outcome of a mood.'

But however frivolous and trivial the words, the very use of those words rendered speech increasingly serviceable and pliable

---

[1] This does not mean that Jespersen believed in ' a golden age' of idyllic happiness.   [2] Difficult to understand; profound.

and versatile—increasingly suitable to the expression of all that touched the heart and mind and spirit of mankind.

When we speak of singing, however, we must remember that the singing of primitive man was, like the singing of birds and the crooning of babies, 'exclamative, not communicative': that is, it expressed emotion, did not seek to make other human beings *understand* the singing, though doubtless it did soon—comparatively soon—seek that end. It is extremely probable that our very remote ancestors had not the least notion that it was possible to communicate ideas or even feelings to someone else, although they may soon have hoped to communicate feelings. It did not occur to them that, in singing or chanting, they were gradually preparing a language whereby they might convey delicate shades of thought; similarly, they did not perceive that their crude pictures would grow into an art. Writing and drawing began by being one and the same thing, and 'in primitive picture-writing, each sign meant a whole sentence or even more—the image of a situation' (static) 'or of an incident' (dynamic) 'being given as a whole; this developed into an ideographic writing[1] of each word by itself; this system was succeeded by syllabic methods, which had in their turn to give place to alphabetic writing, in which each letter stands for, or is meant to stand for, one sound.' The advance is caused by a progressive analysis of language, ever smaller units of speech being 'pictured' or represented by single signs; so, too, though not so obviously, the history of language shows an increasing tendency to analyse into ever smaller units what, in the earlier stages, had been taken as an unanalysable or indissoluble or inseparable whole.

'One point must be constantly kept in mind' as being of the utmost importance. 'Although we now regard the communication' or sharing 'of thought as the main object of speaking, there is no reason for thinking that this has always been the case; it is perfectly possible that speech has developed from something which had no other purpose than that of exercising the muscles of the mouth and throat and of amusing oneself and others by the production of pleasant or possibly only strange sounds. The motives for uttering sounds may have changed entirely in the course of centuries without the speakers being at any point conscious of this change within them.'

---

[1] Writing by ideographs; an ideograph being a character (whence, ultimately, an alphabetic letter) or a figure (elementary picture) expressing and symbolizing the *idea* of a thing, without expressing the name of the thing; as in the Chinese characters, for example. A *graph* is something drawn, hence something written.

Language (in its modern sense) is approached when our ancestors uttered sounds in order to tell others of something. But *how* did sense become connected with sound? How did meaningless sounds, often in a sequence that formed a jingle, come to be the tool or instrument of thought?

In echoic words like *bow-wow* and in interjections like *pooh-pooh*, the association was both immediate and easy: such words were at once used, and understood, as the signs for something—that is, for the corresponding idea. But echoic words comprise only a small part of language. In virtually all language, the association of sound with sense and of sense with sound must have been reached by many different and devious or indirect ways; but this is exactly what we should expect, for, even in the historical period, it is only by devious and roundabout ways that many words, many devices of syntax (the arranging of words into sentences, hence the study of that arrangement), have got their present meanings or, indeed, have got *any* meaning where, previously, they had no meaning. Language, which is complicated, has—like many of the other human inventions—come about in a way far from simple or direct: 'mankind has not moved in a straight line towards a definitely perceived goal, but has muddled along from moment to moment and has thereby now and then stumbled on some happy expedient which has then been retained in accordance with the principle of the survival of the fittest'.

We can nevertheless make an attempt to solve the problem of the association of sound with meaning. The first words were doubtless concrete and objective and specific in the highest possible degree. Now, the most concrete and specific (or specialized) words are proper names—'proper names of the good old kind, borne by and denoting' an individual—one person and one person only. 'In the songs of a particular individual there would be a constant recurrence of a particular series' or sequence 'of sounds sung with a particular cadence . . . Suppose, then, that "in the spring time, the only pretty ring time" [Shakespeare] a lover was in the habit of addressing his lass "with a hey, and a ho, and a hey nonino". His comrades and rivals would not fail to remark this, and would occasionally banter him by imitating and repeating his "hey-and-a-ho-and-a-hey-nonino". But when once this had been recognized as what Wagner would term a person's "leitmotiv" '—or theme associated with him, as it were his musical or chanting brand or catch-phrase—'it would be no far cry from imitating it to using the "hey-and-a-ho-and-a-hey-nonino" as a sort of nickname for the man concerned; it might be employed, for instance, to signal his arrival. And when once proper names had been bestowed, common names or nouns would not be slow in following; we see the transition from one to the other class in constant operation . . . , as when we say of one man that he is a . . . "Rockefeller", and of another that he is "no Bismarck" . . . From the proper name of *Caesar* we have both the Russian *tsar* and the German *kaiser*, and from *Karol* (Charlemagne) Russian *korol'* "king" . . . and Magyar *király*. . . . Compare also the history of the words *bluchers*, . . . *pantaloon* [from *San*, i.e., Şaint, *Pantaleone*, a favourite saint of the Venetians], *hansom* [from an English architect's surname], *boycott*, . . . to name only a few of the best-known examples.'

Thence we pass easily to the origin of sentences. We have already seen that, the further we went back in the history of the known languages, the more the sentence was an indissoluble, inseparable whole, in which those elements which we think of as separate words were not yet separated. It is neither wild nor very difficult to imagine, as the origin of our modern sentence, something that can be *translated* into our present languages by a sentence but was not articulated—broken up into distinct and separate syllables—in the same way as we articulate or separate the words of a modern sentence. We can translate 'the dental click' (*tut!*) as 'That is a great pity', but *tut!* is not in other respects a sentence; it has, for instance, no arrangement, however incomplete, of words. Or take a telegraphic code: if *prab* means 'please reserve a bedroom' or *cof* means 'coming on Friday', we have, in *prab* and *cof*, unanalysable, indissoluble, inseparable wholes, which, though capable of being turned into complete sentences, are not in every way similar to those sentences.

Although not with quite the same degree or kind of meaning as those two code words possess, speech units of this character have an origin and a development easily imaginable if we grant that there was 'a primitive period of meaningless singing'. Thus, if a group of people have witnessed an incident and accompanied it with an impromptu refrain or song, the two ideas (song and incident) are connected, the one with the other; later, that song or even that refrain will tend to evoke, in the minds of those who were present, the picture-idea of the incident and its setting. Let us suppose that some formidable enemy has been defeated and slain: the victors will dance round the corpse and strike up a joyful, exultant chant of triumph and relief, with a refrain of (say) *tarara-boom-de-ay!* This refrain will easily become a kind of name for that fight and victory and might mean 'The dangerous man from beyond the mountains is slain' or 'We have slain the terrible foe from beyond the mountain' or, later, 'Do you remember when we slew that horrible fellow from beyond the mountain?' The refrain, which to us is a sentence but was by the savages regarded as an indissoluble expression (in fact as a speech-unit), will then be applied, as a proper name, to the slayer or, more significantly, be transferred to similar incidents and situations ('There is another warrior of the same tribe: let us slay him as we did that other warrior from beyond the hill'); if there is a different, but not utterly dissimilar, chant applied as a proper name to the victim then the combination of this with the chant-name of the victor—or the singing of the one chant immediately after the other —would lead to several possible meanings, for such a combination or such a blending might end in certain, probably the most emphatic, parts of these melodic phrases, these extremely expressive chants, being disentangled and becoming something distantly resembling our modern words; when those parts have become separate, therefore always separable, wholes or units and have fairly definite meanings attached to them (though nothing may have been said about the matter), then the remaining or at least some of the remaining parts of these chants may be separated and given an at first vague meaning. From even vague meanings it is a long but inevitable journey to real language. Jespersen has summarized the possible genesis thus: There are 'ways by which primitive "lieder ohne worte" [songs without words] may have become, first, indissoluble rigmaroles, with something like a dim meaning attached to them, and then gradually combinations of word-like smaller units, more and more capable of being analysed and combined with others of the same kind'. He gives a very effective example: 'If one of our forebears on some occasion accidentally produced a sequence of sounds, and if the people around him were seen (or heard) to respond appreciatively, he would tend to settle on the same string of sounds and repeat it on similar occasions, and in this way it would gradually become "conventionalized" [i.e. accepted and acceptable] as a symbol for what was then foremost in his and their minds.' And a no less effective and illuminating generalization: 'As in agriculture primitive man reaped before he sowed, so also in his vocal outbursts he first reaped understanding, and then discovered that by intentionally sowing the same seed he was able to call forth the same result. And as with corn, he would slowly and gradually, by weeding out (i.e. by not using) what was less useful to him, improve the quality, till finally he had come into possession of the marvellous, though far from perfect, instrument which we now call our language.'

. . . . . .

In conclusion we cannot do better than quote Jespersen's concluding words: 'Language . . . began with half-musical unanalysed expressions for individual beings and solitary events. Languages composed of, and evolved from such words and quasi-sentences are clumsy and insufficient instruments of thought, being intricate, capricious and difficult', though we must remember that, to us finite and, as yet, far from fully developed human beings (gods potentially, not actually), many thoughts are intricate and difficult.

But from the beginning the tendency has been one of progress, slow and fitful progress, but still progress towards greater and greater clearness, regularity and ease, and pliancy. No one language has arrived at perfection; an ideal language[1] would always express the same thing by the same, and similar things by similar means; any irregularity or ambiguity would be banished; sound and sense would be in perfect harmony; any number of delicate shades of meaning could be expressed with equal ease . . . : the human spirit would have found a garment combining freedom and gracefulness, fitting it closely yet allowing full play to any movement.

* * * * *

To add anything may be an impertinence, yet it is human to 'gild refinèd gold'. There can be very little doubt that Jespersen's explanation of the origin of speech is the correct explanation.

Echoic and ejaculatory words present no difficulties: imitation is inherent in man and monkey; ejaculations are common to all living things. All non-echoic, non-ejaculatory (or non-exclamatory) words do present problems. But we can immediately dismiss derivative words—words more or less obviously drawn from or built on others. It is only the non-echoic and non-exclamatory among the basic words which present a difficult problem: but that these arose from the association of a sound (or, more usually, of a number of sounds conglomerated into one speech-unit) with an object or situation, incident or action, we can hardly doubt. Originally these associations were accidental, but some of these accidentals were frequently repeated and thus became regular or

---

[1] Compare the following statement made by Bertrand Russell in his Introduction to the English edition of Ludwig Wittgenstein's *Tractatus Logico-Philosophicus*, 1922: 'A logically perfect language has rules of syntax which prevent nonsense, and has single symbols'—for all practical purposes, words—'which always have a definite and unique meaning. . . . Not that any language is logically perfect, or that we believe ourselves capable, here and now, of constructing a logically perfect language, but that the whole function of language is to have meaning, and it only fulfils this function as it approaches to the ideal language which we postulate.'

habitual; the regular or habitual became the rule—became conventional.

We see, then, that the 'Why is a dog called a *dog*?', 'a horse a *horse*?', 'a table a *table*?' questions of the uninitiate are, ultimately, unanswerable, for we cannot, except with echo-words and ejaculations, say why a certain speech-unit (one syllable or many; potential word or potential phrase or virtual sentence) was uttered in respect of some nameless object, action, incident, situation, condition that, as a result of this utterance, if it was repeated, finally arrived at the status of having a designation—an indicator —a name.

But we can go some of the way. In English, a table is called a *table* because the French word for the same object is *table*; the French comes direct from Latin *tabula*; the Latin may be traced to an Aryan original: but the proto-Aryan form (the earliest possible form) was caused by some accidental circumstance. *Dog*, on the other hand, was in Old English *docga*; *docga* does not come from any European language, however early, nor do we know its Aryan original. *Horse* is in Old English *hors*, which is traceable to the Gothonic stock. But nobody knows why the earliest possible forms of *dog* and *horse* were whatever they were. Nevertheless, even though we do not know, presumably never shall know precisely why any primitive name was given, yet we at least have a tolerably good idea of the psychology of names and the origin of language.

Postscript.—An extremely interesting—though rather advanced —book on language in general is Karl Vossler's *The Spirit of Language in Civilization* (English translation, 1932). Besides being interesting, it is valuable for its reinforcement of Jespersen's contention that, in linguistics, there is no generalized 'logical syntax' (see Rudolf Carnap's implications in *The Logical Syntax of Language*, 1937), no 'natural grammar'[1] (as John Wilkins upheld so long ago as 1668), and no 'general language nature ... an illusion arising from the abstractions of reason'; for, 'apart from the individual language usages that are continually being modified in space and time, there is no general norm or "nature of language", except in the minds and textbooks of philological enthusiasts' (Vossler). This particular linguistic will of the wisp, this *ignis fatuus* of world words and world grammar has, since the War of 1914–18, been pursued mostly by 'the Vienna Circle' and its disciples, i.e. by the Logical Positivists; compare the footnote on p. 136.

[1] Or 'universal grammar', as certain 19th–20th Century grammarians have called it.

CHAPTER FIVE

WHY WORDS GET NEW MEANINGS AND WHY LANGUAGES CHANGE

To keep the horse before the cart, we had better consider the second question first: by doing this, we make it easier to understand why it is that words do take on new meanings.

I. WHY LANGUAGES CHANGE

How and why do languages change? What forces lead, in the long course of time, to such great differences as we find between (say) Sanskrit and Latin or, much later, between Latin and French? So far back as 1821, a Dane, J. H. Bredsdorff, who examined linguistic changes in the light, and explained them in terms, of human activity and psychology, enumerated the following causes: 1, Mishearing and misunderstanding; 2, defective memory; 3, imperfect speech-organs; 4, laziness; 5, tendency towards and influence of analogy and real or fancied similarity; 6, the desire to be distinct in utterance; 7, the need of expressing fresh ideas. He recognized that there are certain changes—e.g., the Gothonic sound-shift (treated in the next two or three paragraphs)—that cannot be explained in any of these seven ways; and he emphasized the various manners in which foreign nations and foreign tongues may influence a language.[1]

Bredsdorff's seven explanations are so basic that they do not need elaboration, though they are touched on incidentally in the course of this chapter; and should be committed to memory as the Seven Pillars of Wisdom in the matter of linguistic change; and the Gothonic sound-shift represents, not a change within any one language (or at least within any one language known to us), but a change taking place in transition from one known language to another. Still, we must glance at both the consonant-shift and the stress-shift.

The consonant-shift is frequently, in English books, called Grimm's Law, though the merit of the discovery belongs to the Danish philologist, Rasmus Rask (d. 1832). The consonant-shift,

[1] Bredsdorff is cited by Jespersen, to whom I owe much in this chapter.

which must have taken centuries, is most easily seen in operation between Latin and English. A *p* was changed to *f*, as in L. *pater* compared with the Old Gothonic *fader* and the English *father*; *t* was changed to *th*, as in English *three* compared with L. *tres*; and *k* (= hard *c*) was changed to *h*, as in *horn* compared with L. *cornu*.[1] And as any *b* (and *bh*), *d* (and *dh*), or *g* (and *gh*) in Greek or Latin (and/or in still older languages of the Aryan family) were similarly shifted, the difference between most Greek or Latin words on the one hand, and the corresponding Gothonic words (in, e.g., German or English) on the other is so great that the relationship—if one doesn't know this consonant-shift—is almost unrecognizable.

The stress-shift, known as Verner's law, is held by many philologists to have affected the general character of the Teutonic (or Germanic or, better, Gothonic) languages as much as, if not more than, the consonant-shift did. This shifting of the position of the stress or accent took place rather later than the consonant-shift. 'Where previously the stress was sometimes on the first syllable of a word, sometimes on the second, or on the third, etc., without any seeming reason . . ., a complete revolution simplified matters . . . : nearly all words [became] stressed on the first syllable; the chief exceptions [being] where the word was a verb beginning with one out of a definite number of prefixes, such as those [which] we have in modern English, *beget, forget, overthrow, abide*'.[2] The change may have been effected by a purely mechanical process, but more probably it was effected by a psychological process, 'by which the root syllable became stressed because it was the most important part of the word'—and the root syllable is usually the first.

We now pass to changes *within* a language; changes for which, as we have already noticed, Bredsdorff's reasons hold good. It has been asserted that sound-changes must spring from changes in the organs of speech: but any teacher of languages by the phonetic method can get his pupils to learn virtually every speech-sound, including those which their native language has lacked for centuries; besides, many phonetic changes do not result in new sounds being developed or old sounds being lost but merely in the old sounds being used in new places or being disused in places where they formerly existed.

---

[1] In these examples, the English words are not to be taken as originating in the Latin words.

[2] Jespersen, *Growth and Structure of the English Language*. But all the other Jespersen quotations in this chapter are from his *Language: Its Growth, Structure and Origin*.

It has also been asserted that geographical or climatic conditions influence the various sound-systems. But what of the fact that far-reaching linguistic changes have, in historical times, taken place in countries whose climate has not noticeably changed; and, to choose one from among many examples, how comes it that the Eskimos, living in a most forbidding environment, have a quite agreeable phonetic system?

One of the causes of language-changes probably resides in the character of the national psychology. But it is very difficult to *prove* that any particular change arises from this factor: and quite impossible to prove that the Gothonic sound-shift was caused by a revolution in national culture or by the resultant increase in the speed of utterance—an explanation far too extravagant.

Besides, why all this pother and bother about the consonantal shift accounted for by Grimm's Law? There are other shifts of some importance. 'Our main endeavour', as Jespersen pertinently remarks, 'must be to find out general reasons why sounds should not always remain unchanged.' Nevertheless, should we find a period very rich in linguistic changes, it is natural and advisable that we should pay attention to the community's social condition, in order to discover any unusually favouring circumstances. 'In the history of English, one of the periods most fertile in change is the fourteenth and fifteenth centuries: the wars with France, the Black Death . . . and similar pestilences, insurrections such as those of Wat Tyler and Jack Cade, civil wars like those of the Roses, decimated the men and made home-life difficult and unsettled.'

Turning to the general principles governing changes in speech-habits, we see that there is a constant struggle of the individual towards freedom and of the state towards conformity. There is certainly a tendency (not by any means unopposed) towards greater ease, towards economy of effort; a tendency caused by laziness, easy-goingness, inertia; a tendency to follow 'the line of least resistance': there are certain word-forms explainable only by lazy pronunciation. Witness *ma'am* for *madam*, and the complete change from *mistress* to *miss* in addressing an unmarried female. Such changes cannot be explained by the fact that these and similar stock-words are so very frequently used: frequency might equally well lead to fixation. Such changes, however, can be explained by 'the ease with which a word is understood in the given connexion or situation, and especially in its worthlessness for the purpose of communication'. The 'ease' principle operates 'when a word has little significatory value and the intention of the speaker can therefore be vaguely, but sufficiently, understood if the proper sound is merely suggested or hinted at': cf. *ready'm!* for *ready, madam!*

It has been asked why the very elaborate case and gender systems in Old English have virtually disappeared—have, indeed, entirely disappeared in their original form. The answer does not rest in some 'Open, Sesame!' phonetic law; a phonetic law, so called, does not constitute an explanation, for it must itself be explained: it is merely a statement of facts, 'a formula of correspondence', which does not set forth the causes of change. The cause of decay of the Old English declensions of nouns and, to a lesser extent, of the less difficult Old English conjugations of verbs—this cause lies both in the very numerous inconsistencies and irregularities in those two grammatical apparatuses and in the excessive differentiations, more especially in the declensions. To take but one example: the ending *u* denoted the nominative singular in both the masculine (as in *sunu*, a son) and the feminine (*duru*, a door[1]), or the accusative singular or the dative singular, or, if a neuter, the nominative plural or the accusative plural (as in *hofu*); and there are several other instances quite as notorious. Look at it in another way: the nominative plural, for instance, is indicated by the endings[2] *-a, -an, -as, -e, -u*; or by a change[3] in the body of the word, but without a case-ending, as in Old English *fot*, a foot, with plural *fet*; or even by the unchanged kernel—compare the unchanged plural *fish* existing, in modern English, beside *fishes*. 'The whole is one jumble of inconsistency [and incongruity], for many relations plainly distinguished from each other in one class of words were but imperfectly, if at all, distinguishable in another class. Add to this that the names used above, dative, accusative, etc., have no clear and definite meaning in ... Old English, any more than in ... kindred tongues; sometimes it did not matter which of two or more cases the speaker chose to employ: some verbs took indifferently now one, now another case, and the same is to some extent true with regard to prepositions. No wonder, therefore, that speakers would often hesitate which of two vowels to use in the ending, and would tend to indulge in the universal inclination to pronounce weak syllables indistinctly and thus confuse the formerly distinct vowels *a, i, e, u* into the one neutral vowel [phonetically represented as ə—the vowel in '*a*bout' or 'col*ou*r'], which might even be left out without detriment to the clear understanding of each sentence. The only

---

[1] Moreover, 'door' was in Old English not only feminine *duru* but neuter *dor* with plural *doru*!
[2] 'Terminations' is equally common in grammar.
[3] 'Mutation' is the term preferred by many philologists.

endings that were capable of withstanding this general rout were the two in *s*, *-as* for the plural and *-es* for the genitive singular'—endings that, in modern English, became respectively *-es* (or *-s*) and *'s*; 'here the consonant was in itself more solid, as it were, than the other consonants used in case endings (*n*, *m*), and, which is more decisive, each of these terminations was confined to a more sharply limited sphere of use than the other endings [were], and the functions for which they served, that of the plural and that of the genitive, are among the most indispensable ones for clearness of thought. Hence we see that these endings' tended from the very beginning 'to be applied to other classes of nouns than those to which they were at first confined . . . , so as to be at last used with practically all nouns.'

We pass to stress. Now, stress is energy in pronunciation: an intensive muscular activity not of any one speech-organ but of all the speech-organs simultaneously: for, in pronouncing a stressed (or 'accented' or 'accentuated') syllable, all the speech-organs (vocal chords and lung muscles and lips and tongue and palate) are exerted to the utmost. Stressed syllables, as a result, are loud (audible at a considerable distance) and distinct (easy to perceive and distinguish in all their components[1]). Unstressed syllables, on the other hand, are much more easily produced. All this has a primary importance in the history of language in general and languages in particular.

It is the psychological importance of the various elements which forms the chief factor in determining stress in either phrase or clause or sentence. Sentence stress plays a very important part in the development of any language: it has, for instance, differentiated between the demonstrative (*that* person) and the relative (a person *that* does so-and-so), between *one* and *a* (or *an*)—originally the same word; between French *moi* and *me*, *toi* and *te*. Value is influential also in settling which syllable among several is stressed most in long words; and in the Gothonic languages, whether old or modern, value has revolutionized the entire stress-system,[2] for we now have the stressing of the root syllable (psychologically most important syllable), as in *wishes* and *desires*. Psychological principles are as potent in language as in life.

The principle of ease influences all departments of language-development: and in this respect it is important to remember that often it is impossible to draw a sharp line between 'phonetic and syntactic phenomena', i.e. between word-sounds and the

---

[1] Elements; constituent parts.
[2] Cf. earlier in this chapter, the paragraph on the stress-shift (Verner's Law).

word-arrangements of connected speech. When a person begins to articulate, or merely thinks he does, but produces no audible sound until one or two or even more syllables after the beginning of what he imagined he was saying, this, in phonetics, is aphesis[2] if only a short unaccented vowel is lost, as in *squire* for *esquire*, or aphaeresis,[1] which is a term applied to the loss of any letter or syllable or, less often, to the loss of more than one syllable or whole words as in (Good) *morning*! or (Do you) *see*?, and the French (Je ne) *peux pas* or (Je ne me le) *rappelle plus*: syntactically this linguistic feature (in such set phrases as these it is a speech habit) is known as prosiopesis. Aposiopesis, on the other hand, results when a speaker leaves a phrase or a sentence unfinished, either because he notices that the hearer has already grasped the meaning or because he is at a loss which word to use: '*At Brown's* (house or shop)'; 'The *grocer's* (shop) was closed'; 'There's nothing on at *the Haymarket* (theatre)'. Some of these shortenings have become so common that the original is forgotten: how many persons realize that *rifle* is short for *rifle gun*, i.e. a gun with *rifles* (spiral grooves cut on the inner surface of the barrel—grooves now collectively called *rifling*)? Or that *landau* abbreviates *Landau carriage*, a vehicle of the sort made originally at *Landau* in Germany?

But in opposition to the principle of ease is the influence of emphasis: the emphasis of strong emotion; the emphasis of military commands; that of pomposity and self-importance; of amiable banter, delicate irony, scathing sarcasm; that emphasis which arises from a scrupulous articulation of syllables and an almost meticulous spacing of words—the emphasis employed by actors and orators. Notice how *lovely* becomes, among both the illiterate and the jocular, the long drawn out *loverly*; how *God* becomes *Gord* (or *Gawd*); how, as an interjection, *wallop* becomes *kerwallop*; how *delightful* changed to *délightful* ('Dee-lightful couple!' in George Bernard Shaw's *The Doctor's Dilemma*); *beautiful* is distorted to *bē-yewtiful*. Better than these examples from unconventional speech are examples from the most irreproachably correct speech: compare the quick, light pronunciation of 'I didn't wish to go to sleep' with the slowly articulated 'Will—you—go—to—sleep?!' of an exasperated parent; 'The morning wasn't particularly quiet' with a threatening 'Will you be quiet?'; French 'Je me taisais pendant ces moments-là' with 'Mais taisez-vous donc!', where, moreover, the *c* of *donc* is

---

[1] These are well-known symptoms of aphasia in its early stages; *aphasia* is that loss of speech which is caused by an affection of the brain.

pronounced; the German 'Danke schön, Herr Schmidt', with a rasped 'Nein, Schweinhund!'

Euphony results sometimes from the desire for ease of pronunciation; and sometimes from a desire for distinctness of utterance. Since people tend to deem good or pleasant that to which they are accustomed, considerations of euphony more often than not make for a language's being kept unchanged: nevertheless, what is hard to pronounce and what, when pronounced, is indistinct are felt to be ugly and will, in time, disappear.

One thinks more often of what one *has* to say than of how one pronounces what one says. This occasionally leads to an assimilation of two sounds that come together: the Old French *sercher* (whence the English *search*) has become *chercher*. When the two sounds are transferred, we have what philologists call metathesis: as in *third* from Old English *thridda*, *bird* from Old English *brid*, and *wasp* from Old English *waps*.[1]

Such transformations as these lead us to understand that 'it is a natural consequence of the essence of human speech and the way in which it is transmitted from generation to generation that we have everywhere to recognize a certain latitude' or variation 'of correctness, alike in the significations in which words may be used, in syntax and in pronunciation. . . . The latitude of correctness is very far from being the same in [all] languages.' In a given language, 'some sounds . . . move within narrow boundaries, while others have a much wider field assigned to them; each language is punctilious in some, but not in all points'.

It is important to remember that there is a very close connexion between phonetic latitude (permissible variation) and the meanings of words. If, in a language, there exist numerous pairs of words identical in sound except for a difference in vowel (e.g., *bit* and *bite*) or in consonant (as in *cab* and *cap*, *bad* and *bat*, *frog* and *frock*), those words are pronounced distinctly.

The significative side of language—meaning—has, therefore, influenced the phonetic side—sound. But this fact does not imply the supposition that, in those pairs of rather similar words (and there are many of them), the speaker is on his guard because of a phonetic law: all that is required is that he should realize, or be made to realize, that when he speaks indistinctly, his hearers do not understand him. Nor need he be on his guard *against* one. Not every irregularity is due to the operation of sound-laws, for in all languages there are numerous survivals of the confused way in which ideas were arranged and then expressed by primitive man. On the other hand, there are many sound-changes ('phonetic

---

[1] To which children unconsciously revert by the same process.

changes' is the grammarians' term) which make for congruity and regularity—in short, for a simpler system—by discarding phonetic distinctions that lacked value of either sense or syntax. 'Convergent changes are just as frequent as divergent ones.'

In the course of time, and by the alchemy of time and circumstance, many a sound-law (phonetic law) undergoes a process of change and is extended to ever more numerous combinations. Take the English vowel u[1] as in *tune* or *new*: that sound was once very much more common than it now is. It is easy to see how difficult it must have been to pronounce this *u* in *true* and *rude*, i.e. after *r*; hence the pronunciation changed long ago to *troo* and *rood*. Then it was dropped after an *l* preceded by a consonant, as in *blue, clue, glue*. After *s* and *z*, there is a strong tendency—not yet an accomplished fact—to drop the [j]: to pronounce *resume* as *resoom, Zuma* as *Zooma*. After *t, d* and *n* (as in *tune, due, new*), the [ju] sound is discarded not only among illiterates in England but also among many educated people in the United States, where *toon, doo* and *noo* are much the commoner pronunciations. 'Now, it is highly probable that many of the [far-reaching] prehistoric sound changes, of which we see only the final result, . . . have begun in the same modest way.'

The spreading of phonetic change, as of any other linguistic change, is due to imitation, conscious and unconscious, of the speech habits of other people. . . . Man is apt to imitate throughout the whole of his life, and this statement applies as much to his language as to his other habits. What he imitates . . . is not always the best. . . . The spreading of a new pronunciation through imitation must necessarily take some time, though the process may in some instances be fairly rapid. In some historical instances we are able to see how a new sound, taking its rise in some particular part of a country, spreads gradually like a wave, until finally it has pervaded the whole of the linguistic area.

Sometimes the change is due to the authority of the cultured: this century has seen the growing popularity of *Tráf-al-gar* at the expense of *Tra-fál-gar*. Sometimes the new pronunciation becomes general because it is easier. Compare the present *ho-rī-zon* with the very old-fashioned *hór-i-zon*.

But occasionally education leads to exaggerated corrections, to 'hyper-correct' forms. 'In the dialect of Missouri and the neighbouring States [of America], final *a* in such words as *America, Arizona, Nevada* becomes *y*—*Americy, Arizony, Nevady*. All edu-

---

[1] Represented phonetically as [ju]; the change to *toon* (or *noo*) is described as 'the dropping of the [j]'. The *oo* sound as in *toon* is represented phonetically as [u].

cated people in that region carefully correct this vulgarism out of their speech; and many of them carry the correction too far and say *Missoura, praira*, etc.'[1] Irish people anxious to speak the correctest of English often go too far: having noticed that the English pronounce *learn* as *lern* (and not *larn* as they themselves pronounce it), they tend to pronounce *darn* (a stocking) as *dern*.[2]

The thought behind this chapter, so far as we have gone, is that sound-changes, to be properly understood, should not be isolated from other kinds of change, for in a living language there is a constant interaction of sense with sound, of syntax with sense, of semantics[3] with written forms and heard sounds. '*Sounds should never be isolated from the words in which they occur, nor words from sentences. No hard-and-fast boundary can be drawn between phonetic and non-phonetic change.*[4] The psychological motives for both kinds of change are the same in many cases, and the way in which both kinds are spread through imitation is absolutely identical.'

But among these causes of change within a language, we must not forget to mention the desire children and many grown-ups have to play with words. 'There is a certain exuberance which will not rest contented with traditional expressions, but finds amusement in the creation and propagation of new words and in attaching new meanings to old words.' This playfulness is seen best in slang, for slang words are often used deliberately in a form or a sense different from those of standard speech, as when we apply *upper storey* to the human head.

II. WHY WORDS GET NEW MEANINGS

From the preceding considerations we have reached a point at which we are comfortably ready to deal with new meanings; indeed we have already touched, more than once, on this question.

The most potent reason for the development of new senses is that language is called upon, and does its best, to cope with and express all the self-enriching and growing branches of human knowledge and aspiration. But we cannot leave the question at this point and say, 'Well, that's *that*!'

---

[1] E. H. Sturtevant, *Linguistic Change*, 1917, cited by Jespersen in *Language*. This and other hyper-correct forms in American English have been very ably discussed by Robert J. Menner in *American Speech*, October 1937.   [2] Patrick Joyce, *English as we Speak it in Ireland*, 1910.
[3] See chapter ix, A, iv.
[4] The italics are mine: these two sentences, but especially the first, should be repeated every day by those who, when they have evolved a phonetic law (something deduced from actual speech-habits, mind you!, not from the inner consciousness), think that they have created something inviolable.

Changes in the meanings of words and phrases are often so very gradual that the different steps of the process are undetectable: we see the original meaning and the latest meaning; sometimes we can distinguish an intermediate meaning; but only very rarely can we discern *all* the degrees of change. In Old English, *soon* meant 'at once', 'immediately'; it now means 'shortly (in time)'; *presently* now means 'soon' whereas formerly it meant 'at present', 'now'. *Hard* was formerly applied to nuts and stones, now it can be used of labour (the 'hard labour' of penal servitude) and words ('hard words' being harsh, hence unkind words); *fair* used to mean 'beautiful', a sense now almost wholly literary—it now means 'blond' and 'equitable', 'morally just'. Formerly, *meat* signified food of any kind, as in *sweetmeats* and *meat and drink*; now, when it is used by itself, it is confined to one kind of flesh among all the kinds of food—that kind of flesh which is known technically and commercially as 'butchers' meat'. *Pretty*, from 'skilful' or 'ingenious', has come to be a general adjective of approbation or approval: compare the American *cunning*, 'sweet', as in 'a cunning child'. With some words, it is impossible to discover intermediate stages between the original and the present meaning, though we can often find a phrase that suggests the link: *bead*, originally a prayer, now a tiny perforated ball of glass or amber, is 'clued' by *count one's beads*, originally 'count one's prayers'; *boon*, originally a prayer, now a favour, is 'clued' by *ask* (or *grant*) *a boon*. 'There are no connecting links between the meanings of "glad"[1] and "obliged", "forced", but when *fain* [originally = "glad"] came to be chiefly used in combinations like "he was fain to leave the country", it was natural for the younger generation to interpret the whole phrase as implying necessity instead of gladness': similar interpretations by younger generations are frequent when those younger generations do not know the original sense—much less the etymology—of the word or phrase.

With this phenomenon of speech, compare that in which the common noun of vague meaning has to serve so many purposes that it acquires a specific meaning—or, in fact, several specific meanings. *Deer* once meant 'an animal'; it now denotes a specific animal. *Corn*, formerly applied to any cereal or its grain, now denotes wheat in England, oats in Scotland, maize in the United States (where originally the term was *Indian corn*), hence in Canada, New Zealand and Australia, though in the last two *maize* is becoming the accepted term, especially among farmers; the

---

[1] Itself originally = 'bright'; a sense that survives in the slang phrase, *give the glad eye*.

reason being that *corn* (cereal) was applied loosely to the principal crop of a region or country and hence became more usual than the original specific name.

Often, however, the changes in sense represent jumps from one specific to another specific sense. *Tripos* is an excellent example. This Cambridge University term means, literally, 'three-legged', hence 'a three-legged stool'; at Cambridge it soon came to be applied to the man that sat on such a stool to dispute with candidates for degrees. Mr Tripos had also to provide comic verses for the occasion; such verses were printed under the name of 'tripos verses' until late in the nineteenth century, despite the fact that Mr Tripos himself had disappeared long before. The examination list, being printed on the back of these verses, was called 'the Tripos list'; *Tripos* came to denote the examination itself, from such phrases as 'He stands high on the Tripos'.

One of the special processes in the development of meaning is radiation. Originally, *radiation* (from Latin *radiare*, to emit rays of light) was applied to the emission of rays of light; hence to radial structure, form, arrangement, therefore to any divergence and diverging from a central point. Of this process, the best account is in Chapter XVIII of Greenough and Kittredge's *Words and Their Ways*. These American professors, whose admirable book appeared first in 1901, give an example so illuminating that I quite shamelessly reproduce it verbatim: that of *power*.

'Everybody has envied the magician's talent'—or *power* (see sense 6)—'of being in two places at once. Words, in the development of their several'—separate—'meanings, seem to have mastered the trick. *Power*, for example, is almost ubiquitous in its special senses. Thus it may signify (1) control over one's subordinates, sway ("the power of the king"); (2) delegated authority ("the energy exceeded his powers"); (3) physical strength ("all the power of his muscles"); (4) mechanical energy ("water-power", "steam-power", "the power is shut off"); (5) one of the so-called "mechanical powers" (as a lever); (6) moral or intellectual force; (7) a person of influence ("a power in the community"); (8) one of the great nations of the world ("the concert of the powers"); (9) a mathematical conception ("the fourth power of 6"); (10) an army or "troop" of soldiers (now obsolete; but cf. *force and forces*); (11) an effective quality of style in writing or oratory ("a writer of great power"). Yet in all these . . . specializations, the "primary meaning" of *power*, "the state of being able" to do something (Old French *pouer*, modern *pouvoir*, "to be able", from Low Latin *potere* [which supplanted the Classical Latin *posse*]), is still present, so that we may almost say that the word accomplishes the feat of being in eleven more or less widely separated places at the same time without ceasing to hold its original position. . . . [As in all the very numerous examples of radiation,] the simplest meaning stands at the centre [of the various senses, which might be arranged in the form of a sun-burst or of a star-fish], and the secondary meanings proceed out of it in every direction like [sun-] rays. Each of them . . . may be traced back to the central signification as if there were no other derivative meaning in existence. . . . Each of the derived senses [of *power*], it will be seen, might easily have developed from the central meaning ["the being able" to do something] without regard to any of the others. Consequently, any one of them might go out of use without affecting the others in the slightest degree.' But 'some of our special meanings might be derived from one or another of their fellows rather than from the central idea [of "the being able"]. Thus "mental or moral power" (No. 6) may be a figurative use of "muscular power" (No. 3), and, more probably, the concrete sense of "lever" or "wheel-and-axle" (No. 5) may come from the abstract "mechanical energy" (No. 4)': but it is also possible that all, it is probable that most, of the subsidiary senses are literally derivative from the primary sense ('the being able' to do something). Another very good example of radiation is afforded by *hand*, for which see Greenough and Kittredge (Ch. XVIII).

Radiation, in some of its features, resembles or is even the same thing as transference[1] of meaning. 'The Romans had the proverb, "Everything has two handles"; and nowhere is this more true than in mental conceptions and the words that express them. Almost every conception has two aspects; (1) that of the person or thing that possesses or exercises it; (2) that of a person or thing that is affected by it. This difference between the active agent and the effect produced, between the cause and that which it causes, between the subjective and the objective, is very great indeed.' Yet even in Latin, one of the most logical of languages, 'little account is made of this fundamental distinction . . . Thus the Latin *opinio* means both *opinion* (from the point of view of him who *has* it) and *reputation* (from the point of view of him concerning whom it is held) . . . Nothing could be more natural, for "my opinion of Richard Roe" is of course identical with "Roe's *reputation* with me". The difference is simply in the person from whose point of view the conception is regarded.' Nevertheless, 'the distinction . . . seems so important that we feel the need of

[1] Greenough and Kittredge, *Words and Their Ways*, ch. xix: well worth reading carefully and in full.

making it clear in the vocabulary'. We separate *opinion* from *reputation* and limit their meanings.

So with many, very many, other words. 'In "*shame* kept him silent", the subjective feeling of the person who is ashamed is meant; in "*shameful* treatment" the character of the act is objectively described. *Honor* [English *honour*] may be the sentiment which a man cherishes in his own heart and which keeps him true to his better nature, or it may be the tribute of respect which others pay to such a man.' *Odium*, by itself, in English signifies 'marked unpopularity', but in *odium theologicum* we revert to the sense ('hatred') of the Latin original, for this phrase means 'that hatred which proverbially characterizes theological discussions'—a phrase that has generated *odium medicum* (the contentiousness of medical debate), *odium philologicum* (the heat caused, among philologists, by philological discussion), *odium psychologicum*, and the like.

'The same confusion between subjective and objective may be seen in the uses of [grammatical] cases and prepositions, and in other linguistic machinery for expressing the relations of ideas. The Latin *amor Dei*, and our "the love of God", may mean either God's love for us or ours for him. . . . Such phrases as "the Fontenoy forgery case", "the Williamson assault" are equally ambiguous.'

Transference may take place at any moment. Adjectives are particularly exposed to transference: *unexpressive* equals either 'inexpressible', 'ineffable', or 'lacking expression', 'deficient in expressiveness'; *awful* means either 'awe-inspiring' or, though this sense is now rare, 'filled with terror'; *hateful* means either 'full of hate' or 'odious'; a person may be *doubtful* concerning a *doubtful* question or a *doubtful* (disreputable) character; *pitiful* means either 'compassionate' (rare in modern usage) or 'contemptible' (or 'pitiable'); *curious* means either 'inquisitive' or 'odd', 'strange'; *peculiar* itself means either 'characteristic of, or belonging to, one person or thing' or 'odd', 'strange'; and *odd* means 'uneven' or 'strange'. It is all very odd—yet quite natural.

Transference operates also in other parts of speech. *Prove*, 'to test' (Latin *probare*), may signify 'to turn out' (so and so, under the test of time), as in 'His attempt proved unsuccessful', whereas, in the proverb 'The exception proves the rule' *proves* bears the etymological sense, 'to test'.

That 'English is full of happy misapplications of words' is Greenough and Kittredge's happy comment.

CHAPTER SIX

WHY SOME WORDS LIVE, SOME DIE; FASHIONS IN WORDS

IF one were high-handed and high-hat, one might dismiss the reason for the long life of some words, the early death of others, with the statement that words live so long as they are useful and viable (able to maintain a separate existence), whereas those words will die which are more or less useless—or which are superfluous —or which, through sheer unpronounceability, are phonetically impractical. But usefulness and viability and their opposites are not the only factors: and of these others, fashion is the chief.

Linked with viability (the capacity of living or the ability to live in given circumstances) and usefulness on the one hand and with fashion on the other, is elevation; its opposite, degeneration, is correspondingly linked with the death of words.

Sir James Barrie, in *When a Man's Single*, 1888, records a London grocer's price-scale: 'Eggs, new-laid, 1*s*. 3*d*.; eggs, fresh, 1*s*. 2*d*.; eggs warranted, 1*s*.; eggs, 10*d*.' (per dozen). In May 1914, Professor G. H. McKnight noticed in a London grocer's stall a price-scale, in which he espied 'New-laid eggs, 10*d*.; Selected 12*d*., Warranted, 16*d*.' In that short period, the value of words had changed much more than the value of eggs had: the superlative *new-laid* of 1888 had gone to the bottom of the scale.

'Words, like eggs, may degenerate.[1] In fact, degeneration of meaning is a conspicuous phenomenon in semantics'—that portion of philological science which deals with development in the senses of words. 'The figurative force of euphemism and hyperbole . . . fades with continued use, and faded euphemism and faded hyperbole result in degeneration of meaning. . . . The word *insane* is obviously no longer euphemistic'—except perhaps when set alongside *stark, staring mad*—'but the effect of its euphemistic use has been to lower the word from an earlier meaning of "not

[1] In this chapter, until further notice, the 'unacknowledged' quotations are from G. H. McKnight, *English Words and Their Background*, 1923; in the latter half of the chapter I have drawn freely on Greenough and Kittredge.

well" (Latin *in* + *sanus*) to its present terribly direct meaning. *Vulgar*, . . . originally meaning "belonging to the throng" (Lat. *vulgus*), has permanently taken the meaning of "low", "debased". The words *common* and *ordinary*, from [constant] use [in a] euphemistic attempt to avoid the harshness of *vulgar*, are themselves well started on the same downward course'; compare 'Oh, she's a dreadfully common woman!' with 'They're very ordinary people, I'm afraid', usages too frequent on the lips of snobs. *Homely* has, in America, come to mean 'ugly'; *plain* is, in England, rapidly coming to mean the same thing. *Degraded*, literally 'reduced in rank' (Latin *gradus*, a step, a degree, rank), now connotes 'evil'.

A similar result follows from irony and persistent innuendo. 'What less complimentary', McKnight asked in 1923, 'may be said of one than that he is *good-hearted* or *means well*?' As a friend of mine once exclaimed, 'God spare me from being known as *a good fellow*!' Compare the fate of *worthy*: from the thirteenth to the nineteenth century it signified 'entitled to honour or respect for one's good qualities'; since the 1880's, it has generally been used slightingly, as in 'She's a very worthy woman'. And that of *silly*: in Old and Middle English, its predominant sense was that of 'happy'; in the sixteenth century it took on the sense of 'unsophisticated, simple, ignorant'; not long after, it also acquired that of 'foolish, empty-headed', a sense that had, by 1800 at the latest, become the usual one: and *simple* has been, in part, subjected to the same ill-treatment; 'Oh! he's a bit simple' now connotes mental defectiveness.

'The effect of hyperbole is the same in kind': compare the *new-laid* (egg) conspicuous earlier in this chapter. The proverb informs us that 'procrastination is the thief of time'; it is also the thief of meaning, as in '*soon, anon, presently*, and *by and by*, all of which originally meant "at once" [i.e. "immediately"]. The use of such expressions as *doubtless, in fact* and *as a matter of fact*, as means of strengthening assertions, has led to similar degeneration.' Sir James Barrie once said that *the fact is* usually preludes a lie.

Consider, too, the effect of pretentiousness and moral pretence. *Grandiloquent*, 'majestically eloquent', very soon took on the senses, 'bombastic' and 'pompous'; *grandiose*, in addition to meaning 'characterized by grandeur', has acquired the sense, 'flaunting', 'vulgarly showy'; *specious*, 'beautiful', now means 'ungenuine'; *sanctimonious*, 'holy', now signifies 'affecting the appearance of holiness' or, occasionally, 'pharisaical'; *charity* has weakened to 'benevolence'; and *prude*, related to *proud* and etymologically reminiscent of chivalry, is now applied to a person of affected modesty.

It is noticeable that in many of the words here cited (apart from those tainted by faded euphemism and weakened hyperbole), degeneration has sprung from specialization. The connotation of a word gradually comes to admit a new denotation,[1] which, colouring the original meaning, often overshadows that original signification. Thus *adulterate*, literally 'to alter' (Latin *ad alterum convertere*, 'convert to something else'), has, to the connotation of 'to change in whatsoever way', admitted the denotation, 'to corrupt, especially by base admixture'; *alter* itself, from denoting or meaning 'to render different, to modify', has in addition to its connotation of 'changing only in a minor way or in minor ways', long possessed the connotation of 'change thus, but for the worse', a nuance that may easily become, and quite likely will become, a new denotation.

Sometimes 'the element joined to the original meaning is absorbed from the context. A clear case of this is the word *enormity*', which, from meaning 'that which is abnormal', has come to mean 'a monstrous offence' and 'monstrous wickedness' because of its constant association with crime and offence: '*enormity* has absorbed qualifying elements of meaning from associated words'. Another good example is *asylum*, for, 'derived from the Greek *asulos*, ... "inviolable", "free from right of seizure", the word, through constant association with *insane* and [to a lesser extent] *orphan*, has come in popular speech to mean a place of confinement rather than a place of refuge'. *Villain*, originally a *villein* or 'a peasant occupier or cultivator entirely subject to a lord or attached to a manor', has, by an unwarrantably supposed connexion with *vile*, deteriorated so far as to signify a scoundrel; and *vile* has similarly, from 'inferior', 'of poor or bad quality' (itself a deterioration from the Latin sense, 'cheap'), slipped into 'morally despicable'.

'Degeneration of meaning ... has long occupied the attention of the student of language. A corresponding elevation of meaning has attracted less attention, but has played in the development of language a part hardly less important.' McKnight has unconsciously—for at the time he could not have foreseen the change—provided us with a particularly illuminating example. Writing

---

[1] *Connotation* is the attribute or attributes implied—not actually stated—by a term; *denotation* is the signification of the term itself. (A signification is that which is *denoted* by a term; an implication is that which is *connoted* thereby.) Connotation is the including, in the meaning of a term, something that the term does not specifically denote or designate.

in 1922 or 1923, he said: 'In the language of the present day, ... the term *socialist* is degenerating under the influence of an imagined relation with anarchy'. But already by 1930, if not indeed by 1928 or so, *socialist* was a term of honour when opposed to *communist*.

Some of the present names for the highest and the noblest aspects of and elements in human life were, at their origin, applied to things of trivial or, at best, comparatively slight importance. '*Splendid* goes back to the simple meaning "bright". *Magnificent* is made up from the two simple Latin words, *magnus*, "large", and *facere*, "to do" or "to make". *Distinction* goes back to a Latin verb, *distinguere*, which meant literally "to prick off". The word *virtue* is built on an insecure foundation, since it goes back to the meaning "manliness" (Latin *vir*, "a man"), expressing only a nobler aspect of frail human nature. [Note, however, that in Classical Latin it bore the sense, "courage".] *Fame*, a prize much striven for, goes back to the Latin *fama* (from *fari*, "to speak") and meant originally only "report", "common-talk" [or even "gossip"].'

Degeneration and elevation are closely connected with, at times inextricably involved in, fashions in words. And under the head of fashion we may include not only passing vogues, momentary fads and whimsicalities, most of which are very sectional (restricted to a class or a city), but also general tendencies and even movements. If these vogues and tendencies occur in our everyday speech, we are apt to brand them as slang or, from another angle, as affectation; but if they occur in literature, as they do in schools of writing, in movements, and even in 'ages' or epochs, we speak of them as 'stylistic tendencies'.[1] The principles are the same in the trivial and in the cultured: the attraction exercised by novelty, the very odd fact that it is fashionable to do what is in the fashion, the fear of appearing less wise and less alert than one's neighbour, such are the factors leading to widespread imitation of the arresting, the distinctive, or the merely popular.

Fashion introduces new words; gives a not always easily explainable prominence to certain words or phrases, or to groups of words and phrases, already in existence and perhaps, in a quiet way, fairly familiar to a large section of the people or even, in very rare instances, to the larger part of an entire population; or banishes others—and banishment spells death after no very long interval.

Such words as we are constantly hearing, especially the words

[1] Greenough and Kittredge, *Words and Their Ways*: whence all quotations until further notice.

associated with our trade, profession and hobby, slip the most readily on to our tongues. 'That a physician should speak of "dissecting" a subject, a chemist of "analysing" it, a preacher of "expounding" it, is as natural as that an ordinary man should speak of "explaining" it or "making it clear". A calamity [or an unexpected or unpleasant set-back] may be called "a cropper" by the horsey man, "a knock-out" by the amateur of pugilism, "a lost case" by a lawyer.' Such differences, as the quotation exemplifies, will happen as frequently in ordinary as in colloquial speech.

Moreover, an individual comes under various linguistic influences in the course of his lifetime: the speech of the nursery, if he is fortunate enough to have had a nursery; school—the language of teachers, the talk of one's schoolfellows, the game-vocabularies having, perhaps, the most enduring influence; the slang and the greatly increased vocabulary acquired at a university; the special terms necessary in one's trade, business, or profession; the jargon of one's favourite newspaper; the various word-scopes and word-scapes of one's favourite authors. Those are the normal influences, but all of us are subject to the special influences exercised by an unusually important or bitter political campaign, a religious revival, a war (the Great Wars have been especially influential), a rapidly advancing science—especially if it is being popularized: and those special influences may affect either the nation as a whole or, at the least, a large or powerful section of a nation. For instance: late in the nineteenth century, such political-economy terms as *the law of supply and demand, medium of exchange, standard of living, unearned increment, unproductive consumer* became familiar to, and used by, even those who had never read a page of political economy; World War I gave currency to terms hitherto known only by experts or by (say) soldiers or sailors—*camouflage, demobilize, communiqué, liaison, ordnance*, etc., etc., and many colloquial and slangy words and phrases; and the growing interest shown in psychology after that war (and partly because of it) has introduced into ordinarily educated and ordinarily intelligent, or unintelligent, conversation such terms as *subconscious, libido, the ego, psycho-analysis* and, for the most part horribly misused, *complex*.

The same kind of thing that befalls an individual or even the public in general, happens also to the nation as a whole in the lifetime of a language. Here are some of the instances cited by Greenough and Kittredge for the period from the ninth to the end of the nineteenth century.

'The style of the Anglo-Saxon translator of Bede's Ecclesiastical History is marked by a peculiar trick of repetition. Again and again he uses two synonymous nouns or verbs or adjectives, where one would suffice to convey his whole meaning. This may be called, then, an English literary habit of the ninth century . . . The habit survived in English prose until the end of the eighteenth century. And, though out of favour at the moment, it has left a number of idiomatic . . . phrases in the language: as, "end and aim", "lord and master", "without let or hindrance", "act and deed", "pure and simple", "really and truly", . . . "toil and delve" '—not that they all come down from King Alfred's time, but simply that the tendency does.

The Elizabethan age is characterized not so much by any one literary mannerism (even Euphuism) as by the prevalence of every mannerism devised or approved by the fertile Elizabethan mind. The Euphuist's language was not, as is so often stated ignorantly, full of words either intolerably affected or even strange, but it did show an excessive resort to antithesis, to clauses delicately poised, and to often childish tricks of alliteration[1] and assonance.[1] Witness this from Lyly's *Euphues* (of which the hero is one *Euphues*, the name signifying 'well-grown' or, derivatively, 'well-charactered'):—'It fareth with me, Psillus, as with the ostrich, who pricketh none but herself, which causeth her to run when she would rest; or as with the pelican, who striketh blood out of her own body to do others good; or with the wood-culver, who plucketh off her feathers in winter to keep others from the cold; or as with the stork, who, when she is least able, carrieth the greatest burden. So I practise all things that may hurt me, to do her good that never regardeth my pains, so far is she from rewarding them.'

Other very marked characteristics of the Elizabethans were excessive Latinization, the borrowing of terms from Greek as well as Latin, the coinage of strange words, and punning; this last being, not a national habit but a literary convention. If a modern were to be so richly and fantastically free with words as the Elizabethan writers were, his reputation would be shattered on the score of vocabulary alone—unless he went to the lengths of James Joyce, the Playboy of the Western Word, who owes his reputation as a stylist to his adoption and exaggeration of all the neological tricks from the most extravagant eccentricities of the Elizabethans to the haphazard felicities of Spooner and the carefully calculated

---

[1] '*A*pt *a*lliteration's *a*rtful *a*id' *s*ometimes *s*eems to exa*s*perate *e*rudite *E*nglishmen, who, moreover, g*l*ance at the pra*n*cings of asso*na*nce as at a ja*n*gling and cla*n*gour or at *p*ipes and *f*ifes *f*leering and scr*ee*ching over *b*ounds and *t*owns, in *m*ud and *fl*ood.

vagaries of Dodgson, and to the introduction of such mere typographical devices (both of omission and of commission) and syntactic shorthandings as the Elizabethans would have regarded as extra-stylistic. Joyce has, in effect, generated a school more eccentric but much less influential than that of the Elizabethans; but then the Elizabethans' school was so widespread as to be a national education, whereas Joyce's is restricted to Joyce, who, with all his faults, towers above his disciples, and to those few disciples themselves—Jolas and the other Transitionists (would not Transients be an apter name?), and Gertrude Stein, who seceded early from the reJoycing fold to become the apostle of effect-by-repetition and of apotheosis-by-aphasia. The Joyce school was a peculiarly 1919-1939 phenomenon: after a disruption of the world by Mars we had the dislocation of the language by Joyce. And the odd thing is that Joyce had written some admirably restrained, pellucid English, Stein some crystal-clear essays and studies, Jolas some pleasantly intelligible and provocatively intelligent criticism. If these writers had, even in the whirlpools of the most flood-like 'stream of consciousness', remained as lucid as Virginia Woolf or Ernest Hemingway, they would have been justified: and if they had suffered from such a mass-neurosis as forced them to write only Joyceëse, and indeed, prevented them from writing anything else, they would have had an excuse in compulsion: but is enduring fame likely to be the lot of those who deliberately ape the juggler, who joy in word-mutilation, who consider obscurity a virtue? Such writing is easy, much too easy, and this lexical levity and this lexicographical licentiousness are available to all who are good linguists or who have much Latin and more Greek or who merely have the patience to mine in exhaustive dictionaries of various languages. The Elizabethans were artificial, but easily intelligible to the averagely intelligent; the Joyceans are artificial, but, except at the cost of a highly gymnastic cerebration, unintelligible—and, when one has solved the puzzle, one feels that the result does not justify the effort. (I do not wish to imply an opinion that *Ulysses* is not a remarkable and important book, but merely to hint my belief that it would have been much more important if it had been more intelligibly written.)

But, to return to the literary fashions of an earlier time, we see that after the Elizabethans came the Puritans, who indulged in an excessively religious and theological phraseology, based mainly on the language of the Bible. 'In New England these forces worked with peculiar power' and 'the intellectual history of Massachusetts was practically unaffected by the Restoration', which in England promoted both licence and lucidity, which latter became, in the eighteenth century, merged with a Classical simplicity and, even where—as in Johnsonese—simplicity was lacking, clarity. The reaction from Puritanism was seen in the widespread fear both of 'enthusiasm', at that period almost synonymous with 'fanaticism', and of 'the romantic', a term applied in that century to anything (very) fanciful or (highly) imaginative or (excessively) emotional, the ideal being that 'easy elegance of language which befits a cultivated man'—or woman—'of fashion': an ideal that made for, and for the most part achieved, grammatical correctness and syntactical regularity and (comparative) simplicity and lexical purity.

'Of course, this schoolmastering tendency could not last for ever ... There is such a thing as pedantic dread of pedantry, and as soon as the Eighteenth Century reached that stage, its work had been done, and another readjustment began.' The Romantic Revival, which owed much to the Elizabethans, began late in the eighteenth century. 'There was a revolt against French neatness and "correctness" of style, a return to the older models of English—to Spenser, and Shakespeare, and Milton. Obsolete and half-obsolete[1] words were revived ... Variety and striking effects were sought after. Metaphor became bolder. . . . The easiest catchword [or label] for the revolt is "individualism" ... We have a feeling that "the style is the man",[2] and that every author is therefore entitled to use that form of language which best expresses his individuality.'

In the present century, the most marked phenomenon is the preponderance of thought and matter over style—the subjection and subordination of style to content. The opponents of this tendency seem, at the moment, to be fighting a losing battle: yet soon there may come a reaction against this tendency. There is also a strong tendency to glorify science and the machine at the expense of art, culture and man himself: to this the reaction will probably come even sooner, for there are already many writers (O'Neil, Dos Passos, Faulkner, Steinbeck) who, perhaps more in America than in England, strive to render artistic the findings and workings of science and, it may be added, of that social consciousness which has grown so rapidly since the War of 1914–18.

---

[1] 'Obsolescent' is the philological term. The obsolete is dead; the obsolescent is moribund, i.e. dying.

[2] Better '. . . the man himself' or '. . . the essential man', for the French original is *Le style, c'est l'homme même.*

The explanation of those movements and national fashions is that
in long lapses of time the continuance of similar impressions produces in one speaker a mode or habit of thought consonant with that of others. The several impressions in the mind as a particular word is constantly used act somewhat like objects in a composite photograph: all that is alike is constantly accumulating, while that which is individual or peculiar is as rapidly dissipated. Thus there arises a regular and persistent mode of thought, and consequently of expression, which more or less dominates [and determines] the form of the language in the mouths of all its speakers, whether they mean to be guided by it or not. To this tendency the Germans have given the expressive name *Sprachgefühl*, or 'speech-feeling',

which is itself partly determined by the *Zeitgeist*, 'time-spirit', the thought and feeling peculiar to a generation or a period. The *Sprachgefühl*, feeling for speech, exercises a pervasive influence in a language so long cultivated as English: and it has kept English true to itself through all those changes and fashions with which we have been dealing. 'No author, however eminent, can disregard this subtle and pervasive "feeling for language". Men of genius may take great liberties with their mother tongue . . . , but let them once run counter to its characteristic tendencies, let them violate the English *Sprachgefühl*, and their mannerism becomes, as it were, a foreign language. They are writing not English, but—say Carlylese.'[1]

These literary-linguistic considerations, besides being intrinsically important, possess a great extrinsic importance in that they enable us to come well-prepared to those instances of degeneration and elevation which are connected not only with fashion but also with changes in the social and political lives of the people. 'A classic instance[2] is the adjective *doughty*. The word is derived from the Old English noun *duguth*,[3] the native English equivalent of the later French derivative *Court*. The word expressed the courtly ideals of the early English. The present meaning reflects the Norman English contempt for Anglo-Saxon ideals. *Churl*, also, which in the English before the Conquest, was a term of respect (. . . *ceorl*, "freeman"), under the influence of Norman contempt for Anglo-Saxon manners, acquired its present meaning' of 'a rude,

---

[1] Even Carlyle, however, could write English: witness his contribution to his edition of Cromwell's letters.
[2] From here, the 'unacknowledged' quotations are from G. H. McKnight's *English Words and Their Background*.
[3] This derivation is open to grave suspicion: see, e.g., *The O.E.D.*

low-bred fellow'; and its doublet *carl* has suffered a similar fate.

'There are certain occupations and certain conditions in life the associations of which are the reverse of noble or distinguished. Rural life... until recent times has been associated with ignorance and dullness. Hence the names associated with agriculture have in general declined in dignity. *Peasant*, from a French word meaning "countryman", conveys the idea of a lower social class. The English *boor*, which once meant "farmer", is now associated with bad manners' in the male: compare *churl*. '*Rustic*, as a noun, suggests lack of social graces, and the word *farmer* itself, in the colloquial speech of the city, stands for slowness of wit': compare the English slang *hay-seed* and the American slang *hick*, both meaning a rustic, especially a farmer or a farm-labourer. The decline of *villain* offers a parallel case. 'The teacher shares, to a [rapidly lessening] extent, the contempt felt for the farmer, since his earlier name, *pedant* [from either French *pédant* or Italian *pedante*, both = "teacher"], is now associated with contempt, and its derivative, *pedantry*, has come to stand for misapplied learning.'

Degeneration is linked very closely, too, with terms designating servants: as in *slavish* (from *slave*, which is cognate[1] with *Slav*, a person of Slavonic race) and *servile* (Latin *servus*, a slave) and *menial*, which, from 'belonging to a household', has descended to meaning 'servile' or 'sordid'. *Wench*, a maiden or a young woman early came to signify 'a girl of the rustic or working class' and has, in the United States since ca. 1760, signified 'a coloured female servant'; during 1914–18 and after, it has, however, been much used jocularly by the English middle classes as an affectionate term of address. '*Knave* (Old English *cnafa*, "boy") has gone even farther. Not stopping at the first stage in the downward course, with the meaning "servant", it has descended to the meaning "rascal". In more recent times the spirit of democracy, which leads to the euphemistic avoidance of such terms of inferiority as *servant*'—as though we were not, even all of us, servants of the state, slaves of the life-force, and subjects of that ultimate power and destiny which is God!—'has led to the euphemistic use and consequent degeneration of words like *domestic* and *help*.'

On the other hand, elevation has busied itself with words of lowly origin. The word *court*, which dates back to the Latin *cohors, cohort-*, meaning 'enclosure' or 'poultry-yard', has, partly

---

[1] *Cognate*, in philology, is applied to words 'coming naturally from the same root, or representing the same original word' but developing independently: thus English *five* is cognate with Latin *quinque*. (*O.E.D.*)

by royal influence and partly by the influence of Latin *curia*, risen considerably in dignity. *Knight* (Old English *cniht*), which, like *knave*, originally signified 'a lad', has developed in the direction opposite to *knave*: contrast also *knightly* and *knavish*. *Esquire*, later *squire*, once meant 'shield-bearer'; because the esquire was a shield-bearer to a military knight, the term has been elevated. *Marshal* has gone far since it stood for 'horse-servant' (Old English *mearh*, horse and *scealc*, servant); and *seneschal* once denoted the 'senior servant'. *Chamberlain* at first meant 'one in charge of rooms'. *Steward*, which originally was a 'sty-ward', attendant to an enclosure for pigs, came to be a royal surname with variant *Stuart*.

For 'if change in fashion has served to cause degeneration in meaning, it has also at times had the opposite effect. The name *Gothic*, applied contemptuously, in the days when the taste for the classic prevailed, to a form of architecture that had its origin in the late Middle Ages, with change of fashion has come to designate something highly admired.' *Quaker* has come to be a term of honour for a member of the Society of Friends. *Methodist* was originally a nickname applied, by students at Oxford and with humorous contempt, to the followers of John Wesley: the sect is, and long has been, proud of the name. *Yankee*, originally a term of ridicule, is now, and long has been, taken in good part; and, by the way, this name[1] is, by Americans, applied to natives of New England, hence to inhabitants of the northern States generally, and, during the War of Secession, by the Confederates of the Federal soldiers, and by the English since ca. 1780 to a native (loosely any inhabitant) of the United States—to any American, in short. 'Names of political parties such as *Whig* and *Tory* and *Mugwump*, [bestowed] in ridicule, have been proudly adopted and elevated to the rank of cherished names.' But perhaps the most significant instance of all reversals is that afforded by *the Contemptibles*, which, applied scornfully and derisively by the Kaiser to the English expeditionary force sent to France in August 1914, soon came to be a most honourable, admiring, distinguished name, which in present English use generally takes the form *the Old Contemptibles*, often employed in a slightly more comprehensive way as a synonym for what is still referred to as *the First Hundred Thousand*, as in Ian Hay's fine book so titled.

Also it is interesting to note a few of the many instances of the divergence to degeneration, on the one hand, and to elevation on the other hand, among associated pairs and groups of words. 'If *rind* has been lowered in dignity by being too intimately related

[1] For etymology, see ch. ix, B, iii.

with the flesh of a beast not associated with elegance, *bristle* (originally belonging to pigs exclusively) and *sward* (Old English *sweard*, "skin", "bacon-rind") have risen, through association, from their [humble] origin. If *childish* and *puerile* have been lowered to the expression of an unattractive aspect of early life, *boyish* and *youthful* have been correspondingly elevated', to which statement I must add the rider that the neutral, but also the elevated, term corresponding to *childish* is *childlike*. A similar case is that of *senile* and *old* (or even the jocular *ancient*). 'If *cheap* and *vile* have been turned to the expression of related ideas of one kind, *costly* and *precious* have turned in the opposite direction': note, however, that the true opposite of *cheap* is *dear* (or *expensive*) and that *costly*, though admitting the cost, stresses the kind or the quality of the goods or article, whereas *precious* (Latin *pretiosus*, expensive, from *pretium*, price) is now felt, even in *precious stones*, to refer almost wholly to quality. 'If *rash*, which originally meant "quick", "swift", has been turned into the meaning "foolhardy", *sturdy* (Old French *estordi*, "reckless") and *stout* [in the sense of 'brave' and, though of Gothonic origin, probably from the Latin *stultus*, 'foolish'] have counterbalanced the change. While the names of [some] parts of the human anatomy have descended to the class of unmentionables, *pluck*,[1] originally a butcher's term [for the heart, liver and lungs of a beast], has come to express [courage], one of the most admirable elements in human nature, and *frill*, originally "belonging to the mesentery", has come to apply to one of the ornamental features of dress.'

---

[1] Cf. the almost exactly parallel development of *guts*, itself still, as *pluck* was at first, slang.

PART THREE

CHAPTER SEVEN

ENGLISH: GOOD; BAD; AND WORSE

I. STANDARD ENGLISH

ORIGIN

IF we take the definition, 'Standard English is the speech of the educated classes' when not speaking slangily, as adequate for the time being, we may yet wish to know how, and where, Standard English arose; indeed, its rise makes an interesting story.[1]

Old English had a standard for use in literature, but it disappeared with the Norman Conquest. Some three centuries later, there was a strong growth of national feeling: in the victorious reigns of Edward I and Edward III—that is, in 1272–1307 and 1327–77—national consciousness was accompanied by (probably it was in part responsible for) an increasing hostility to the use of French and consequently an increasingly favourable attitude to English. 'In the second half of the Fourteenth Century, the English language came once more to its own, into use not only in Parliament and the law courts and in schools, but in the literary productions composed for English cultured society.'

In this renewal of English as a literary language, the particular kind of English adopted was the East Midland dialect. The reasons for its adoption are these:

'The dialect of the East Midland district lay between Northern and Southern dialects and, as the Northern differed considerably from the Southern, the Midland served as a midway compromise understandable by all; it formed the speech of Oxford and Cambridge, the two great centres of higher education and of a culture more profound and mellow than that of London; it formed also the dialect of London itself, the centre of the political, official and commercial life of the country. And thus it was the speech of Chaucer, who, the greatest English writer until the 16th Century and, during the 11th–14th Centuries, the only great writer to employ English at all, passed most of his life in London; as the dialect spoken at Oxford, it was used by Wycliffe, who discarded

---

[1] For the more advanced student, Professor H. C. Wyld's books are invaluable; but for those who are less advanced I have seen no clearer account than that of Professor G. H. McKnight, whose arrangement I follow and whom I often quote.

his native Yorkshire for this smoother speech; as the dialect of London and hence of the Court, it was used by Gower, who might have been expected to employ the Kentish dialect.'

Gower was a much lesser poet than Chaucer, but his influence was almost as great: most of their best work appeared in the last twenty years of the fourteenth century: and so in the next century, their disciples (including Lydgate and Occleve) and other writers followed their lead and wrote in the East Midland dialect. Standard English,[1] then, began in the second half of the fourteenth century as the East Midland dialect for the reasons given above; and in the fifteenth century that dialect was established as the correct one to use for general literary purposes. It was the more readily adopted because it lacked the harshness of the Northern dialects and had very little of the slightly drawly softness of the Southern. So rapid was its progress that its supremacy was unquestioned by the great dramatists and the melodious poets of the Elizabethan Age.

The language of the sixteenth century, however, was far from being as fixed and regularized as that of the twentieth or, perhaps still more, that of the nineteenth century. Spelling was irregular, grammar experimental, and vocabulary a glorious uncertainty: but these defects were counterbalanced by 'the freedom enjoyed by writers of that period in the adoption of new words and the combination of existing words in word-compound and in phrase'. Regularity in spelling and vocabulary, along with order in grammar, came in the approximate period, 1660–1800. 'In the eighteenth century, especially near the end, the influence of grammars and dictionaries made itself fully felt. Words admissible into literary use were registered with their meanings in dictionaries, which also more and more undertook to indicate the pronunciation. English grammar became a subject for school study, and conformity to the use authorized by dictionary and grammar became the test of [culture] in language.'

RECEIVED STANDARD; MODIFIED STANDARD; LITERARY STANDARD

These are varieties of *good* or *pure* or Standard English.

The East Midland dialect, more especially that variety spoken

---

[1] It may be noted that Wyld's view is just slightly different: he narrows the incipient Standard English down to the speech of the Court in the 15th Century; a speech, he adds, which was primarily that of the upper classes in London. It was, he holds, not a pure speech, for it combined the dialect of the Midlands with that of the South: though this is almost the same as saying that it was the East Midland dialect, especially as spoken in London.

at the Court, 'spread among all those who came into contact with the Court, and was adopted by custom as the best and most polite form of English. For more than 300 years this dialect, at first, no doubt, merely held to be the fashionable mode of speech, has gained in prestige, until, at the present day, it is spreading all over the country, and among all classes.'[1] This Standard English is a matter of the choice of words and phrases, of syntax, and of pronunciation. Of Standard English as we know it in the twentieth century, we may say that it 'is a kind of English which is tinged neither with the Northern, nor Midland, nor Southern peculiarities of speech [and] which gives no indication . . . of where the speaker comes from . . . It is the ambition of all educated persons in [Great Britain and Northern Ireland] to acquire this manner of speaking, and this is the form of our language which foreigners wish to learn.'

But it is important to remember, with Wyld,[2] that 'no form of language is, *in itself*, [originally] better than any other form. A dialect'—and Standard English was, as we have seen, originally a dialect—'gains whatever place of superiority it enjoys solely from the estimation in which it is commonly held. It is natural that the language of the Court should come to be regarded as the most elegant and refined type of English, and that those who do not speak that dialect naturally'—that is, by circumstance of birth and environment—'should be at the pains of acquiring it. This is what has happened, and is still happening, to the dialect which is called Standard English', although Standard English is not, in its present stage, to be regarded as a dialect properly so called. 'Of course, since this form of English is used in the conversation of the refined, the brilliant and the learned, it has become a better instrument for the expression of ideas than any other [variety of speech] now spoken. This is the result of the good fortune which this particular dialect had to reach its position of pre-eminence over the others.'

'When we speak of Good English, or Standard English, or Pure English, as distinct from . . . Provincial English [the dialects proper], we must remember that there is nothing in the original nature of these other dialects which is in itself inferior, or reprehensible, or contemptible. In a word, the other dialects are in reality, and apart from fashion and custom, quite as good as Standard English, considered simply as forms of language; but they have not the same place in general estimation, they have not been so highly cultivated' nor rendered so subtle and delicate,

---

[1] This quotation, like the next, comes from Professor H. C. K. Wyld's *The Growth of English*. [2] In the same valuable book.

'and they have not the same wide currency.' (With dialect in general, we shall deal in a later section of this chapter.)

To come now to the different kinds of Standard English: The best of these is Received Standard,[1] for it conforms to all the requisites of good speech; Modified Standard is Standard English that differs from Received mainly in pronunciation; and Literary Standard lies beyond any consideration of pronunciation and is confined to written English—when it is used in speech it is too bookish to be Received.

'Of Literary English'—Literary Standard—'we need only say that it is the more conventional and dignified, more accurate and logical, sometimes the more beautiful form that standard'—that is, Received Standard—'English assumes, like evening dress, for important occasions; it is also more rhythmical and musical. With slang [and colloquialism and cant and dialect] it has nothing to do, unless [they have] a long pedigree, and then only in very rare instances.'[2]

What then of Received Standard[3] and Modified Standard?[3] 'It is proposed to use the term *Received Standard* for that form which all would probably agree in considering the best, that form which has the widest currency and is heard with practically no variation among speakers of the better class all over the country. This type might be called Public School English.' (The stress here, as you see, is on pronunciation.) 'It is proposed to call the vulgar English of the Towns, and the English of the Villager who has abandoned his native Regional Dialect'—his dialect in the ordinary sense of the term—'*Modified Standard*. That is, it is Standard English, modified, altered, differentiated, by various influences, regional and social. Modified Standard differs from class to class, and from locality to locality; it has no uniformity, and no single form of it is heard outside a particular class or a particular area.' As Professor Wyld remarks, all this is very obvious—yet it is very important.

THE LIMITS OF PURE (OR RECEIVED STANDARD) ENGLISH[4]

But there is a considerable difference between pure English and the English spoken by the uncultured. In the American *Them guys*

---

[1] 'Received Standard' and 'Modified Standard' are terms coined by Professor Wyld; 'Literary Standard' is a term coined by myself, after due thought.

[2] From my *Slang To-day and Yesterday*, revised edition, 1935.

[3] The ensuing quotation is from Wyld's *Short History of English*.

[4] In this section, I draw very extensively on G. H. McKnight's *English Words and Their Background*.

ain't got no pep or the English *Them blokes ain't got no go*, not a single word would pass the standard exacted by pure (or Received Standard) English, whether American English or British English: for, in both versions, the first word is ungrammatical, the second is slang, the third is ungrammatical, the fourth is unnecessary (and colloquial), the fifth is illogical (sense demanding *any*), and the sixth is slang. True, both versions are examples of illiteracy, yet the meaning is unmistakable, the speech is direct.

There are, however, inestimable advantages to be gained from uniformity of vocabulary and regularity of syntax. Since the seventeenth century English has gained tremendously in precision. Language has not been created to be the sport of the illiterate, any more than to be the private plaything of the high-brow or the chopping-block of the journalist: whether collectively or individually. Language is a means of communication, not merely between two gangsters or two Cockneys, nor even between two high-brows, but among all the members of a nation. 'It is important that the language medium should offer as little as possible resistance to the thought current, and this end is attained only when the symbols of language are ones that convey precisely the same meaning to all who use the language.'

But we may raise a question concerning the degree to which a language can be healthily standardized. Rather too often are spoken English and spoken American criticized as though it were impossible for them to have their own laws—or, at the least, a freedom not shackled at every turn by the rules implicit in Literary Standard.

A language cannot be at the same time entirely standardized and vital: a rigorously regimented language would die from stiffness of the joints and boredom of the spirit. 'Ideas inherited from the past, to be sure, may find adequate expression in the fixed idiom of the past', though the modern attitude towards those ideas will require language that is modern. 'The shifting, developing forms assumed by living thought, however, demand the plastic medium of a living language.' After all, it is only natural that new systems of thought and new modes of living should, by the very strength of their processes and by their widespread currency, generate new words, new compounds, new phrases and even new modes of expression: in linguistics, as in politics, the will of the nation is all-powerful; it is of no use for the pedants to deplore and lament the misuses implicit in (say) *aggravating* or *the psychological moment*, for usage has consecrated the original errors and made them correct currency.

An entertaining and valuable discussion of this question of

the limits of pure English (Received Standard) was contributed by the late Logan Pearsall Smith, who, an American long resident in England, had made a profound study of the English language. 'Since our language seems to be growing year by year more foreign, abstract and colourless in character, it stands in greater need than ever of this vigorous and native reinforcement'[1] which we could obtain from dialect in particular and popular speech in general. This reinforcement could be enlisted and profitably used by all of us, 'were we not paralysed by that superstitious feeling of awe and respect for standard English [i.e. Received Standard] which is now [1925] being spread by the diffusion of education'. We are being enslaved by the tyrant Correctitude.

But why should Standard English have to resort to dialect and popular speech for the elements of vitality and picturesqueness instead of drawing them from its own resources? 'It is inevitable that when any form of speech becomes a standard and written language, it should as a consequence lose much of its linguistic freedom. All forms of speech have of course their rules and usages, but in a written language these rules and usages become much more settled and stereotyped': so that, finally, words and phrases are adjudged to be good or bad, not by their power, clarity and aptness of expression, but by the external criterion of correctness—that is, by their conformity to the standards of Public School English.

'Such an attitude ... tends ... to fix grammar and pronunciation, to discourage assimilation [of picturesque or vigorous outsiders], and to cripple the free and spontaneous powers of word-creation.' Then, too, 'a standard language, in modern conditions, tends to be rather a written than a spoken language'.

'The printed word becomes more and more the reality, the spoken word an echo or [a] faint copy of it. This inversion of the normal relation between speech and writing, this predominance'—almost tyranny —'of the eye over the ear, of the written symbol over its audible'— i.e., spoken—'equivalent, tends to deprive the language of that vigour and reality which comes, and can only come, from its intimate association with the acts and passions of men, as they vividly describe and express them in their speech. Freed from the necessity of using terms which can be easily spoken and understood, and more concerned with abstract thought than feeling, the written language, when it finds new terms are necessary, supplies its needs by borrowing learned words, or by making long compounds out of Greek or Latin elements. It is by means of these mechanical or dead words that it tries to make up for its lack of original power; and their abundant use, and the mechanical

---

[1] 'Popular Speech and Standard English' in *Words and Idioms*.

ease [with] which they can be formed, tend in their turn to cripple still further what creative powers the language may still possess.'

This, however, is not to attack or to depreciate Standard English. This accepted form of English, with its national scope and its national use, with its rich and varied vocabulary, with its often subtle and, for the most part, flexible grammar, with all the historical associations inevitably and naturally garnered in the course of centuries, and with these and other associations enriched by successive generations, is the inestimably precious inheritance of the English people, as any such language is of any ancient people. It is an inheritance that we rightly feel should be guarded and safeguarded: and that feeling and that accompanying instinct are essentially healthy which cause us to hesitate before —and often to refrain from—offending against its well-tested rules and its native growths of usage. But the position of good English is, in essentials, impregnable: for as it arises from, so does it serve, a social need. It is necessary for a person to be intimately familiar with this good, this pure, this Received Standard English if he wishes to share in the privileges and to understand the aims of the ruling and the cultured classes. The danger, then, lies not in its being disregarded and set aside (with the consequence of linguistic chaos and hence of a lack of national unity), but in its being so unthinkingly and blindly respected and, as it were, deified, that we may forget the very existence of popular speech and widespread colloquialism, of slang and dialect, and thus lose sight of their value in themselves and of their value as readily available sources of freshness and invigoration.

Obviously, as we see when we do come to think about the subject, no standard language (English, American, French, German and the others) exists on its own capital; indeed, it cannot—if it is to continue to be a language and not a graveyard. Standard English has arisen from a dialect, but it has never, for long, disregarded those other dialects over which, through a geographical and political accident, it has been exalted: those others have always had too much to offer in potential enrichment of the triumphant dialect. Like dialect, popular speech may—and does— abound in uncouth phrases and low words and absurd or, at the least, hasty perversions and inaccuracies; but it also abounds in vivid phrases, in words racy of the soil and vigorous on the ear, in strong monosyllables and picturesque compounds, and also in ancient words that have, unluckily for us, dropped out of cultured speech: how useful, how valuable, how right it would be if many of these words and phrases were to be admitted (or readmitted) to the standard speech and were to become, in their turn, Received Standard, whence there would duly be expelled those learned terms which had become synonyms of these racier or stronger or more musical words adopted from dialect and from the popular speech of the towns. Their adoption would not only enrich (enrichment is hardly necessary) but improve the material stock, hence the spiritual value and potentialities, of Standard English: they would strengthen Standard English; but more, they would render it less standardized.

The present trend, however, is in the direction of standardizing the language still further and of making it, not more aristocratic but more democratic. Linguistic fashions spring from the educated: it is therefore the duty of the educated to relax their guard over the language and to welcome democratic words and phrases instead of snobbishly excluding them with upraised hands and an appalled sideward glance.

'For human speech[1] is after all a democratic product, the creation, not of scholars and grammarians, but of unschooled and unlettered people. Scholars and men of education may cultivate and enrich it, and make it flower into all the beauty of a literary language', but they should not, in their efforts to keep the language pure, forget that it should also be kept vigorous; they are too apt to forget that the 'rarest blooms [of any language] are grafted on a wild stock, and [that] roots are deep-buried in the common soil. From that soil it must still draw its sap and nourishment, if it is not to perish [from inanition], as the other standard languages of the past have perished, when, in the course of their history, they have been separated and cut off from the popular vernacular'—from that popular speech which (as we see best in the survival of Low as compared with the virtual disappearance of Classical Latin) has ultimately displaced their outworn words and forms.

Nevertheless, as another distinguished American writer[2] on the English language has excellently said:

'The standardization of modern English is not as nearly complete as is sometimes supposed. The language ideal of philosophers like Locke has never been realized. Idealistic efforts . . . have been only partially successful. The English language has not been subjected to absolute rule . . . In other words, English is not yet a dead language . . . "Law", says Roscoe Pound, "must be stable and yet cannot stand still." The statement applies with little modification to . . . language.

[1] Logan Pearsall Smith.
[2] G. H. McKnight, in the Preface to *Modern English in the Making* (a very good book indeed).

Language, though regulated, is not fixed for all time but must change in company with changing conditions of life. Like human nature, of which it is a mirror, language has imperfections; and like human nature, its prospects of absolute perfection are distant and uncertain.'

Purity, so far as possible; but not to the detriment of vigour and raciness. And, after all, the garden of English is far more likely to remain an essentially English garden if we admit the flowers of popular speech instead of constantly introducing foreign plants and, often, foreign weeds.

STANDARD ENGLISH IN THE DOMINIONS

Except among English Public School men resident there, the Dominions do not speak with a Received Standard pronunciation though the vocabulary is, among the cultured and the well educated, that of Received Standard: they must, then, be said to speak Modified Standard. Inhabitants of the Dominions are, all in all, less inclined, when engaged in literary work, to rise to Literary Standard than are their peers in Great Britain and Northern Ireland. Most Dominion writers are independent in their attitude to style; but less independent than are non-academic Americans; yet such Australian and Canadian writers as are bitten with the nationalistic bug are almost as independent as the most lawless Americans, the former because they exalt popular speech, the latter because, the less English they are, the more do they tend to be indistinguishable from Americans.

Nationalism, separatism, independence—these are excellent in their spirit and essence: but they can easily be carried too far. Nevertheless, it is perhaps not too optimistic to hope that, as in England popular speech may revivify and enrich Standard English, so in the Dominions (more especially in Canada and Australia[1]) the clarity and subtlety of the best Standard English will always exercise their rightful charm and influence: and it is idle to think that these Dominion writers will be unduly cramped thereby, for, if anything, they are (most of them) perhaps a shade too self-righteous in their sturdy self-reliance; self-reliance, however, is an excellent thing when tempered with a mellowing experience; and, in those sunny lands, experience should generally be mellowing, not embittering.

But English scorn of Colonial accents and Colonial contempt of Public School English might well die out! There is an excuse for Colonial accents; and in Public School English resides much virtue.

[1] I do not ignore the virile writing of Roy Campbell and several other South Africans; but the statement, I think, is substantially correct.

STANDARD AMERICAN SPEECH AND WRITING

In the United States we have a knottier problem, affecting a much larger population than that of the English-speakers in the Dominions.

In writing, there is an American Literary Standard, which so closely resembles the English Literary Standard as (with the exception of the few very minor points mentioned in the last paragraph but one of Chapter III) make no basic, no important difference.

But, in American speech, is there a Received Standard? Or is there nothing but a number of Modified Standards? On first thoughts, one might be tempted to say that the latter supposition is correct, although one would add that perhaps some of these Modified Standards are more pleasing to the ear, or more close to good English speech, or more widely used than others. But the fact remains that, whereas there is, in the United States, no speech that can be called Received Standard to the same degree, and with the same certainty, as Public School speech is said to be the Received Standard in England, nevertheless the speech taught and learned at Harvard and Yale, Bryn Mawr and Vassar, and at certain other American universities and colleges, the speech (moreover) of the cultured portion of American society, is as close to a Received Standard as can be expected in a vast, many-peopled country like the States. That the criterion is not so severe, nor so rigid, as that of English Received Standard does not make it any the less a genuine criterion; the speech any the less Received Standard American. But as in Great Britain, so in America are the speakers of Modified Standard far more numerous than the speakers of Received Standard. Both the accent of Chicago and the more musical accent of the South are a feature in two of the most marked Modified Standards in America; it just so happens that the pleasantest accent does not belong to what we have agreed to call Received Standard, yet the Southern vowels have had a not quite negligible influence on the vowel system of the Received American Standard.

It must, however, be remembered that the differentiation between Standard and popular speech, between Standard and slang, between slang and cant, is, on the whole, less marked in the United States than in the British Empire; perhaps even the 'deepest' dialects of America present fewer differences from American Standard than the deeper of the English and, especially, the Scottish dialects do from English Standard.

STANDARD ENGLISH AND STANDARD AMERICAN IN THEIR RELATIONS TO NON-STANDARD SPEECH

What holds good for British English holds good—here at least —for American English. Nothing in the following verdict by the late Sir James Murray[1] is less true of American than of English.

'The English vocabulary', he says, 'contains a nucleus or central mass of many thousand words whose "Anglicity"'—Englishness—'is unquestioned; some of them only literary, some of them only [spoken],[2] the great majority at once literary and [spoken]—they are the Common Words of the language. But they are linked on every side with words that are less and less entitled to this appellation and [belong] ever more ... distinctly to ... local dialect, ... slang of "sets" and classes, ... popular technicalities of trades and processes, ... the scientific terminology common to all civilized nations [and] the actual languages of other lands and peoples. And there is absolutely no defining line in any direction: the circle of the English language has a well-defined centre but no discernible circumference ... The centre is occupied by the "common" words, in which literary and [spoken] usage meet. "Scientific" and "foreign" words enter the common language mainly through literature: "slang" words ascend through [spoken] use; the "technical" terms of crafts and processes, and the "dialect" words, blend with the common language both in speech and literature. Slang also touches on one side the technical terminology of trades and occupations, as in "the slang of the Stock Exchange", and on another passes into true dialect ... Dialects similarly pass into slang, colloquial, and literary use';

and so on. 'It is not possible to fix the point at which the "English Language" stops, along any of these diverging lines.'

But what of those two terms, *idiom* and *familiar English*? *Familiar English* is generally applied to that Standard English— the same holds for Standard American—which is not quite formal or dignified or beautiful enough to be used on very formal occasions or in lofty or unremittingly dignified or beautiful writings.

Idiom is that English or American which, without being either low or slangy, is the very essence of English or American; idiomatic English or American is much the same thing as 'familiar English' or 'familiar American'; but the term *idiom* is applied chiefly to phrases (e.g., *lock, stock and barrel*) and grammatical

---

[1] In vol. I (1888) of *The Oxford English Dictionary*.
[2] Sir James has 'colloquial' = 'characteristic of, or belonging to, speech'. But throughout this little book, I use 'colloquial' only in the sense of 'characteristic of, or belonging to, that speech which is less respectable than standard but more respectable than slang'.

constructions (*yours sincerely* for *believe me*, or *I am, yours sincerely*). There are two nuances attached to the word *idiom*:— 'The specific character, property, or genius of any language; the manner of expression which is natural or peculiar to it'; and the usual one, 'a form of expression, grammatical construction, phrase, etc., peculiar to a language; a peculiarity of phraseology approved by the usage of a language' (*The Oxford English Dictionary*). English and American idioms go to make up English and American idiomatic speech.

II. DIALECT[1]

A dialect is that variety of a language which prevails in a district and has local peculiarities of vocabulary, pronunciation, and phrase.[2] These peculiarities of what Professor Wyld calls 'regional dialects' and most of us call simply 'dialects' are constantly being adopted by colloquialism. At ordinary times, the adoption is slow, but on special occasions, as during a war (when countrymen mingle at close quarters with townsmen), numerous dialect terms become part of the common stock, and some few of them pass into formal speech and into the language of literature, whether prose or poetry.

More fully than slang and much more fully than colloquialism, dialect has been charted and mapped. 'Of all the forms of non-[Standard] English, the local dialects have been most carefully documented and studied', as Logan Pearsall Smith has remarked. This accessibility of dialect words and phrases affords a ready mine for the enrichment of Standard English: but few are the miners. American dialects have not been so fully dictionaried as English dialects and, if we except the New England dialect, they have been less utilized in literature: but it is only fair to add that Standard American (in its Modified forms), has less need of reinvigoration from this particular source.

The virtues of dialect, as related to a country's speech in general, are that it abounds both in pithy words, including vigorous and apt monosyllables (*croon*) and delightful compounds (*winter-proud* for 'cold', *will-led* for 'mentally deranged', *star-glint* for 'star-light', and *teeth-haler* for 'dentist'), and in happy phrases (*want all the water to run in one's own ditch*, to be self-willed; to be covetous); it has a surprising number of picturesque words as well as picturesque phrases. Logan Pearsall Smith has pointed out that English dialect has provided not only English Standard but

---

[1] This section very closely follows the corresponding section in my *Slang To-day and Yesterday*.

[2] This is a slightly changed form of H. W. Fowler's definition.

European Standard ('There ain't no sech animal') with *coke*, *snob* and *tram*—possibly also with *lunch*.

We might receive again into Standard English, as generally spoken, these words which once belonged to it or at least to good English before there was a Received Standard: *fain*, glad; *fey*, fated; *bide*, to wait; *thole*, to suffer or endure (a thing); *nesh*, delicate or physically soft or out of training; *kemp*, a fighter; *speer*, to inquire; *bairn*; *weird*, fate; *dree*, to suffer. In other senses, the first two and the last two of these words are known to all; and *bairn* is familiar to most of us: yet these five words form no exception.

III. COLLOQUIALISM[1]

'Colloquialism' and 'the colloquial' and 'colloquialisms' are but three names for the one thing: that speech which, although not accepted as Standard English, is yet above slang and far above cant, and standing apart from vulgarisms and low language. As is well said in Greenough and Kittredge, 'every educated person has at least two ways of speaking his mother tongue. The first is that which he employs in his family, among his familiar friends, and on ordinary occasions. The second is ... the language which he employs when he is "on his dignity" as he puts on evening dress when he is going out to dine. The difference between these two forms consists, in great measure, in a difference of vocabulary.' True; yet it must not be forgotten that there are other features, some of which occur very frequently. For instance, syntax so flexible as to become at times ungrammatical or, worse still, ambiguous; a fondness for sentences with only one verb; the omission of *I* at the beginning of a sentence or clause; sudden leaps from one subject to another; the use of such words and phrases as, unintelligible or, at least, obscure in print, are in speech made clear and sometimes arresting by tone or gesture, pause or emphasis. But to continue with Greenough and Kittredge: 'The basis of familiar words must be the same in [Standard and in colloquial speech], but the vocabulary appropriate to the more formal occasion will include many terms which would be stilted or affected in ordinary talk. There is also a considerable difference between [colloquial] and dignified language in the manner of utterance'—in pronunciation and enunciation. 'In conversation, we habitually employ such contractions as *I'll*, *don't*, *won't*, *it's*, *we'd*, *he'd* ... which we should never use in public speaking, unless with set purpose, to give a markedly colloquial tinge to what we

[1] Here again I follow closely the corresponding section in *Slang To-day and Yesterday*.

have to say'; though it must be added that colloquialisms are used much more freely nowadays than they were fifty years ago.

The colloquial varies tremendously from class to class, clique to clique, group to group, family to family, individual to individual; and even the individual uses different sets of colloquialisms according to the person or persons he is addressing. The difficulty of confining the colloquial within practical limits is rendered still more marked by the fact that, as Dr Henry Bradley once remarked, 'at no period . . . has the colloquial vocabulary and idiom of the English language been completely preserved in the literature' or even in the dictionaries.

Bradley mentions 'phrases of contemporary currency'; catch phrases. These have some topical reference to history, to events (mostly recent), to well-known characters and much-advertised things. They are less idiotic than they seem, for to the most inane catch phrase, there is a pointed meaning, sun-clear if you know the origin; but they get repeated so often that they end by ruining our nerves. Think of the Victorian *all serene* (early), *get your hair cut* (late), and *does your mother know you're out?* (from ca. 1840), the 1914–18 *Belgium needs you*; and the more general twentieth century *won't you come home, Bill Bailey?* (Edwardian) and *I hope it keeps fine for you* (or *him* or *her*, etc.). These are colloquialisms of the most colloquial.

IV. LOW LANGUAGE; VULGARISMS[1]

Low language consists of the coarser part of colloquialism and slang and dialect; cant; and what I call vulgarisms. In many dictionaries *low* and *vulgar* denote the same defect—a defect that qualifies the word or phrase for inclusion in the linguistic class low language; in those dictionaries, *low language* and *vulgarisms* are synonymous.

Perhaps it will clear the air if I define *vulgarisms* (in my sense) before I define *low language* (in everybody's sense). *Vulgarisms* are words that, belonging either to dialect or, especially, to Standard English of the familiar or ordinary idiomatic kind, denote such objects (mostly parts of the body) or actions (especially, bodily processes) as are not usually mentioned at all by the polite and are almost never, under *those* names, mentioned by name in the respectable circles of any social class.

Low language (or vulgar English[2]) is of several kinds: words foisted on one social class by a lower social class or brought from the stress and purlieus of trade into the serenity of the drawing-

---
[1] This section abridges and modifies the corresponding section in *Slang To-day and Yesterday*.   [2] Including American English.

ENGLISH: GOOD; BAD; AND WORSE

room; more importantly, cant and slang and colloquialism and dialect that show, towards feebleness, suffering, and misfortune, an attitude so thoughtless, so inconsiderate as to be cruel or, at best, to be indicative of stupidity and a rhinocerotically thick skin, as in *old codger* and *old geezer*—*to bash*—*cracked* or *bats*, *bughouse* or *nuts* (mad); words that are very trivial, as well as being unnecessary (e.g., *an invite, lolly, a Jane, palooka*, and *to diddle*); and illiteracies, such as *ain't* for 'am not' or 'is not', *don't* (once permissible) for 'does not', *interdooce* for 'introduce', *sech* or *sich* for 'such', *git* for 'get', the double negative ('He ain't never done it'), wrong part of verb ('He done it'), wrong pronoun ('He's the cove as murdered the slop'), and so forth.

V. SLANG

Slang is less respectable than colloquialism, but more respectable than cant. It is defined by *The Oxford English Dictionary* as 'language of a highly colloquial type, considered as below the level of standard educated speech, and consisting either of new words or of current words employed in some special sense'; by the admirable H. W. Fowler of *Modern English Usage* as 'the diction that results from the favourite game among the young and lively of playing with words and renaming things and actions; some invent new words, or mutilate or misapply the old, for the purposes of novelty, and others catch up such words for the pleasure of being in the fashion'.

The two chief reasons for the invention of slang words and phrases are 'the desire to secure increased vivacity and the desire to secure increased sense of intimacy in the use of language' (Henry Bradley).

And slang is employed for one or two or more of thirteen reasons:

1. In sheer high spirits; 'just for the fun of the thing'.
2. As an exercise in wit or in humour.
3. To be 'different'—to be novel.
4. To be picturesque.
5. To be startling; to startle.
6. To escape from clichés and long-windedness.
7. To enrich the language.
8. To give solidity and concreteness to the abstract and the idealistic, and nearness to the distant scene or object.
9. To reduce solemnity, pain, tragedy.
10. To put oneself in tune with one's company.
11. To induce friendliness or intimacy.

12. To show that one belongs to a certain school, trade or profession, intellectual set or social class. In short, to be in the fashion—or to prove that someone else isn't.
13. To be secret—not understood by those around one.

'Slang phrases often possess a greater wealth of association than others because they appeal to recent experiences'—a national or a local incident—'rather than to dim memories' (Sechrist). Slang is racy of the national soil and saturated with the virtues and vices of a people, a district, a city, a trade. It tends to be, in greatly varying degrees, uneducated rather than learned; Saxon rather than Latin; simple rather than abstruse or concealed; to simplify the difficult and the strange; to abridge, not to elaborate; to omit the incidental; to give colour and point; to take nothing too seriously, yet to imply a standard of common sense; not to restrict itself to any one social class; to refer to human nature rather than to Nature; to lash humbug and hypocrisy; to be tolerant and human.

Nearly always originating in speech, slang is much rather a spoken than a written language. In literature, its use is confined to dialogue; if it does happen to occur outside of dialogue, it is usually set off from the other words by quotation marks or italics.

Perhaps the difference between slang[1] and colloquialism and Standard English can best be shown in a few examples. Standard English (or American) *man* is colloquial *chap* and slang *bloke* or *cove* or *guy* or *stiff* or *bozo*; *an old fellow* becomes, in slang, *an old buffer* or *an old geezer*; *money* is colloquial *shekels* and slang *brass* (mostly North Country) or *tin*; *doctor* becomes colloquial *doc* and slang *the vet* or *croaker* or *pill-shooter*; *lawyer's clerk* becomes colloquial *limb of the law*; lawyer, in colloquialism, is *pettifogger*—in slang, either a *mouthpiece* (which is both English and American) or a *fixer* (American); a *clergyman* is colloquial *parson* and slang *sky pilot* or *fire escape*.

VI. CANT

'English: Good; Bad; and Worse': the good English is Standard English; the bad English is illiteracy and such slang as is used by a person ignorant of the fact that it is slang; the worse is cant, or the speech of the underworld.

By the underworld is meant not only criminals and their associates, but also beggars and tramps.

It is not correct to speak of cant as underworld slang: for it is not slang at all. It is a language. A modified language, in that all

[1] By the way, slang is not to be called argot; nor yet lingo.

the small coin of speech—*a* and *the*; *is* and *has*; *and* and *because*; *to* and *from* and *at*—is the same in cant as in Standard English. It is only the key words which are different—but how very different! Only an adept would recognize the meanings of the cant words for taking and stealing; running away; shooting, killing and arresting; house, door, safe, window, ladder, money, jewels, gold, silver; man, girl; policeman, judge, lawyer, advocate; jemmy, glycerine; a drug and a doctor.

It is, in short, a secret language, with only the important words (important, that is, for criminals and policemen) disguised. And in that language, many of the terms have a very long life; comparatively few terms are discarded before it becomes certain that they have got too well known by the general public.

Some cant words have been adopted into general slang and colloquialism: for instance, *bloke* (originally *gloke*—or *gloak*) and *cove*; *booze* and *grub*; *queer* and *rum*, which, in cant, were opposites, *rum* meaning 'excellent, costly, very able or skilful'; *snooze*; *nap* (to take or steal); *hick*.

VII. JARGON[1] OR TECHNICALITIES

Jargon is the generic or collective name for the technical terms used in a profession (e.g., the law) or a trade (e.g., carpentry); in a process or a game or sport. The special vocabulary of cricket or of baseball contains many terms that are purely technical: they are not slang, they are not even colloquialisms: in fact, they belong to Standard English. But if they were used in the drawing-room or at the dining-table they would probably be stigmatized as jargon or, in the better-known term, shop. Employed by and among initiates, they are entirely permissible; transferred to wider circles, they have an unpleasing air and are, obviously, out of place.

There are, between jargon and slang, several notable differences that may be mentioned: jargon consists of words and phrases concerning, or demanded by, the letter of a trade, profession, process or game, whereas slang deals with the spirit of the whole world and with life; jargon treats with respect—sometimes with solemnity—the avocation it serves, whereas slang treats every avocation as a joke; and where jargon prospers, there does slang fare hardly.

Jargon may be and often is an indication of the extent to which one knows one's game or one's avocation. Too often is it also an indication that one's knowledge of good English is embarrassingly small.

[1] *Jargon* is often misused to mean slang or cant or even pidgin English.

PART FOUR

CHAPTER EIGHT
WHAT GRAMMAR IS—AND *WHY*

I. INTRODUCTORY

In one sense, a language may be said to consist of whatever is the number of words and phrases that this particular language possesses.[1] One learns, however, only so many of those words and phrases as one needs to know; at least, that is the ideal, for usually one fails to learn a certain number that might be very helpful, and learns a few that are of no use whatsoever. But if one is learning a language (whether one's own or a foreign), one has to be taught, or to pick up, or, as a child does, assimilate more or less subconsciously those rules which tell us *how* to put those words together into phrases and sentences: this process is taught by grammar; the process itself is applied grammar and is, in fact, the *spirit* of grammar; a spirit that can be helped by the *letter* of grammar or, in other words, by the rules.

It is important to remember that, in the first stage of a language, there are no grammatical rules: no rules informing us how to express our thoughts (that is, form sentences); no rules telling us how, for instance, we may turn a singular word into a plural; not even a rule to warn us that such a change is necessary. The first rules were based on practice; on speech as it already existed. As speech became more supple and subtle—as, for example, it learned to deal with tenses and *if*'s—so did the rules become more numerous. But, at the same time, those rules were soon felt to be extremely useful: it was, to take only one example, convenient and far from unpleasant to know how to grapple with time-changes by availing oneself of the rules of tense (*I am, I was, I shall be*).

Naturally, one does not burden a young child with these rules. The young child picks them up unconsciously or, at best, empirically (by experiment, by trying things out for itself): but not all rules can be learnt thus. Hence the teacher. Hence the grammar book, with its two main divisions: 1, Accidence, or that part of grammar which deals with flexions or changes in words (*me, my, mine; he, him, his; dog's* and *dogs* as compared with *dog*), the term

---

[1] Compare the Postscript at the end of Chapter IV; the point of that Postscript should be borne in mind throughout Chapter VIII.

meaning *accidents* or those things which happen to the word proper (*dog*); and 2, Syntax, or the construction (building) of sentences.

Young children make many mistakes before they learn the correct way of forming plurals and possessives and before they learn how to form sentences—that is, make complete statements. Older children have learnt how to avoid the simpler mistakes and normally they are eager to find out how to avoid making mistakes at all. These older children know how to put words together: how to set them, as though they were pearls, on a string—the string of a simple sentence, such as 'I bought a dog' or 'I shall be an airman when I'm grown-up'. But they are not so sure how to express such a thought as the thought in 'I should have bought a dog long ago if only I had known what it would cost or if I had not feared that if I asked my father for the money, he might say No'.

*Well, in this book you will find no rules of grammar, unless I have occasion, here and there, to give one to illustrate some point. But you *will* find what lies behind grammar; why this rule or that exists, and on what it rests; why this rule or that rule or the other rule has come into existence; and why these rules, collectively, are useful.

If you wish to express yourselves well (first of all clearly; and secondly, neatly and vigorously or even beautifully) you will find that rules of grammar help you to do so. But it is not enough to learn the rules; it is necessary to understand those rules—to see just what they mean, and to discover why they were made. There is an excellent reason for every rule: and generally it is a very interesting reason. There is much fun to be had from grammar if you tackle it in the right spirit and in the right way. In fact, you will (to your surprise, perhaps) find that even learning the rules themselves can be made entertaining and at times funny, if only you remember that grammatical rules have interesting reasons and that they are based on actual practice, not on mere theory, and that they show the common sense of the men and women who have, through many centuries, learnt to speak and write our language. If you know why a rule was formed and what it sought to guard against and in what it planned to be a help, you will certainly understand and probably enjoy the rule.

And now, after that long sermon, I shall show you what grammar is—and why it is. I do not say, 'I shall try to show you', for I know that, if you are willing, you will understand me without wrinkling your foreheads and without giving yourselves a headache; what is more, you will do it easily. But I should like you,

* Adults may skip the next three paragraphs.

later, to read the book that has made *me* see what fun grammar is and the great interest it has for all of us: *The Philosophy of Grammar*, by Dr Otto Jespersen.

II. THE ORIGIN OF GRAMMATICAL ELEMENTS[1]

In any account of the origins of grammar and of the reasons for those origins, this is a necessary chapter—for advanced students. But it cannot be made satisfactory for students below University standard or for those who have not, in English, the equivalent of a University training in the subject: less because the principles involved are difficult, and the examples unavoidably erudite, than because the philologists have not yet succeeded in arriving at certainty on three or four of the main problems. Some of the points are: what, precisely, is a root (radical or stem), and when?; the rise of affixes, and their philosophy; the inner history of grammatical gender; the logical concept of number; why are there flexions?; the rationale of agglutination, coalescence, and secretion: not, you will admit, the simplest of problems, nor questions amenable to easy explanation. We should be wise to defer these problems.

III. THE SOUL—OR INNER HEART— OF GRAMMAR

It is possible to arrive at the secret places of grammar only by the application of 'sound psychology, . . . sane logic, and . . . solid facts of linguistic history', as Professor Jespersen once remarked. True; but, here, the difficulties will be short-circuited or gently set on one side. It is, however, well to realize the following three points: psychology assists philologists, as of course it assists us, to discover and understand what goes on in the minds of speakers and why these speakers break rules and perhaps, by breaking them, help to form new and better rules; the logic employed nowadays in discussions of language is much less narrow and formal than it was formerly, yet logic is of the greatest use and value in forming rules and in devising methods; linguistic history teaches us to be tolerant—for instance, we learn that what was bad grammar[2] in Queen Victoria's day may be the best of grammar to-day.

---

[1] When young people reach the awful maturity of undergraduate status, or when other inquirers-after-knowledge are ready to learn more than they can learn from this little book of mine, they should read ch. xix of Jespersen's *Language: Its Nature, Development and Origin*.

[2] I am thinking of the completely changed attitude to the split infinitive and to prepositions at the end of sentences.

Happenings in and features of grammar—'grammatical phenomena' is the learned term—can be, and should be, examined and considered from various points of view; points of view that are often bound up, one with another, or that assist understanding, this of that, that of the other viewpoint. Take the agreement (technically, 'the concord') between a noun or substantive and its adjective—in some languages an agreement of gender, number, case; or that, in number and person, between a subject and its verb. The old-fashioned grammarian flatly states the rules and treats all deviations or exceptions as blunders or virtual blunders, and he no less flatly declares that these deviations are either illogical or (with a stern look on his parchmenty face) senseless. The genuinely modern grammarian, who brings sympathy and psychology to his study of language, sets himself to discover why the rules are broken in this or that instance: he does not oppose or modify the rules on some high-and-mighty principle nor by some merely abstract, philosophical reasoning; he seeks particular instances and examines and treats these instances separately and on their merits. He sees that if 'the verb comes long after its subject, there is no more mental energy left to remember what was the number of the subject', i.e. whether it were singular or plural; 'or that if the verb precedes the subject, the speaker has not yet made up his mind as to what the subject is to be'. In both these instances, the writer has an advantage: he can go back to the subject or the verb and then correct any error that he may have committed.

The historian examines his texts over various centuries and finds a growing tendency to neglect the forms distinctive of number [, gender, and case]. And then the linguistic philosopher may step in and say that the demand for grammatical concord in these [parts of accidence] is simply a consequence of the imperfection of language, for the ideas of number, gender (sex), case and person belong logically only to primary words [e.g., nouns] and not to secondary ones like adjective . . . and verb. So far, then, from a language suffering any loss when it gradually discards those endings in adjectives and verbs which indicated this agreement with the primary [noun or pronoun], the tendency must, on the contrary, be considered a progressive one, and full stability can be found in that language alone which has abandoned all these clumsy remnants of a bygone past.

If language is studied in this human, sensible and logical way, and especially if grammar is felt as (and taught as) a living organism, then language, whether in its sounds (phonetics) or in its vocabulary or in its accidence or in its syntax, will inevitably become an absorbing subject—perhaps the most absorbing of all. Thus, too, will language be related to life: and by making language a more intimate part of life we shall stand a better chance of making life a success.

IV. CONFLICTS IN GRAMMAR

The aspects of life, the happenings that befall us, the emergencies with which, even when young or inexperienced, we have to cope, are many and various, and some of them perplex us; the variety and the number of objects are, the former considerable, the latter bewildering (if we let them impose on instead of impressing us). With all of these, language has to contend; language has to fit them all; and, especially, language has so to master them all that they fall into clear order, acquire a definite meaning, and become things we understand, not obstacles in the path of understanding. It is not always easy for language to do this: but as things become simpler if our thoughts are clear in our minds, so also do words and phrases become clearer, if we regard the world alertly and see things for what they are. Words do not exist in their own right, though they have rights of their own. Words stand for things, represent things, are the symbols of things; and by things we mean objects and acts and thoughts and feelings. Never think of a word as apart from what it pictures or indicates or symbolizes; not even the most pedantic etymologist can consider a word as only a shape, a form. Dissociation or separation of the word from the thing it symbolizes will certainly lead to trouble; wholly unnecessary trouble. Luckily, it is not easy to sever a word from what it represents.

Now, since words are, in our minds, the things themselves, it is natural that conflicts should occur. The speaker has hurriedly, the writer has leisurely, to make a choice; after hesitating, he may use such a word or phrase or turn of sentence (that is, a grammatical construction) as would not be used by some other speaker or writer. 'In some cases we witness a tug-of-war, as it were, between two tendencies which may go on for a very long period, during which grammarians [and others in their scores] indulge in disputes as to which form or expression is "correct"; in other cases one of the conflicting tendencies prevails, and the question is settled practically by the speaking community, sometimes under protest from the Lindley Murrays [or H. W. Fowlers] or [the] Academies of the time', such pundits and such corporate authorities often preferring 'logical consistency to ease and naturalness' and, even though it seems hard to believe, to the true spirit and healthiest life of the national language. An old saw runs, *Vox populi, vox Dei*, 'the voice of the people is the voice of God': but whereas in politics the voice of the people is too often the voice of the devil, in language the voice of the people (especially if we make 'people' synonymous with 'nation') is the voice of the god presiding over speech and literature; or, if you prefer it, the voice of the people is usually in accordance with the spirit, the very self, of the national language. This is not to exalt the voice of the gutter; nor is it, on the other hand, to suggest that the language of the gutter has nothing to offer standard speech. It is merely to stress the obvious, or what should be obvious: the whole of a nation is not, over a period of years, likely to err, except in a few instances; those instances will always, and rightly, be combated by the H. W. Fowlers of tonic memory.

Some of these conflicts will be mentioned in the course of this chapter, and two may be mentioned here and now: 1. The discrepancy and the rivalry between actual sex and grammatical sex, i.e. gender, have been wholly resolved in English, where, in the modern period (from 1450 onwards), there has been no gender[1] apart from the actual sex (masculine or feminine) or lack of sex (neuter) of the person, animal or thing. 2. A collective noun takes a singular or a plural verb according to whether the noun indicates a unit or a collection: but for a long time there were bitter arguments on the subject.

V. LIVING GRAMMAR

If, instead of regarding it as a dry-as-dust bore, you look on grammar as the result of mankind's attempt to make things as easy (by making them as clear) as possible for the speaker to be understood by the listener and for the listener to understand the speaker, you will not only rid yourselves of a silly prejudice but also realize the main cause of speech; and you will realize that grammar is not always quite so easy as knocking a ball about, for the simple reason that the exchange of abstract ideas and the communication of complicated business and the narration of long, detailed stories are not learnt as quickly as that $1 + 1 = 2$. If you wish to understand the nature of grammar (and who but a fool or a pedant could tolerate ignorance of the instrument he is using?), you must always bear in mind this relationship between speaker and listener or, better, hearer, hence the less important relationship between writer and reader.[2] 'Even in our modern newspaper-ridden communities, the vast majority of us speak infinitely more than we write.'

[1] In dialect, however, sex is continually attributed to inanimate things.
[2] The speaker and the writer are the *producers* of language; the hearer and the reader are the *consumers* or *recipients* of language.

WHAT GRAMMAR IS

We can never hope to understand what language is and how it progresses, or doesn't, if we do not constantly remember that language is primarily the interactivity of speaking and hearing, and that writing is speech at second hand. Grammar is that wonderful and invaluable set of means and devices whereby we can render our words significant and make our ideas pass, from within ourselves, to other persons. If you like to think of it in that way, language is the vehicle of our thoughts and feelings and of our stories, whether true or not, and grammar is the machinery by which that vehicle is set and kept in motion; the motive power (the steam, the electricity) is the mind; and the speech-sounds are the air and space through which the movement of the vehicle takes place.

As a result of this predominantly important relation between speaker and hearer, it is only natural that emphasis and tone play notable parts in the grammar of spoken language. 'In the written language it looks as if the [past tenses] *paid* and *said* were formed in the same way, but differently from *stayed*, but in reality *paid* and *stayed* are formed regularly . . . , whereas *said* is irregular as having its vowel shortened.'

Let us now be psychological: which is much less difficult than it sounds! There is a great, a fundamental difference between formulas (or such collections of words as are run together into virtual units) and variable formations—that is, between fixed groups and free expressions. There exist in the English and American language, as in almost every other language, certain phrases and short sentences that are of the character of formulas; they are unchangeable. *How do you do?*, spoken at a meeting between two persons, differs widely from *I gave the boy a lump of sugar*.[1] In *how do you do?*, no word can be changed: the fact that careless speakers say *how d'you* [jer] *do?*, and many Americans say *howdy do?* or even *howdy?*, does not weaken but rather strengthens the argument. Nor does one, normally, change the stress: if one says 'How do *you* do?' or 'How *do* you do?' or (more rarely still) '*How* do you do?', one renders oneself conspicuous as a would-be humorist or a senseless revolutionary. For all practical purposes, *how do you do?* is as much a formula as *good day!, good morning!, good afternoon!, good evening!* or *good night!*; or as *thank you!*; or as *I beg your pardon*. (It is true that the pedantic or the facetious may say, 'I bid you good day'; the exquisitely polite may declare, 'I thank you!'; the genuinely sorry may exclaim, 'I *beg* your

---

[1] Most of the examples and all the quotations in this chapter are (unless there is a statement to the contrary) taken from Jespersen, as I hope I made quite clear at the end of section I.

pardon'.) But these phrases are formulas suitable to certain occasions: *how do you do?* does not require an answer, and is generally embarrassed when it receives one; and *I beg your pardon!* (or its abbreviation *pardon!*) means 'I did not catch what you said' almost as often as it constitutes an apology.

But *I gave the boy a lump of sugar*[1] is of a wholly different order. This statement can be changed in every one of its members, thus:

> *You gave the boy a lump of sugar;*
> *She lent the boy a lump of sugar;*
> *We brought that boy a lump of sugar;*
> *They sent this girl a lump of sugar;*
> *Tom posted a woman no lump of sugar;*
> *Dick threw, to the man, yonder piece of sugar;*
> *Harry trundled those men the loaf-sugar;*
> *The others passed these fellows that fragment from the loaf.*

There are many other variations: *I never gave the boy a lump of sugar, Should you have made the boy so much sugary cake?, To think that you sent the boy twenty-six lumps of sugar!*, and so on and so forth.

In formulas, one has only to remember; in free expressions, one has to create a new form for every different shade of the same basic thought, and invent as many different expressions as there are thoughts. But most free expressions fall into a few well-known types of phrase, a few not too difficult moulds of sentence. In simple sentences, the mould is used almost automatically: it is obvious that *Jack and Jill went up the hill* is of the same type or mould as *Humpty-Dumpty had a great fall*; *I gave the boy a lump of sugar* is of the same shape as *The boy's parents lent me five dollars.*

'All very nice', you may say; 'but how do these types, these moulds, take shape, or come into existence in the mind of the primitive speakers?' A young child is not told, 'The subject usually precedes the verb', yet that child has no difficulty in learning to set the subject before the verb. He is able, from the scores of sentences heard by him every day, to build sentences for himself. In free expressions then, there are portions and frequently wholes that conform to a type heard and remembered. Sometimes it is not easy to decide, immediately, whether a statement is a formula or a free expression of a well-known type. In *long live the King!, long live the Queen!, long live the President!*, the

[1] I have, in this paragraph, taken the liberty of considerably modifying Jespersen's variations.

sentence-type (adverb preceding verb, verb preceding its subject) is now used much less than it was several centuries ago; *long live* is a formula, the rest is variable. In the sixteenth century, the plurals of *ox, eye, shoe, foe, cow* were *oxen, eyen, shoen* (or *shoon*), *fone, kine*: only *oxen* has remained, although *kine* has survived in Biblical language; the living type of plural has, ever since the fifteenth century, been that in *-s* (as in *kings* and *stones*); so *eye, shoe, foe, cow*, following that vital pattern, have become *eyes, shoes, foes, cows*. This type has become all-powerful; and modern coinings (learnedly, 'neologisms', i.e. new words or new expressions) conform to that type: *aeroplanes, stunts, blurbs*. And this affords another reason why we may expect soon to have *nucleuses* and *phenomenons*; *indexes* is already dispossessing *indices*, except in that stronghold of learned terms, the jargon of algebra.

Consider suffixes. The *-ness* type is living, for we can still form, quite freely, such words as *weariness* and *closeness*; but the *-lock* of *wedlock* and the *-th* of *width, depth, length, breadth, health* are dead, except in fanciful coinings that (*illth*, illness, and *coolth*, coolness) have met with little success. Yet are not *width, depth* and the others very common words? They are; but, because they were common currency, they have survived as units—as formulas. The *-ness* words, being even more abstract, were much less commonly used: therefore they have not come down to us as units, nor *-ness* as a formula. Whereas *-th* could formerly be added to an adjective, to the accompaniment of a change in the adjective's vowel (as in *wide—width, deep—depth, whole—health*), we no longer resort to *-th* as a suffix whereby nouns may be formed from adjectives: *-th* is a dead formula, but *-ness* is a living type or exemplar.

This distinction between formula and free expression is so marked that it can be seen to affect the order of words. 'So long as *some + thing* is a free combination of two elements felt as such, another adjective may be inserted in the usual way: *some good thing*. But as soon as *something* has become a fixed formula, it is inseparable, and the adjective has to follow: *something good*.' To Jespersen's example I should like to add two rather odd ones: *sometime* used to be *some time*, but we still have to say *at some time*, not *at sometime*; *my self, your self, your selves*, etc., etc., have become *myself, yourself, yourselves*, but psychologically *my self* can still be used (in a different nuance, admittedly) and in commercialese we find *yourself* and *yourselves* broken up into their elements (with no change of nuance) in the phrases *your good self, your good selves*, themselves virtually formulas (for only *good* is thus infixed).

This distinction between formulas and free combinations of words (word-combinations formed for the purpose of free expression) constitutes one of the most marked features of grammar—that is, of living grammar; not of grammar so dead that it ought to be forgotten. A formula may be so short, so small, as to be a mere part of a word (as *hus-* in *husband, hussif, hustings*) or just one word; but it may be a group of words (that is, a phrase), or even a sentence. A formula may have been built on a pattern or type that is either dead or living, whereas a free combination (a free expression) must, as a matter of course, be built in accordance with a living type—on a pattern still used. It follows, therefore, that 'formulas may be regular or irregular, but free expressions always show a regular formation'; this regularity does not extend to vocabulary—the range and the choice of words.

'Apart from fixed formulas, a sentence does not spring into a speaker's mind all at once, but is framed gradually as he goes on speaking.' Suppose you wish to tell a friend what persons you met on a certain occasion; if you remember all the names before you start, you say 'There I met Mr X., Colonel Y., Mrs Z., the A. couple, and young Spiffin'; but if you recall the names only one at a time, you will say, 'There I met—hem! let me see—oh yes, Mr X. and Colonel Y. and Mrs Z., and—er, er, the A. couple, and, of course, young Spiffin.' And your pronunciation of the names will be more deliberate in the latter than in the former instance.

In writing, one thinks (or should think) beforehand; in speech, one must, unless one is content to be a dreadful bore, go straight ahead and make the best of the sentence. Hence many irregularities and mistakes of syntax: permissible and, except to the crusted pedant, not unpleasing in speech; but less pleasant, and often downright intolerable, in all writing except that which repeats conversation and that which purports to reproduce the unedited musings of a halfwit or an illiterate. It is at once natural and yet surprising to come on Ruskin at his ease, thus: 'But if the mass of good things be inexhaustible, and there are horses for everybody,—why is not every beggar on horseback?' And in speaking, one often begins the sentence with such and such a subject and then switches to another; or gets as far as the verb and decides to put the statement differently: these breakings-off and resumptions form an interruption that is called anacoluthon when it occurs in writing. Sometimes anacoluthon is employed deliberately.

But whereas the instances of imperfect sentence-building could be multiplied, the important thing is to remember that a language is not merely a collection of words manipulated in accordance with dull and exasperating rules, but a mass of utterances, a set of habits, that require more than rules to render them intelligible. Sentences and sometimes even words do not flow automatically from a speaker: they are complex actions, which require his attention if he desires to avoid making a fool of himself. He may and usually does remember a type of sentence that will be suitable for that thought which he wishes to express or that statement which he wishes to make: but he has to find the right words. He has constantly to vary the types he knows and occasionally to devise a new type: mental exercises that are very exciting and most beneficial. The more willing he is to adventure among new words, new phrases, and new types of sentence, the more skilled does he become in his use of speech. From ready he becomes fluent, from adventurous he becomes rich, from fearless he becomes powerful; and in writing he may be enabled to develop his gift to a very high pitch. He will not so develop it, however, if he regards syntax as a bore and composition as a joke: if he does consider them thus, it will be he who is the bore—and the joke, though perhaps a rather poor one. Grammar is not a matter of mere words; it is based on psychology and it deals with that large part of life which consists of, or depends on, talking and writing. Grammar cannot be taught by, or adequately learnt from, a pedant; it cannot be explained or treated dogmatically, for there are many exceptions and many variations or possibilities.

VI. SYSTEMATIC GRAMMAR

Formerly, aspects of language were always treated descriptively; now they are usually treated historically. Grammar, treated historically, has yielded important results. 'Where formerly we saw only arbitrary rules and inexplicable exceptions', we can now appeal to sensible rules and show the reasons for the exceptions. For instance, 'the plural *feet* from *foot* was' formerly mentioned only 'as one of the few exceptions to the rule that plurals in English substantives were formed in -*s*'. What was an isolated fact is now shown to be 'related to a great number of other facts in the older stages of the same language and in other languages of the same family. Irregularities in one stage are in many instances recognized as survivals of regularities in older stages.' Nevertheless, it is to be remembered that although we can explain most irregularities, yet we cannot explain them away, as Jespersen has pointedly remarked. 'The distinction between the regular and irregular always must be important to the psychological life of language, for regular forms are those which speakers use as the basis of new formations, and irregular forms are those which they will often tend to [dis]place by new forms created on the principle of analogy.'

Apart from phonetics, linguistic facts fall into two great divisions: (1) vocabulary or dictionary (lexicology) and (2) grammar; the former dealing with special facts (e.g., the definition of *cat*), the latter dealing with general facts of language (the plural in *cats* is a general fact, many other words being made plural by the addition of *-s*). The plural *oxen* would be mentioned in a dictionary, because that is now an extremely rare form of plural; but the formation *-en* would be mentioned in a grammar, for otherwise we should be entitled to assume *ox* to have plural *oxes*. In some instances, it is both doubtful and arbitrary to include a feature in grammar or in dictionary, for that feature may belong to both; moreover, grammar and dictionary sometimes overlap.

In treating of specific sounds, we should do well to keep in mind (preferably at the back of our mind) the meanings of the words in which they occur; but in building up a theory of sounds, it is best to concentrate on the sounds themselves. 'It is a simple consequence of the nature of the spoken language that it is possible to have a theory of human speech-sounds in general, the way in which they are produced by the organs of speech, and the way in which they are combined to form syllables and higher units' (words, phrases, etc.): this may conveniently be called *phonetics*. 'By the side of this we have the theory of what is peculiar to the one particular language with which the grammarian is concerned': this may conveniently be called *phonology*, though *phonetics* is more widely used in this sense too.

But phonetics and phonology are not—or should not be—learnt from a book: or rather, general phonetics should be taught in actual demonstration by one who has an elastic mouth and an indiarubber throat, and particular phonology should be imparted in the same way, in respect of its elements; phonology in its entirety belongs to the course taken at a university by an aspirant to honours in English Language.

Systematic grammar, if we set aside phonetics, is usually divided by the professional grammarians into: accidence; word-formation; syntax. Jespersen proposes a simpler and more logical division into two: 1, morphology, in which we take a form for granted and inquire into its function (its activity or duty, the work it does) and into its meanings, though obviously the work it does depends on the meaning it has; and 2, syntax, in which we accept the meaning and then inquire how that meaning is expressed in form. In morphology,[1] we proceed from without (the form) to within (the meaning); in syntax, from within (the meaning) to without (the form).

A. MORPHOLOGY

Morphology classes together such grammatical features as the ending in -*s* (plural), the ending in -*ed* (indicating either the past participle or the past-definite tense, the preterite), and various kinds of mutation (changes in the form of a word). But since we have to discuss the function of—the work done by—the endings -*s* and -*ed*, we also, by that discussion, state or imply the meaning of -*s* and -*ed*. To say that -*s* denotes the plural is to give a syntactic definition; yet the grouping of forms in -*s* is a feature of morphology. Whence it appears that it is, ultimately, impossible to treat form and meaning separately. 'It should be the grammarian's task'—as it is certainly the pupil's necessity—'always to keep the two things in his mind, for sound and signification [the technical term for 'meaning'], form and function, are inseparable in the life of language, and it has been [to] the detriment of linguistic science that it has ignored one side while speaking of the other, and so lost sight of the constant interplay of sound and sense.'

Jespersen's divisions of morphology are not only convenient and sensible; they are illuminating. As in phonetics he takes, first sound-elements, then sounds, and then sound-combinations (words, formula phrases and sentences), so in morphology he takes first word-elements, then words, then word-combinations. He admits that the boundaries are not always clear: *not* in *could not* is a separate word; so (probably) is *not* in *can not*, despite the modern English (not American) practice of printing it *cannot*; but the *nt* in *can't, don't, won't, shan't* is rather a word-element than a word: a probability strengthened by the fact that the addition of *nt* to *can, do, will* and *shall* has been accompanied by a change in the vowel sound in all these words. Inversely, *'s* as the sign of the possessive ('genitive' is the usual term among grammarians) has, for many years, tended to become increasingly independent of the preceding word (the word to which it belongs), as in *the King of England's power, the Emperor of India's privileges, the President of America's private life, someone* (or *somebody*) *else's hat*—a phenomenon known as 'the group genitive'.

In considering word-elements, we deal separately with each affix, whether *pre*fix, coming before the radical, root, or stem, or

[1] Jespersen's use of *morphology* differs somewhat from the general sense ascribed to it. Yet he does include word-formation, and *morphology* means the science of word-forms.

*suf*fix, i.e. *sub-fix*, fixed at the end of the root, or *in*fix, an addition within a word, this last being very rare in English; we state the form or forms of the affix; and we define its function (activity or work) or functions. We do not, like the old-fashioned grammarians, examine the parts of speech ('word classes', as Jespersen calls them) one by one as though they were watertight compartments: what, much more logically, we do, is to take the suffix *-s* and note that one of its functions—the chief one—is to serve as the sign of the plural of nouns (substantives); that another of its functions is to indicate the genitive (possessive) of nouns, a closely related function being its use in the genitives of pronouns, as in *ours* and *yours* and *theirs*; and that it has a fourth function—to denote the third person singular of the present tense, as in (he) *hits* (the ball). Then there are some very interesting word-elements that are noticed only by the person with the alert eye and the ready ear: in *half* and *breath*, the final consonant is 'voiced' to form the verbs, *halve* and *breathe*; in *foot* the vowel sound undergoes that change which modern philologists call 'mutation' and old-fashioned ones call 'umlaut' in order to form the plural *feet*, and in *food* the vowel sound undergoes the same process to form the verb *feed*; and there is apophony ('ablaut' is the old-fashioned word), which is such a deviation of sound as we see in *sang* and *sung* as compared with *sing*.

It may be—indeed, it sometimes is—objected that in doing this, we mix things that belong to accidence with things that belong to word-building. But why shouldn't we? 'It is hard, not to say impossible, to tell exactly where the boundary has to be drawn between flexion'—the endings in *him* and *his*, compared with *he*, are flexions—'and word-formation'. Thus, *-ess* (*shepherdess* from *shepherd*) is an element in word-formation, and the French *-ne* (*bonne* from *bon*, and *paysanne* from *paysan*) is a flexion and therefore placed under accidence: but is there any essential difference between forming *shepherdess* from *shepherd* and forming *paysanne* from *paysan*? Morphology covers both accidence and word-formation: the same kind of process is at work in both accidence and word-formation: it is not only convenient but revelatory to consider accidence and word-formation as branches of the same tree, phases of the one phenomenon, sub-divisions of the one subject.

After word-elements, words themselves. Not words as 'separates' in a dictionary, but in so far as they are parts of grammar—that is, 'general expressions'. These general expressions are the auxiliary or grammatical words: words that assist the sense, but have less dictionary meaning than *man* or *war* or *food*, or than (to) *live* or *find* or *get*: words comprised of pronouns (auxiliary to nouns), auxiliary verbs ('I *have* lived in Yonkers', 'He *will* find himself in a zoo if he isn't careful'), prepositions (*in* and *at* and *to* and *by*) and conjunctions (*and*, *but*, *because*).

In word-combination, we have to consider each kind or class or type of word-order and see how it works; to discern the part it plays in that comedy which we call speech. One word-order (a sequence of words in a sane statement, not the succession of barely related words in the babblings of a lunatic) plays a humdrum, everyday role; another plays a poetic or an eloquent or an arresting role; one word-sequence shyly hints a timid question, another advertises an arrogant assertion; and so forth. You can discover these differences, play these parts, for yourselves. But for your guidance, here are a few suggestions; suggestions of an elementary nature, so that you can proceed from them to slightly more difficult, but vastly more interesting ones. In the combinations of noun + noun, whether in *Admiral Nelson* (or *General Pershing*) or in *stone wall* and *wine-glass* and *mankind*, you will find it worth while to examine the relations between the two components (i.e. parts making up the whole), not only for stress (emphasis) and spelling but also for the meaning. In the combinations of adjective + noun, you will notice at least three kinds: 1, *red coat* or *black chimney* or *new arrival*; 2, ordinary compounds, as *blackbird* or *newcomer*; 3, special compounds, as *redcoat*, one who wears a red coat, i.e. an English soldier of the period between the doffing of armour and the donning of khaki. Of the combinations of noun (or pronoun) + verb there are many varieties: *rain came; came the rain; did rain come?; and so the rain came; rain beat on the roof; I heard the rain; had rain come, I should not have gone to the theatre.*

'Many people', remarks Jespersen, 'probably will wonder at the inclusion of such things in Morphology, but I venture to think that this is the only consistent way of dealing with the grammatical facts, for word-order is certainly as much a formal element in building up sentences as the forms of the words themselves. And with these remarks I shall leave the first main division of grammar in which things [are] looked at from without, from the sound or form [to the meaning].'

B. SYNTAX[1]

In the second main division of grammar—syntax (the marshalling of words into a sentence-army)—we are occupied with the

---

[1] 'Given the syntax of a language, the meaning of a sentence is determinate as soon as the meaning of the component words is known', Bertrand Russell in his Introduction to L. Wittgenstein's *Tractatus Logico-Philosophicus*, 1922.

same phenomena—features and processes—as in morphology, but from a different angle or viewpoint. In syntax we regard these phenomena from within; from that interior which is meaning, sense, signification.

One important division or section of syntax is Number: singular, collective (*committee*, *herd*), and plural. The various methods of forming the plural (*dog—dogs, ox—oxen, foot—feet, I—we, that—those, loaf—loaves*) are dealt with most easily by morphology, in which each ending (*-s, -en, -es*) or other formative (for instance, the vowel-change in *feet*) is treated by itself. It is helpful to discover what is 'common to all singulars and to all plurals, no matter how these latter happen to be formed'; to note the plural in 'a thousand and one *nights*', the singular in 'more than one *man* has thought his country to be worth dying for' (where the connotation is of plurality), 'the "generic" use of singular and plural to denote the whole class' ('*The cat* is a four-footed animal'; '*cats*'—not 'the cats'—'are quadrupeds'):—all these are things that cannot be placed under morphology.

The possessive case deserves a section to itself. The genitive ('King *George*'s death') has an equivalent in the *of*-phrase ('the death of King George'). But these equivalent usages cannot always be interchanged: thus, 'I bought it at *the baker's*' and 'the date *of* his birth'. Then there is the subtle distinction between 'a friend *of mine*' and 'a friend of President Truman'.

In Comparison, we examine *sweet—sweeter—sweetest; good—better—best; evident—more evident—most evident;* and such positive superlatives as *perfect* and *unique*, which, in good English and good American, admit of neither comparative (*more perfect*) nor superlative (*most unique*). We see why it is preferable to say *the better of two* and *the best of three* or more: three degrees are not needed for two things, whereas two degrees would be insufficient for three or more things.

In Tense, the grammatical device whereby we cope with the varieties of time, it is worth remarking on the difference between *I go* and *I am going*; *I went* and *I was going*; *I shall go* and *I shall be going*; between *I go* and *I have gone*; *I went* and *I had gone*; *I shall go* and *I shall have gone*. Look at the ways in which we can express futurity: '*I* shall (or *he will*) *depart* to-morrow'; '*I am going to depart* to-morrow'; '*I am to depart* to-morrow'; '*I am about to depart* to-day'; '*I may depart* to-morrow'; '*I depart* to-morrow': the first is the simplest form of expressing the fact, the second a softening of the statement (a hardening of the statement is 'I *will* (or he *shall*) *start* to-morrow', indicating resolution or strong purpose); the third hints that one is under orders or compulsion to depart then; 'I *am about to depart*' connotes instancy, is therefore hardly suitable to a time so far off, and has a variant 'I *am on the point of departing*', which connotes such instancy, such urgency, that 'to-morrow' would cause the sentence to become grotesque; 'I *may depart* . . .' conveys that there is no certainty of departure on that day; and 'I *depart* to-morrow' shows the speaker to be visualizing the deed as belonging to the present, or to be understating with a quiet dignity.

These few observations will perhaps suggest that if you regard syntax or, indeed, any other section of grammar as a living organism, you will find it much easier to express yourselves clearly and adequately; and much easier to understand what the other fellow is saying. Indeed, if we compare syntax with morphology, we notice that, in conversation, 'the hearer encounters certain sounds', precisely as the reader encounters certain forms: the hearer and reader have to assign a meaning to sound or form: they proceed from the exterior to the interior. 'The speaker' or the writer, on the other hand, 'starts from certain ideas, which he tries to communicate; to him the meaning is the given thing'—the thing with which he begins—'and he has to find out how to express it: he moves from within to without.'

If we look at syntax from a distance, we notice that it falls into two sets of categories:

i, the categories of the parts of speech (noun, verb, adjective, adverb, etc.): nowadays called, quite often, word-classes.

ii, the categories that are aspects or phases in the life and nature of those word-classes or parts of speech, thus:

1. The singular and the plural (to which might be added the dual, which does not exist in English): the category of number.

2. The nominative (or subjective), the accusative (or objective), the genitive (or possessive), etc.: the category of cases.

3. The present, the past, the future: the category of tenses.

4. The indicative, the subjunctive, the imperative, etc.: the category of moods.

5. The active and the passive: the category of voices (or 'turns', as Jespersen cleverly proposes).

6. The first, the second, the third person: obviously the category of persons.

7. The masculine, the feminine, the neuter: the category of genders.

Jespersen's remarks thereon are invaluable. 'We are able', he says, 'to establish all these syntactic ideas and categories without for one moment stepping outside the province of grammar, but as soon as we ask the question, what do they stand for, we at once pass from the sphere of language to the outside world' (for the outside world is mirrored in the human mind, and, in any case, words are symbols representing things, acts, desires, etc.) 'or to the sphere of thought'; this is where syntax and logic meet.

Now, some of the categories enumerated above bear evident relations to something that is found in the sphere of things: thus the grammatical category of number evidently corresponds to the distinction found in the outside world between 'one' and 'more than one'; to account for the various grammatical tenses, present, imperfect, etc., one must refer to the outside notion of time; the difference between the three grammatical persons [first person, second person, third person] corresponds to the natural distinction between the speaker, the person spoken to, and something outside of both.

In others of the categories, the correspondence must not be too closely pressed; in one or two of them, there may be no correspondence whatever. Human language, moreover, has never quite been able to march level with the universe.[1]

Both of those sets of categories are syntactic categories; there exist also certain categories based on notions, and these are called notional categories. Take gender or sex. In grammar, there are three genders (masculine, feminine, neuter), which are syntactic: in nature there are two sexes (masculine and feminine beings, whether human or animal), to which we may add things, which are sexless. But the syntactic category of the gender does not follow the notional category of sex, although beings that are male are usually of masculine gender and beings that are female are usually of feminine gender; sexless things are always neuter in English, except in personifications (*she* of a ship, *he* of the sun), whereas in French, German, Spanish, Italian (and other Aryan languages), as in Greek and Latin, the gender of notional (or natural) neuters may be masculine or feminine (in the Romance

---

[1] In 1668, the Rev. Dr (later Bishop) John Wilkins published his abstruse work, *A Real Character and a Philosophical Language*, wherein, disgusted with the fact that many important words had come to bear several or indeed many senses, he attempted to set forth a system of such signs or characters as stood for one thing (or feeling or thought, etc.) and only one thing; he is thus a forerunner of the Logical Positivists—M. Schlick, Ludwig Wittgenstein, Rudolf Carnap, K. Gödel, A. J. Ayer, to name only a few of them. In Wilkins's book, there is much relevant matter in Part iii, 'Concerning Natural Grammar': but his views and the views of the Logical Positivists on a Universal Grammar (a grammar common to, and applicable to, *all* languages), though interesting, do not emerge with credit from a searching examination. (Cf. the Postscript on p. 75.)

languages) or masculine, feminine or neuter as in Greek, Latin, German.

This brings us to the fact that, in grammar, there are three points of view, three stages of treatment: a word has form (the combination of sound or sounds with the letter or letters representing that sound or those sounds); function (its role or activity or work in syntax); and notion. Jespersen gives a brilliant example, which I modify only slightly: the English preterite or past definite tense. Its function is that of indicating past definite time; it may have seven different forms; and it may and does express five different notions. A preterite may be formed in *-ed*, as in *landed*; *-t* as in *whipt*; *-d* as in *did* or, for the sound, in *showed*; *-t* with inner change, as in *left* (from *leave*); root or kernel unchanged, as in *put*; with an inner change but without *-t*, as in *drank*; with a different kernel, as in *was*. Even more remarkable is the number of senses or, rather, notions that can be expressed by this one tense: the primary notion, past time ('we walked'); unreality in present time ('If only we knew'—'I wish we knew'); future time ('It is high time you told us about it'); shifted present time, in reported or indirect speech ('He said that I was a fool'); timeless notion, all times ('Men always thought themselves wonderful').

'Syntactic categories thus ... face both ways, towards form, and towards notion. They stand midway and [constitute] the connecting link between the world of sounds and the world of ideas.' The speaker or the writer proceeds from the notion, via the function, to the form; the hearer or the reader proceeds from the form, via the function, to the notion.

In the next section, we shall, in dealing with the parts of speech, keep in mind the notional categories so far as they bear on the subject.

VII. THE PARTS OF SPEECH

Parts of speech are a convenience, not a necessity of language; language is so very great a convenience that it is virtually a necessity. Take apples. There are millions of them, none exactly like another: but it would be slightly inconvenient to have a separate name for each apple: so we apply *apple* to every apple that ever existed, is now existing, or is to exist. So with other things: there is only one Earth, but there are countless Worlds. Pain is everywhere: it varies tremendously in kind and in degree: yet to all the variations (past, present, potential) we give the name *pain*. 'The world is in constant flux around us and in us, but in order to grapple with the feeling of reality, we create in our thought, or at any rate in our language, certain more or less fixed points, certain averages' or norms. 'Reality never presents us with an average object', and 'the average man' of the journalists is a myth; 'but language does, for instead of denoting [one, single] thing, a word like *apple* represents the average of a great many objects', a word like *pain* the average of numerous states 'that have something in common'.

In the same way, an adjective (e.g., *green*) denotes a quality that differs according to place and circumstance; a verb denotes an action or a state that is, or can be, done or perceived in very many ways; an adverb fits many shades of meaning; a preposition has many nuances, and occasionally we find '*from under* the table', '*from above* the level of the water'; a pronoun is used not merely to refer to a person or thing previously mentioned but also to render a noun unnecessary, and *they* may, in its function, be rather a noun than a pronoun, as in 'They say . . .' (French *on dit*), where no persons have been named and no persons need be named; a conjunction has various shades of meaning; even an interjection can convey now this, now that, and then the other shade of emotion.

There has, of late years, been a certain amount of opposition to the parts of speech: on the ground that they have no counterpart in reality; or on the ground that a word may be either a noun or a verb (*love*), or a noun, a verb, an adjective, an adverb (*round*: 'a round table', 'the round of applause', 'come round to-morrow to see me', 'walk round the table'), a preposition or an adverb ('from London', 'to and from'), and so forth; or on the ground that one can learn a language without hearing of the names or thinking of the meaning of the functions played by these eight word-classes or parts of speech. Actually, they have a basis in reality, despite the difficulties presented by certain words, but there! grammar, like government, legislates for the majority; the word-class of a term is determined not by its form ('he *rose*', 'a lovely *rose*') but by its function, and it wouldn't matter a brass farthing, a red cent, or a pedantic grammarian, if a few words fell, according to their various functions, into all the eight word-classes, for the context (or, if you prefer, the syntax) makes the sense quite clear, and the class quite obvious, as in this sequence, 'I'd like to visit you, *but* I'm unable to get away'—'I like a *but* for its contradictoriness'—'He's a *but* man' (on the analogy of *a yes man*)—'*But* me no "buts"'—'Everyone *but* you'—'He all *but* did it'—'"You're a liar!" "*But!*"', where it is an interjection.

Although it is true that an ordinary person might never feel the lack of parts of speech, yet a language-teacher and a student of language would find things rather easier if they did know of, and understand, these categories.

This, however, is not the place to enter into a disquisition on the word-classes or parts of speech; and presumably you already know the definitions thereof. But here are several points that are worth considering. Certain persons, who ought to have known better, say that there is no essential difference between a noun and an adjective; that almost any noun can become an adjective, and that many adjectives have become, and all could become, nouns: these *becomings* are irrelevant, and there is no reason why they shouldn't exist; moreover, it is silly to speak of a noun being used *as* an adjective, for when it is used adjectivally it *is* an adjective. And there is an essential difference between a noun and an adjective, for the latter can be applied to far more things than a noun can, an adjective possesses only one quality, a noun many qualities—or, put it another way, a noun has to fulfil many conditions or requirements, an adjective only one; that is Jespersen's penetrating distinction, to which I should like to add another. If there were no difference between (say) *red*, noun, and *red*, adjective, in what a strange situation we should find ourselves. 'He is white' (-coloured) is very different from saying 'He is white' (the colour): obviously we would not mean the latter, unless we were qualifying for a lunatic asylum.

Jespersen's treatment of the word-classes is, basically, philosophic, as you have seen in his differentiation of noun from adjective: but many of his reasonings, being as abstruse as they are acute, are hardly suitable to this book. Yet it may comfort you to know that it is on syntax that he bases his philosophizing; and that he bases syntax on practice. The great thing is to use your common sense. Try your intelligence on: 'He looks *fine*', 'He cut it *fine*, running for his train', ' "How are you getting on?" "Oh, I'm doing *fine*" '; or on 'I'm *so* busy!', ' "He thinks you're a fool"—"*So!*" ', 'I believe *so*', 'He is poor, but his brother is still more *so*'. If you examine what *fine* and *so* do in these sentences, you will see what they are syntactically—hence, what parts of speech they are (which word-class do they belong to?). Indeed, Jespersen himself warns us that the categories named 'parts of speech' or 'word-classes' cannot be explained solely by reference to the outer world, and that, in other words, these classes are not wholly notional: they are also grammatical or, more precisely, syntactical.

If ever you are in doubt, remember that, although a word set by itself can rarely be explained satisfactorily, almost every word can be explained when it occurs in a sane phrase or a sane sentence; that is, in its context. You have only to examine where a word comes in a sentence and what it does, or apparently does, there. It is well known that you can guess the approximate meaning of almost any word if you know the meaning of the other words, whether the sentence is in your own language or in a foreign one: so, you will find, you can tell what part of speech a word is, by examining the sentence.

In all grammar, you must use your head; in fact, you will find that grammar is easy if you retain your head on your shoulders and not let it slink to the cinema when it's supposed to be in a class-room or engaged in study. You can make up a sentence? 'Of course!' 'Sure!' Well, well; then you can also see what its parts mean—and, seeing that, you will learn how to express more clearly what you wish to say, and thus save time for yourselves and others.

VIII. A GLANCE AT THE HISTORY OF ENGLISH GRAMMAR[1]

In English grammar, as in English word-formation, there has been a most noticeable trend towards unity and simplicity: a very general tendency away from either disorder or lack of order and towards orderliness and order: 'from chaos to cosmos', as Jespersen neatly phrases it. From a very large number of flexions, especially of endings (case, number, gender; suffixes), we have progressed to few flexions, and those few are more definite; in general, the irregularities, once so numerous, are now few. Perhaps the most remarkable simplification has been at work in the adjective, which has, throughout Modern English (say from 1450), had only one form, whereas in King Alfred's time there were eleven different forms. A backward movement is rare. All in all, the increase (hence the gain) in clarity and simplicity has been tremendous.

But this development has taken hundreds of years and is due to many causes. The Old English declensions of nouns and adjectives, and the conjugations of the verbs, were highly irregular in their conduct; if, therein, a vowel did not everywhere indicate the same function or the same meaning, speakers naturally tended to pronounce weak syllables (especially at the end of words) indistinctly—and all flexional endings were unstressed in Old English; 'thus *a, i, u* of the endings were levelled in the one colourless vowel *e*, and this could even after some time be dropped

---

[1] This section is based on Otto Jespersen: *The Growth and Structure of the English Language*.

altogether in most cases'. The ending *-s* (or for euphony, *-es*), indicating a plural, and *'s* (from *-es*), indicating a genitive, were obviously very useful and, in the context, perfectly clear: hence they were retained, to the rapid exclusion of other endings that served the same purposes. The power of preponderance and the beneficent tyranny exercised by the advantages of regularity, of clarity, of simplicity are seen even better in the genitive (the possessive) than in the plural, for now the position of the *'s* or the *s'* marking the genitive is always immediately before the governing word, the word that *causes* the genitive: thus, not only *my hat* and *the dog's leg*, but also *the Justice of the Peace's privilege, the King of England's power, the bride and bridegroom's return, the Mayor and Council's vote*.

Very convenient, too, is the total disappearance of word-gender. All nouns in English are now neuter except those which stand for the male or the female sex in nature: a feature in which English and American are infinitely superior to French, Italian, Spanish, Portuguese, with their two-gender differentiation, and German with its three-gender differentiation, of actions, conditions, and lifeless things. The English dichotomy (two-fold division) into animate and inanimate has been responsible for the rise of *its* in distinction to *his*, which, until ca. 1580, was used of things as well as of males, and for the limiting of the relative *which*[1] to things.

The pronouns, which in Old English were clumsy and confusing, have become clear and comparatively simple and regular; here, the loss of flexions is less noticeable than in nouns, but a genuine system has grown up—by no means perfect, yet tolerably elastic and adaptable. An increase in subtlety, hence also in clarity, has resulted from the addition, to the monotonous *that*, of *who* and *which* as relative pronouns. Modern English has formed compounds in *-self*, and *self* has taken to itself a plural, which hardly antedates the year 1500. Only since the sixteenth century have we possessed *one* as a substitute or convenience or prop-word ('I saw a big lion and a little one'); only since the fifteenth, *one* as 'evasive *I*' or 'modified *they*' ('One doesn't always know, does one?'—'One says that a libel action is impending').

The ending *-ing* originally belonged only to nouns and was formed only from nouns; it was not until ca. 1400 that the ending *-ing* had become so firmly established that an *-ing* could be formed unhesitatingly from any verb whatever ('apart from the auxiliaries *can, may, shall,* [*must*], etc.) . . .' And in the later seventeenth century the *-ing*, from being noun only, completed

---

[1] Cf. 'Our Father which art in Heaven'.

its development by becoming a gerund (partly noun, partly verb in its function), as in 'His saying so makes no difference' or 'She didn't like her brother's departing so abruptly'. In short, *-ing* 'has clearly become a most valuable means of expressing tersely and neatly [certain syntactical] relations that must else have been indicated by clumsy dependent clauses', e.g., 'She did not like that her brother departed . . .'

In the conjugation of verbs, English has developed towards a system that, though less simple than that affecting nouns, is at least much simpler than the verb system of Old English and even Middle English. In most verbs, there are in the present and the imperfect and the future, two different forms; in the past definite and the pluperfect, only one. The verb *to be* is a little more difficult, but then it consists of three different stems. In all normal verbs, the third person singular is (except in the preterite and the pluperfect) the only dissentient to uniformity; but even there, the *-th* form has disappeared except in Biblical and poetic language, and in the latter it is now an archaism. Moreover, the English system of tenses has, from something inadequate and often hazy, developed into the subtlest tense-system to be found in the Aryan family of languages. But the moods have, since ca. 1820, tended to grow less distinct: we still have a subjunctive mood, but we use its forms less and ever less.

The negative (*not*) represents a convenient simplification of the cumbrous old form (*ne . . . noht*); and the number of conjunctions has increased—to the advantage of vividness and subtlety.

These few indications may serve to show or, at the least, to hint that such changes are continually going on and that it would be a gross error to suppose that any deviation from the established rules of grammar is necessarily a corruption. 'Those teachers who know the least . . . are generally the most apt to think . . . evil', whereas genuinely knowledgeable teachers 'will generally be more inclined to see in the processes of human speech a wise natural selection, through which—while nearly all innovations of questionable value disappear pretty soon—the fittest survive and make human speech ever more varied and flexible and yet, ever more easy and convenient to the speakers . . . Let us hope that in the future the more and more [powerful] schoolmaster may not nip too many beneficial changes in the bud' and that the B.B.C. will not, in the United Kingdom, throw too much cold water on the warm-hearted babes of linguistic naturalness, spontaneity and picturesqueness.

To Jespersen's wise plea and my trifling addition thereto, one must enter a demurrer: there may come a stage when, too late, we see that overmuch has been sacrificed on the altar of simplicity, for it would not be to the advantage of the English language and the American language if simplicity were gained at the expense of variety, subtlety, richness: still, human beings—or many of them—are too impatient of a niggling, prying standardization to allow it to wither the language and render it juiceless and insipid.

PART FIVE

CHAPTER NINE

THE FUN OF WORD HISTORY[1]

A. GENERAL: SYMBOLISM; ETYMOLOGY; FOLK ETYMOLOGY; SEMANTICS

I. SOUND SYMBOLISM[2]

FOR the purpose of word history, it is convenient to divide words into two classes: echo words (words that echo, words that are echoic), which formerly were called, not so well, onomatopoeic words; and the far more numerous class consisting of non-echoic words.

Echoic words may have quite as long a history as the others, and that history is far easier to trace, for they show a close relation of sense to sound, whereas non-echoic words do not show any such relationship. In echoic words there is 'a natural correspondence between sound and sense' and these words acquire their meaning by sound-symbolism; that is, their sound symbolizes—represents or recalls or suggests—the sense. That certain sounds are not symbolic of sense in all words is not to say that these sounds are not thus symbolic in *some* words: those words which *are* echoic.

The simplest kind of echoic words is that in which there is direct and obvious imitation, as in *clink*, *clank*, *tinkle* employed to represent metallic sounds; the *boom* of cannon and the *bang* of a gun; the *rumble* of thunder and *thunder* itself; the *bubble* of gushing water, the *splash* made by the impact of an object or a body on water or by water falling on to something, the *sizz*, *sizzle*, *sizzling* of boiling water; the *whistle* of the wind; the *rustle* of leaves—often called *susurration,* from the equally echoic Latin word *susurrus*; the *murmur* of a shell or of quiet, distant voices; the *bow-wow* or *woof-woof* of a dog, the *miaow* of a cat, the *baa-baa* of a sheep, the *moo* of a cow, the *roar* of a lion, the *hiss* of a

---

[1] My debts in this chapter are to Jespersen; Greenough and Kittredge; G. H. McKnight; Owen Barfield's *English History in Words*; and, above all, to several books by Ernest Weekley.

[2] Here I follow, closely yet not slavishly, the corresponding chapter in Jespersen's *Language: Its Nature, Development and Origin.*

serpent, the *hum* of bees; the *snort, snore, sneeze, snigger, whisper, grunt, grumble* of sounds made by human beings. Less obvious but fairly certain is the theory that continuity of sound is produced in *clatter* and *rattle*, in *jingle*, and in *chatter* and *jabber*.

Almost as simple is that kind of echoic words in which the sound produced gives its name to the producer (the originator) of the sound: the birds *peewit* and *cuckoo* and *whippoorwill* (often written *whip-poor-Will*) take their name from the cry they make. A special sub-division of this kind of echoic word consists of the names given to various nations from a word or words occurring constantly in their speech: thus a Frenchman is called *Parleyvoo* (i.e., *parlez-vous*) by the English and *deedonk* (i.e., *dis donc*) by the Americans.

Sound is produced by vibrations (rapid movement, especially to and fro); you hear sounds because of the impression made on your ears by those vibrations; the kind of impression determines you to name the sound *clash* or *crack* or *smack, bubble* or *sizzle*. 'Human actions may therefore be denoted by such words as to *bang* the door or (with slighter sounds) to *tap* or *rap* at a door.' Sounds less loud and less distinct are conveyed by *l*, whether as *fl* (*flow, flutter, flicker, flurry, flit*), or *gl* (*glide*), or *sl* (*slide, slip*).

Sound-symbolism may be applied to things: here there is some relation between what is visible and what is audible. There is an association between high tones (made with very rapid vibrations) and light, and between low tones and darkness: contrast *gloom* and *murky* and *obscure* with *gleam* and *glitter*.

From such associations 'it is no far cry to words for corresponding states of mind', and sometimes the same words are used (e.g., *gloom*). In showing dissatisfaction, one *grumbles*: *grumble* is echoic for the sound one makes, *grumbling* indicates the mood that causes it; perhaps the person is *grumpy*. And there is a whole group of dull-*u* words expressive of contempt or scorn, dislike, disgust; for instance *bungle* and *blunder* and *muddle, clumsy* and *slovenly, muck* and *slush, juggins* and '*mug*' and *numbskull* and '*dumb-bell*' and *dunderhead, humbug* and *humdrum*.

Then, too, there is the fact that short words are suitable to certain feelings and emotions, long words to others. In imperatives, the general tendency is to use short words: *go!* (not *depart!*); *run!* or *scram!*; not *assist me!* but simply *help!* Emotional effect is sometimes obtained by lengthening a word or by substituting a long for a short word: thus *vex* is more effective if it is pronounced *aggravate*; dialect has both *gumption* and *rumgumption*; slang lengthens *splendid* to *splendidious* and *splendacious* (both virtually obsolete) and *splendiferous*, and makes *to beat* more impressive by changing it to *spiflicate*. Occasionally the intention is to create a humorous effect, as in *terminological inexactitude* for a *lie*. That the tendency is rooted in human need appears further in the fact that, 'under the influence of strong feeling and in order to intensify the effect of the spoken word', one is naturally apt 'to lengthen and strengthen single sounds' and to articulate more distinctly and levelly: ' "Is it cold?" "Co-o-o-ld?!" '; ' "Very good, isn't it?!" "Ve-ry!" '; ' "Do you think you're right?" "Ab-so-lute-ly!" '; ' "May I see you?" "Get—out—of—the—room!" '

The points we have considered are both interesting and useful: and to them we need add only a very few general considerations.

No language uses sound-symbolism (more concretely, echo words) to its full extent,[1] and every language contains a vast number of words unconcerned with this symbolism—and some words that run counter to this symbolism. It is well known that the English short *i* occurs very often in words either indicating or implying smallness (*little, piccaninny, kid, chit, imp, pigmy; bit, chip, whit, tip, pin*); but that vowel does not always imply smallness, nor is smallness always conveyed in words containing that vowel, for the opposite of *thin* is *thick*, one of the synonyms for 'large' or 'great' is *big*, and one of the synonyms for 'little' is *small*.

Some words that were originally examples of sound-symbolism have ceased to be so, either because of a phonetic development (a sound-change). as in the bird *crow*, which used to be, with more apt symbolism, *crawe*, or because of a sense development, as in Latin *pipio*, any bird that cries 'peep', which has come to designate a particular kind of bird, the *pigeon*.

'On the other hand, some words have in course of time become more expressive than they were at first. . . . *Husky* may at first have meant only "full of husks, of the nature of a husk" [*The Oxford English Dictionary*], but it could not possibly from that signification have arrived at the current sense "dry in the throat, hoarse", if it had not been that the sound of the adjective had reminded one of the sound of a hoarse voice.'

And echoic words are—have since the sixteenth century been

[1] Rather late in the day, John Wilkins, in his *A Real Character and a Philosophical Language*, 1668, lamented thus: 'It were exceedingly desirable that the *Names* of things might consist of such *Sounds*, as should bear in them some Analogy to their *Natures*; and the Figure or Character'—sign or symbol—'of these Names should bear some proper resemblance to those *Sounds*, that men might easily guess at the sence or meaning of any name or word, upon the first *hearing* or *sight* of it. But how this can be done in all the particular species of things, I understand not.'

—on the increase, partly because 'life moves at a more rapid rate, and people are less tied down to tradition than in former ages, consequently they are more apt to create and adopt new words of this particular type, which are felt ... to be significant and expressive': there has been a steady progress 'towards a greater number of easy and adequate expressions' in which sound and sense are closely related and even inseparably united. *To biff* and *to slosh*, *tosh* and *slush* (both in the sense of 'nonsense'), *to skedaddle* and *oodles of boodle*—to take but a few from many examples—are comparatively recent.

II. ETYMOLOGY[1, 2]

'Nowhere have I found any reason to accept the theory that sound-changes always take place according to rigorous ... laws admitting no exceptions', remarks Jespersen. He adds that 'it has been repeated over and over again that without strict adherence to phonetic laws, etymological science is a sheer impossibility': with this compare the epigram, made by Voltaire, that etymology takes no account of vowels and very little of consonants—but it might very well have been expressed the other way about! *Etymology*, literally, means a discoursing on *etymons* or primary words, i.e. roots or radicals or stems; yet, in practice, it also concerns itself with word history. Now, there are numerous instances in which, despite the rupture of the so-called phonetic laws, the etymological connexion is clear: Gothic *azgo* is obviously related to Danish *aske*, German *asche*, English *ash*; Modern English *pebble* to Old English *papol*; English *flagon* to French *flacon*; Latin *cor* (heart) to Greek *kardia*. In fact, it would be better to discard the untenable severity of phonetic laws and to speak of phonetic rules: to which, as to other rules, there are many exceptions.

But that is dangerous ground! It is more amusing to note that philologists often burst into dignified praise of the achievements of modern etymology. In 1910, somebody ('No names, no pack-drill!') so far forgot himself as to assert that 'nowadays etymology has got past the period of more or less "happy thoughts" and has developed into a science in which, exactly as in any other science, serious persevering work must lead to reliable results'.

[1] This section also is based on the corresponding section in Jespersen's *Language*; but again not slavishly.

[2] Etymology refers properly to the origination of a word from another language or from an early form of the same language (e.g., Modern English *crow* (the bird) from Old English *crawe*); derivation is origination from a stem in the same stage of the same language—thus *horsey* is a derivative of *horse*.

THE FUN OF WORD HISTORY

Unfortunately work is not enough, even when it is allied to erudition: the best etymological results are obtained by those who, to labour and learning, add imagination and either good sense or shrewd ingenuity. And as Jespersen has said: 'From English alone ... it would be an easy matter to compile a long list of words, well-known words of everyday occurrence, which etymologists have had to give up as beyond their powers of solution'. No; it wouldn't be fair to tease and tantalize you with even a short list. Besides, they are not particularly entertaining words. One may have a guess: many philologists do guess: some guess with the most delightful freedom; it is, however, incorrect to say that one man's guess is as good as another's. But let us leave guesses until we reach our particular examples.

It is an odd fact that many philologists, barbarously and sometimes ludicrously strict about a word's obedience to phonetic 'laws', will presume and manufacture a proto-Aryan form and compare that probably imaginary form with some other word found in a language different from that to which belongs the word they are trying to solve: and they will even manufacture a proto-Aryan word that does not look too different from that other-language word which forms so powerful a corroboration of their theory. Some—indeed many—philologists are so rigorous in their administration of the 'laws' *they* have formulated that they ignore common sense or, rather, good sense. The great Kluge and other eminent persons refute any connexion between English *nut* and Latin *nux* (a nut): Jespersen is rightly scornful of this 'phonological pedantry', as he calls it; this 'phoneticians' purblindness', as I venture to name it. The truth is that phonetics will often prove insufficient, and semantics, to which we shall come shortly, quite satisfactory except to proto-Aryan last-ditchers and phonological intransigents.

Two minor means of solution are provided by echoism (see the preceding section) and blending. The blending of synonyms, or else of two words not grossly disconnected in meaning or in the world about us, plays a much greater role in the development of language than is generally recognized, says Jespersen. 'Many instances may be heard in everyday life, most of them being immediately corrected by the speaker ..., but these momentary lapses cannot be separated from other instances which are of more permanent value because they are so natural that they occur over and over again until speakers will hardly feel the blend as anything else than an ordinary word.' American philologists call these words 'blends' and so, now, do certain English ones; but the usual English name is 'portmanteau-words'. Lewis Carroll's portmanteaus are famous; let us pass to some less known blends, cited by Jespersen: *blot* is *blemish* (or *black* or *blob*) + *spot*; *flush* = *flash* + *blush*; *good-bye* = *good-morning* and *good-night* + *godbye* (*God b'ye*, God be with ye!); *twirl* = *twist* + *whirl*. Slang contains many blends, as *tinner* (*tea* and *dinner* taken together), *brunch* (*breakfast* + *lunch*), and the Harrow School *tosh* (either *tub* + *wash* or, less probably, *toe* + *wash*).

But it must not be assumed that to say 'etymology' is to say 'word history'. Etymology tells us nothing about the things symbolized by words, though the nature, the qualities of things often help us to hit upon the etymology; sometimes not even about the present meaning of a word, though this statement does not apply to simple things and creatures—*cat*, *dog*, *tree*, *sea*, *ground*, etc., etc., etc.: but by telling us what *has* been true, by telling us the original meaning, it helps us to understand the modern sense or senses of a many-sensèd word and it gives us an immediate clue to the basic or essential meaning of scientific and technical words such as *telegram* and *microphone* and *gastro-enterotomy*; it enables us to discern the poetry of (say) *comet*, which comes from Latin *comes*, hair—a comet thus being likened to a lovely creature, with hair streaming back over her shoulders, in a fleet traversing of windy space; 'the long-haired one'. Word-history goes further: it deals not only with the origin of words but with the development of their meaning; it relates things and facts in which it may never have occurred to you to find or even imagine a connexion; it illuminates history—the history of physical progress, mental improvement, spiritual values; the history of common things, the story of things uncommon. And it provides the most entertaining and profitable exercise for your faculties (brain, imagination, sense of fitness and of beauty).

III. FOLK ETYMOLOGY[1]

This progress and feature of languages is also known as Hobson-Jobson, from the fact that British soldiers, hearing Mohammedans in the religious procession of the Moharram, cry *Ya Hasan! Yu Hosain!*, turned the rhythmic wail into the familiar English sounds *Hobson-Jobson*. The process is continually at work: when the English and the Americans adopt a foreign word, they usually change its pronunciation and make it look as English as possible. The results are sometimes odd. But the term 'folk etymology' is properly applied only when the foreign word or phrase is given a

[1] Based on the corresponding section in G. H. McKnight's *English Words and Their Background*.

wholly English dress, as when the English soldier converted *Ploegstert* into *Plugstreet*, the American into *Plow Street*, or as when the English sailor renamed the *Bellerophon*, *Bully Ruffian*, or the American renamed the *Miantonomoh*, *My Aunt Don't Know You*.

There is a constant tendency, sometimes unconscious, sometimes deliberate and humorous, to give strange words a familiar form, to link the unknown with the known. Thus *asparagus*, so oddly Latin in its appearance, became *sparrow-grass*, especially among speakers of dialect; the perversion of *artichoke* to *hearty choke* was too obviously a pun to succeed for any length of time. The tendency has been, and is, so constantly at work that it has made the search for the true origin or etymology more difficult than it would otherwise have been: and vastly more interesting. Thus *ravenous* has nothing to do with ravens; *pantry* is not connected with pans but with bread (Old French *paneterie*, where bread was kept, from Latin *panis*, bread); and *buttery* had originally no connexion with butter, its origin being Middle English *botery*, from Old French, *boteillerie*, a place for bottles (of liquor), therefore a bottelry.

The attempt to explain the puzzling, the unknown, by the well-known, and even the known by the better-known, is seen in the form of many English words; often, if the early form exists and we know it or have the good luck to run it to earth, we can discern the origin. Thus *buzzard*, from Old French *busart*, became *buzzard* through the influence of *buzz*; Old French *soverain* became *sovereign* through the influence of *reign*; Old French *riban* became *riband* because of a supposed connexion with *band*; Old English *aecern* became *acorn* because of a foolish linking with *corn*; *cutlet* has nothing to do with *cut*, but, via French, derives from Latin *costa*, a rib, and means a little rib, just as *cuplet* means a little cup. The American *cold-slaw* derives from Dutch *kool*, cabbage, and therefore is not, as the artless suppose, even a distant relation of *cold*; *buckwheat* originated in the Dutch *boekweit*, 'beech-wheat', and was changed by the American settlers, who, as their descendants are still, were fond of the word *buck*; *musk-rat* is an ingenious American solution of the problem set by the Algonquin Indian *muskwessu*, precisely as *woodchuck* is a most creditable attempt at another Amerindian word, *wuchak* or *ojeeg*.

In many instances, folk etymology has led to a compound in which the second (or the first) part or element means the same as the first (or the second) part or, more often, renders the total meaning tautological (excessive). Thus, the Old English *h·an* (like *hreinn*, its Norse cognate or perhaps original) signified a reindeer, but because it was used as a beast of burden and, especially, draught (cf. *draught horse*), *hran* became *rein* and *deer* had to be added; in other words *hran*, that kind of deer which we now call reindeer, has acquired an additional, would-be explanatory, but actually useless element (*deer*, Old English *deor*). *Cellar* represents the process by which a word was tacked in front: for *cellar* represents Latin *saliaria*, a receptacle for salt, and etymologically *salt-cellar* means 'a salt salt-cellar'.

Two of the best examples occur in the vocabulary of food: *Welsh rarebit* and *sponge cake*. *Welsh rarebit*,[1] which one sees on so many menus, is an explanation of a phrase that greatly puzzled its devotees: *Welsh rabbit*, born early in the 1760's, occurs in C. Johnston's entertaining novel, *Chrysal*, 1768, and is recorded in Grose's *Classical Dictionary of the Vulgar Tongue*, 1785; the *rarebit* form hardly, or never, appears until the nineteenth century. Properly, *Welsh rabbit* is an indivisible term; and to coin *buck rarebit*, as the twentieth century has done, is a gastronomic desecration. *Welsh rabbit* is only one of many such jocularities: English has *Bombay duck* (which is a fish), itself a piece of folk-etymology on *bummalo* and likewise an eighteenth-century term —*Digby chicken* or *Gourock ham* (and several other synonyms), a smoked herring, the live variety being *Atlantic ranger*—and many others; Australian has *Colonial goose* for a leg of mutton; American has *Alabama wool* for cotton, *Alaskan sable* for skunk, *Hudson seal* for musk-rat fur, and almost as many others as English has.

Sponge cake[2] is—to be Irish—a different kettle of fish. The *Oxford English Dictionary* refers it to *sponge* (with which one douches oneself), and I never thought of doubting that simple and obvious explanation until Mr Julian Franklyn happened to mention to me that not only does the Japanese for *sponge cake* mean, literally, 'bread of Spain', but the Italian name is *pan di Spagna*, which means exactly the same thing. My theory is that *sponge cake* is folk etymology for *Spanish cake*. I cannot prove it, but here is the rest of the evidence: The term *sponge cake* is not recorded before 1843, when it occurs in a cookery book; but in a cookery book of 1769[3] (Mrs Elizabeth Raffald's *The Experienced English House-keeper*, in Chap. XI, 'Observations upon Cakes'),

---

[1] The 18th Century had several derogatory *Welsh* terms: e.g., *Welsh comb*, the thumb and four fingers; *Welsh fiddle*, the itch—as also was *Scotch fiddle*.

[2] To be fair to Professor McKnight, I must mention that he has no responsibility in this paragraph.

[3] The *O.E.D.* supplies these two dates.

there are, among the biscuit recipes, two that concern us, the former for *Spanish biscuits* ('bake them on Papers'), the latter for *Spunge biscuits* ('bake them in Tin Moulds buttered, or Coffins'), the point being that, except for the method of baking and a slight difference in the proportions of the ingredients, the two so-called biscuits are virtually the same, one with the other, and, for all practical purposes, the same as the two modern kinds of culinary sponge (sponge fingers and sponge cake), which differ from each other in little except the baking and the size; the term *Spanish biscuit* appears not to have survived the 1830's or 1840's; simple housewives, puzzled by *Spanish biscuit* applied to a cake, would have called it a cake and then, since it was a spongy cake, changed apparently senseless *Spanish* to the so very obviously sensible *sponge*, on the analogy of *sponge biscuit*, which already existed. Hence, I surmise, comes the *sponge cake*,[1] beloved of Victorian hostesses and not disdained by modern girls and fellows.

But even the learned have fallen into folk etymology; for instance, sixteenth- and early seventeenth-century writers often spelt *abominable* as *abhominable*, on the assumption that it came from Latin *ab homine*, 'from man', and Middle English *iland*, 'water-land', has become *island* simply because certain scholars wished to prove a connexion with *isle* (from Latin *insula*). On the other hand, *rime* has become *rhyme* on the analogy of *rhythm*: yet those of us who retain *rhyme* have reason on our side.

The folk-etymology process is a phase of the very general tendency (manifest among the learned and the unlearned, the lettered and the illiterate) to effect—or, at the least, to try to effect —uniformity and to introduce system into our speech. '*Donkey* is formed after the analogy of *monkey*, *parsnip* after the analogy of *turnip*, *benignant* after *malignant*'; odd-looking words, whether native or foreign—for the natives escape no more than do the foreigners—are reshaped, to resemble something more familiar.

IV. SEMANTICS[2]

Semantics, which used to be and still is sometimes called *semasiology* or *sematology*, may summarily be defined as the science of meanings: and it is often opposed to phonetics or phonology, the science of sound. More fully, it[3] is that branch of

[1] By the way, the French name is *gâteau de Savoie*; the Dutch, *moscovisch gebak*, lit. 'Muscovite baking', i.e. Russian cake.

[2] In general outline and most of the examples, I follow the chapter on this subject in Weekley's *Romance of Words*: not parrot-fashion but Partridge-wise, 'though I says it as shouldn't'.

[3] Originally, like *mathematics*, a plural, *semantics* is now, like *mathematics*, used often as a singular.

philology which deals with meanings both in themselves and in relation to the senses from which they derive or the senses to which they lead; its application in etymology depends partly on a wide erudition and a sympathetic knowledge of life and the world around one, and partly on an alert mind that seizes on parallels and analogies and is able to see the wood as well as the trees; it is psychological etymology. *Semantics* is the English form of *sémantique*, coined by the great French philologist Bréal, and it comes from the Greek *semantikos*, 'significant', itself a derivative of *semainein*, 'to show', hence 'to signify, to mean'.

'One phenomenon which seems to occur normally in language', remarks Weekley, 'results from what we may call the simplicity of the olden times. Thus the whole vocabulary which is etymologically related to *writing* and books has developed from an old Germanic verb that means to *scratch* and the Germanic name for the *beech*. Our earliest books were wooden tablets on which inscriptions were scratched. The word *book* itself comes from [Old English] *boc*, beech. ... Latin *liber*, a book, whence a large family of words in the Romance languages, means the inner bark of a tree, and *bible* is ultimately from Greek *biblos*, the inner rind of the *papyrus*, the Egyptian rush from which *paper* was made'; and 'when the supply of papyrus failed', man substituted *parchment*, originally or notably made at *Pergamus* in Asia Minor, the word travelling to England via France (*parchemin*).

'The earliest measurements were calculated from the human body. All European languages use the *foot*, and we still measure horses by *hands* . . . *Cubit* is [from the] Latin for *elbow*, the first part of which is the same as *ell*, cognate with Latin *ulna*, also used in both senses [arm; ell, also fathom]. ... A further set of measures are represented by simple devices: a *yard* is a small stick [the 'stick' meaning survives in the *yards* of a ship], and the *rod, pole*, or *perch* . . . which gives charm to our arithmetic is a larger one. A furlong is a *furrow-long*'; in the same way, a tenth of a furlong is a *chain* (22 yards), a measure adopted early in the seventeenth century because it happened to be a length of standardized chain consisting of 100 links. 'Our decimal system is due to our possession of ten *digits*, or fingers, and *calculation* comes from Latin *calculus*, a pebble.'

Semantics has many branches, whose enumeration and exhaustive treatment belong to the language course of an honours-degree student; but we may notice that one of the most interesting branches is that which deals with parallel metaphors in different languages. For instance, 'the names of flowers show that the same likeness has been observed by various races. The spice called

THE FUN OF WORD HISTORY

clove and the *clove*-pink both belong to Latin *clavus*, a nail. The German for pink is *Nelke*, a ... diminutive ... of *Nagel*, nail.' The same applies to proverbs, though often with a variation of symbols: to the pig of *buying a pig in a poke*, a cat is preferred by the French and the Germans; and the English cat and the king at which it may look become dog and bishop in French and German, which latter has ten birds on a roof, whereas we have two in a bush, when odious comparison is made to the bird in the hand.

Even from these few remarks, you will have seen—or guessed—that semantics is of great service to the etymologist and of considerable entertainment to the word-lover. Let us take a few examples in which it is tolerably clear that, without the sensible and sensitive help of semantics, the etymologist would have been stumped, gravelled, and stymied: but then your true etymologist, whether professional or, like most of us, amateur, is nothing if not a sportsman, one who looks for game and takes a risk among the strange, capricious, rarely dangerous but often incredible adventures of words: and he imperils his leisure—for, as 'once a policeman, always a policeman', so 'once a word-lover, always a word-lover' (and you might travel further and fare very much worse)—he imperils his leisure only if, and only in so far as, he is a semanticist, whether made (if ever he is!) or in the making. Once you wander from the beaten track, phonetics will not take you far; though, mind you, phonetics will often prevent the semanticist from wasting his fair youth or his mellow age in a wordy welter of alternative possibilities stretching from *A* to *Z* and from Alpha to Omega, or afford him a clue to the right tree-root in a jungle of psychological doubt. Take *antlers*. 'The *antlers* of a deer are properly the lowest branches of the horns, what we now call brow-antlers. The word comes from Old French *antoilliers*, which answers phonetically to a conjectured Latin *ante-oculares*', literally '(things) before the eyes': only a semanticist would have thought of 'that which hangs before the eyes'; only a phonologist could have said that Latin *ante oculares* would—or could—become *antoilliers* in Old French. 'This conjecture is confirmed by the German *Augensprosse*, brow-antler, literally eye-sprout.' Another good example, in which, however, phonetics need not be summoned to our assistance, is *pips*. 'The *pips* on cards or dice have nothing to do with apple pips. The oldest spelling is *peeps*', which occurs in Shakespeare. 'In the Germanic languages they are called "eyes", and in the Romance languages "points"; and the Romance derivatives of Latin *punctus*, point, also mean "peep of day". Hence the *peeps* are connected with the verb to *peep*.' To Weekley's admirable exposition, I shall (though there is no need to) add that the seventeenth to eighteenth-century underworld spoke of the human eyes as *peepers*.

To those examples, let us add *grog*, which serves to warn us that 'no human ingenuity', no phonetic skill, can solve the etymological puzzles in certain words 'if we do not happen to know the historical facts'. As Jespersen says, 'Admiral Vernon, known to sailors by the nickname of "Old Grog" because he wore a cloak of grogram (this, by the way, from French *gros grain* [coarse thread]), in 1740 ordered a mixture of rum and water to be served out instead of pure rum, and the name was transferred from the person to the drink'; he did it 'to prevent the sailors intoxicating themselves with their allowance of rum or spirits' (Captain Grose) and became very unpopular as a result; the naming was therefore intended as an insult to this insulter of the navy's hard heads. And from the liquor *grog* comes *groggy*, drunk; hence *groggy*, shaky on one's pins.

B. PARTICULAR: ENGLISH HISTORY IN ENGLISH WORDS; AN ASPECT OF OCCIDENTAL CIVILIZATION, SHOWN IN ENGLISH WORDS; AMERICAN HISTORY IN AMERICAN AND ENGLISH WORDS; WORD HISTORY RATHER THAN HISTORY IN WORDS

I. ENGLISH HISTORY IN ENGLISH WORDS[1]

In the words of every language, there is much of the history of the people that speak it: and history can, in English and American, be deduced on the one hand, on the other exemplified, better than in any other language, whether ancient or modern; the very fact that English is much less pure[2] than (say) Greek or Italian explains why it is, at the same time, much more revelatory of the influences that have affected it, hence of the influences to which the English people have been exposed, hence of the phases and periods of its history. Hence, too, of the English mind and morals at these periods. Hence of the development of, and changes in, the English character and outlook throughout recorded history. This art of reading history in the medium of language—in the rise of some words and the fall of others, in the struggles between competing words, and above all in changes of meaning—some-

---

[1] This section, after the four introductory paragraphs, represents a paraphrased précis of selected portions taken from chs. iii-iv of Owen Barfield's suggestive and fascinating book, *History in English Words*, revised edition, 1933 (Methuen; London); I have, however, made many comments and many additions.

[2] In the sense that it has been profitably influenced by more foreign languages over a longer period.

times so complete that a word comes to mean the opposite of its original sense, as in the adjectives *restive* and *rum*—this deduction of history from language is only in its infancy; and yet, to practise it in its simpler forms (no less interesting and often more significant than its erudite and more difficult forms), one does not need to possess either a degree in English or a maturity of years, for astonishing results can be obtained by any alert person, whether youthful or mature, that is ready to follow a trail, able to recognize a simple clue when it hits him in the eye, and possessed of a good etymological dictionary (say, Weekley's) or a good etymological and historical dictionary (say, *The Shorter Oxford*). Naturally, a working knowledge of English and American history through the ordinary channels provides a very useful basis and a valuable check; and this is a precaution that can be taken by all. A working knowledge of either Latin (or French) or German is a tremendous help: but it is not absolutely necessary. You will be astounded by the way in which one thing leads to another, that other to a third, the third to a fourth, and the fourth, perhaps, to a sidelight or an aspect that is well worth the hare-and-hound chase through the dictionary—a chase diverting enough in itself, even if you do fail to catch the hare, for although you may miss your goal, you will, on the way, have picked up something either amusing or useful, possibly more important than that which you hoped to prove or to find.

But the proof of the pudding is in the plums.

Here I shall stress rather the plums than the pudding, rather the trees than the wood, rather the historically interesting words than the history: for much of the necessary history has already been given in Chapter II and in the latter part of Chapter IV. If, as I hope, you wish to read a connected history of England in English words, you must go to *History in English Words*, by Owen Barfield; but connected history—that is, political and social history—must not be dragged by the heels into a book dealing specifically with language. Here you will find a few selected phases and aspects of English history. Just enough to show that kind of thing which you can do for yourselves, and just enough to give you some idea of the lines along which you might work, the ways in which that work can be done.

And now at last we reach the plums (or examples) with just sufficient pudding (or history) to prevent the fruit from becoming sickly and to prevent the stones (the hard facts) encasing the kernel (or sweet goal) from choking you.

Of the earliest immigration into England—that of the Celts (or Britons or Ancient Britons)—there are few traces; the clearest being in the names of rivers, for many rivers contain one of the three main Celtic terms for 'water' or 'river': *avon*; *dwr*, in the more pronounceable form *der* or *ter*; and *uisge*, in the manageable shapes, *usk*, *ax*, *is*, and *wye*, whereas the other parts of the name, if it is a compound, 'are often composed of words for "water" taken from another Aryan language, as in *Derwentwater, Windermere, Easeburn, Ashbourne*'.

The period of Roman colonization, beginning with the invasion by Claudius in A.D. 43 and lasting some four hundred years, left comparatively little trace. The stock example is that Latin *castra* (a camp) which has given us *Chester* and the endings of *Chichester, Gloucester, Lancaster*, and *Winchester*; almost a stock example is Latin *portus*, whence (sea) *port* and *-port* in such names as *Bridport* and *Devonport*.

'Then, during the Fifth and Sixth Centuries of our era, the Angles and Saxons began to flow in from the Continent, bringing ... old Aryan words like *dew*, *night*, *star* and *wind*, which they had never forgotten, new words which they had coined or developed in their wanderings, and Latin words which they had learnt as provincial subjects of the Roman Empire, bringing, in fact, that peculiar Teutonic variant of the Aryan tongue which forms the rich nucleus of our English vocabulary.' These newcomers were, soon after their arrival, converted to Christianity. 'The Latin and Greek words which entered our language at this period are concerned for the most part with the dogma and ritual of the Church ... Far more important was the alteration which now gradually took place in the *meaning* of many old Teutonic words—words like *heaven*, which had hitherto denoted a "canopy".'

To the Northmen, who were Scandinavian Teutons, we owe some of the basic words of our language: for instance, the pronouns *they, them, their, she*; the genitive and the plural in *-s*; such useful terms as *call, get, hit, knife, leg, same, skin, take, want, wrong*.

Then comes the Norman invasion, the most powerful of all influences (properly so called) on the English language. 'These Normans ... were the descendants of a Teutonic Danish tribe, which had taken possession of Normandy about a hundred and fifty years before'; a tribe that had adopted French as its language. They introduced not only French words, accepted very slowly at first, but also the feudal system: William the Conqueror may be said to have brought *master* and *servant*, *parlour* and *buttery*, *dinner* and *supper*; but it was the feudal system which, to such words as *honest* and *gentle* (originally, 'of good birth'), gave their finer meanings. We may note those lovely flower-names, *dandelion* (French *dent de lion*, 'lion's tooth', describing the leaves) and *pansy* (French *pensée*, 'thought'—hence 'remembrance'); the language of heraldry with its *azure* and *gules*; military terms, such as *banner* and *pennon*, *lance* and *hauberk*, *standard* and *tower*, *battle* and *war*; the titles of *countess*, *baron*, *viscount*, *marquis*, *duke*.

Most of the words that, in the Middle Ages, came from French have descended from Latin: as *duke* from Latin *dux*, through French *duc*; through Old French *maistre* comes *master* from Latin *magister*.

Not only did useful words throughout the Middle Ages, but also literary words during the latter part of the medieval period, get themselves transferred, the former from Normandy and the latter from the whole of France, from French to English. And the invention of the printing press 'fixed the ingredients of our language in a way they had never been fixed before': with the result that it is only a slight exaggeration to say that, 'to-day, if we want to borrow a word directly from Latin, we still give it a shape which tacitly assumes that it came to us through the French language'.

Some of those Latin words may be of Greek origin; and many Greek words have reached us through other channels. The threads of Latin and Greek run all through the history of the English language and the English people. 'The fact, for instance, that *hospital*, *parliament*, and *prison*'—which have arrived via French —'are Latin, while *church* and *school* have only come *through* Latin from the Greek, is symbolical of the two main divisions into which the Classical part of our language falls; for words which are genuinely of Latin origin—unless they have been especially used at some time to translate the thoughts of Greek writers— are very often concerned with the material outer world, but words of Greek origin are more likely to be landmarks in the world of thoughts and feelings.'

English owes much to the Roman art of war and to Roman politics; much also to Roman law. 'Dignified vocables like *justice*, *jurisdiction*, *jurisprudence*, speak [of] the lasting influence of the great Roman conception of "jus"—that abstract ideal of the relation between one free human being and another in so far as it is expressed in their actions . . . A whole chapter might be written on the numerous English words whose meanings can be traced back to the usages of Roman law.' Thus *obligation*, 'duty', comes from Latin *obligatio*, which, in Roman law, connoted the fact that 'a defaulting debtor was literally bound'—Latin, *ligare*, to bind—'and delivered a prisoner into the hands of his creditor'; this crude and cruel practice having been abandoned, *obligatio* came to mean 'the duty to pay'—a duty now enforceable against the debtor's property; hence, by gradual steps, *obligation* has attained to its present high moral stage. More objective is the odd history of *culprit*, which was used in the law courts from the Middle Ages down to the eighteenth century; it is, therefore, a relic of Law French—a fearful though not a wonderful mixture. 'In former days, when the prisoner had pleaded "Not Guilty", the Clerk of the Crown would open proceedings by saying "Culpable: prest",[1] meaning that the prisoner *is* "guilty" and I am "ready" to prove it. In the official records of the case this formula was abbreviated, first to "cul-prest" [or "prist"] and afterwards to "cul-prit", until later clerks formed the habit of running the two words together.'

But at the Reformation, when England finally cast off allegiance, whether political or theological, to the Holy Roman Empire, an end came also to the period of perhaps excessive, certainly potent and pervasive, French influence. The Reformation itself was responsible for 'the confusion of the English *Sunday* with the Jewish *Sabbath* and the consequent fastening upon that day of rest of many of the sombre inhibitions'—or *don'ts*—'entailed by the Sabbatic Law' of the Jews and, in several countries, rendered still more sombre by Calvinism.

Much more important than the linguistic influence of the Reformation was the linguistic influence of the Renaissance (or Revival of Learning), which, by making England aware of the literatures of Greece and Rome, caused a torrent of word-borrowing, at first chiefly from Latin. The importance of this borrowing may be gauged in part by imagining English without *accommodate*, *capable*, *corroborate*, *distinguish*, *estimate*, *experiment*, *investigate*, and scores of words equally common and useful. 'There is indeed good evidence that the stream of new words flowed too fast at this time for ordinary people to keep up with it ... Many of the Latin words that were borrowed have since fallen out of use. ... Francis Bacon, who is not a fantastic writer, was using such unfamiliar expressions as *contentation*, *contristation*, ... *ventosity*.' The tendency to over-Latinize English was parodied and ridiculed; and a Purist movement, which went too far in the opposite direction, helped to check the spate of Latin and Latinized Greek words.

Greek soon began to be freely enlisted in the cause of the English language. The Renaissance introduced *apology*, *climax*,

[1] Or *prist*, the more usual Anglo-French form, with a later variant *prit*.

drama, emphasis, epidemic, episode, hysterical, parallel, physical,
and many others. 'The number of technical terms . . . is particularly noticeable, and it was now that the foundations were laid of that almost automatic system whereby a new Greek-English word is coined to mark each advance that is made in science, and especially in mechanical science. *Automatic* is itself an example, and it is hardly necessary to add *chronometer, dynamo, magneto,* . . . *telescope,* . . . *thermometer.*'

But the English language was settling down, the post-sixteenth-century additions and changes being, some of them important but none of them so far-reaching as the vocabulary influence of the Norman Conquest, the syntactic changes from Middle to Modern English, and the alchemy of the Renaissance. Etymology can no longer tell us the complete story: yet still, from various angles, it can 'light up for us . . . different little portions of the dark, mysterious mass, the past'.

By the sixteenth century, for instance, that (until the twentieth century) 'peculiarly English characteristic, the love of sport, had already begun to make its mark on the language'. *Sport* has been noticed in another chapter. Hawking has bequeathed *allure, haggard, rebate, reclaim* to the language. *Allure* comes from *lure*, the apparatus with which the hawks were recalled; and *reclaim* got its present sense ('to call back') from 'the cries that were uttered to summon the hawk back to the wrist', for the meaning of the Latin *reclamare* was quite different. From fencing we have received *forte* and *foible*, the strong and the weak (*feeble*) point of a sword. Hunting has given us *couple, relay, retrieve, run riot, ruse, scent* ('on the scent of a criminal'), *worry*, and other terms; for instance, 'a *ruse* was a doubling of the hunted animal on its own tracks'. From cock-fighting we have taken the *white feather* of fear and the *crestfallen* look that too often accompanies defeat; from *bowls*, the *bias* of prejudice and 'there's the *rub*'. Few of us know that, either from the game of chess or from the board on which the hour-long struggle takes place, the language has drawn *chess, check* (rebuff, repulse), *checkmate, cheque* (in American, *check*), *chequer,* all of which reached England from Persian via Arabic: *checkmate* is the Persian *Shah mat*, '[the] Shah (or King) is dead', Arabic *Shah mata*, the English term passing through Old French *eshec mat*.

The more modern sports have provided us with comparatively few words but a very fair 'bag' of phrases; these technical terms and phrases have won a place in general use—have become idiomatic. From numerous claimants we choose *put on a spurt* and *the last lap*, from athletics; from cricket, *to stump* (and *take his middle stump*), *caught out*, *not cricket*; *skate on thin ice*; *kick off*, from football; *tee up* and *one up* and *stymied* from golf, which supplies also *caddie*.

Like *cad*, *caddie* is from the French *cadet*, 'a younger son'; and 'when we hear a golfer use this word, when we hear a Scotch person ask for an *aschet*, instead of a dish, or see the queer expression *petticoat-tails* on a tin of Edinburgh shortbread, we are taken back to the close connection between the French and Scottish courts . . . in the days of Mary Stuart' . . . For *aschet* is a form of the French *assiette*, and *petticoat-tails* is perhaps a corruption (by folk etymology) of *petits gastels* (Modern French *petits gâteaux*).

English nautical relations with the Dutch have made a deep impression on the English language. The fourteenth century ushered in *bowsprit* and *skipper*; the fifteenth as many as nine sea-terms, including *buoy*, *freight*, *keel*, *lighter*, *pump*, and *scout*; the sixteenth, at least seven, including *dock* and *reef*; and the seventeenth another seven (including *bow* of a ship, *cruise* and *cruiser*), for this was the period 'when Van Tromp nailed his broom to the mast, the Dutch fleet sailed up the Medway, and William of Orange sat upon the English throne'. And there are such military words as *freebooter*; as *cashier, drill, furlough, onslaught*; and 'the apparently English *forlorn hope*', actually a corruption, again by folk etymology, of the Dutch *verloren hoop*, meaning 'a lost detachment' and therefore having tragically little to do with hope.

The words from Spanish are not very numerous, but some of them are rich in history. Many of the earlier loans travelled to England via France. Of those which came originally from Arabia, a few will be mentioned in the next section of this chapter. *Alligator* (a corruption of *el lagarto*, the lizard), *chocolate*, *cocoa*, *tomato*, words that 'come through Spanish from Mexican, commemorate the Spanish conquest of Mexico, and the poetic *breeze* is a sixteenth-century adaption of the Spanish "brisa", a name for the north-west trade wind in the Spanish Main. Of the other words which come to us through Spanish, *cannibal*, *hammock*, *hurricane*, *maize*, and *savannah*, are Caribbean, whereas *canoe*, *potato*, and *tobacco* are South American. *Cannibal*, like the names *West Indies* and *Indian* (meaning "aboriginal inhabitant of America"), hides a more detailed history. It was brought back by Christopher Columbus who believed, when he reached the islands of the Caribbean Sea, that he had sailed right round the world, back to the east coast of India. The name "Cariba"—a variant of "Carib" or "Caribes"—he took as a proof that the inhabitants were subjects of the Grand Khan of Tartary.'

THE FUN OF WORD HISTORY

But the Spaniards had rivals in the Portuguese and English explorers and settlers. The Asiatic Indian *coolie* and *curry* reached us through Portuguese, which, by the way, has been described as the most Latin of the Romance languages. *Banana* and *negro* came from Africa, perhaps through Portuguese, as *palaver* certainly came. *Coconut*—not, please note, *cocoanut!*—is from the Portuguese *coco*, 'a bogey', the reference being to the monkeyish face of the nut. *Amuck, bamboo*, and *cockatoo* came, through Portuguese, from Malayan, but the tea-*caddy* is pure Malayan. '*Moccasin, tomahawk*, and *hickory* are among the words sent back to us by 17th Century English settlers in North America. *Taboo, tattoo* [an indelible mark stamped on the skin], and *kangaroo* came home with Captain Cook from the Pacific.'

Meanwhile, England had been growing politically. *Politics, political, politician*, as well as *parliamentary*, all arose in the sixteenth century; *Cabinet Council* came with the accession of Charles I; *cabal*, contrary to a hard-dying legend, is a Hebrew word that was popularized in the reign of Charles II. The *army*, i.e. the standing army, arose only during the Civil War, before which there was none; *demagogue* occurred in the famous Royalist pamphlet, *Eikon Basilike*; and 'the expression *to send to Coventry* is probably a gift from the rebellious citizens of Birmingham, who, according to Clarendon, frequently "rose upon small parties of the King's", and either killed them or sent them, as prisoners, to Coventry, which was a Parliamentary stronghold'.

In the seventeenth century, too, appeared some important commercial and financial terms. Among these are *capital*, which certain philologists consider to be a doublet of *cattle* (the oldest Aryan form of wealth), *commercial, discount, dividend, insurance, investment*, and 'the modern meaning of *bank*, which, like the names of so many protective and responsible institutions—the *Assizes* [or county *Sessions* held periodically], the [judge's] *Bench*, the [Roman] *Consulate*, the [Privy or Town] *Council*, the *Chair* at a public meeting, a *Seat* in Parliament, and the *Throne*—is based etymologically on one of the oldest and safest of human occupations', i.e. sitting down (and talking). 'The old Teutonic word which subsequently became modern English *bench* was adopted into Italian, probably from the Teutonic Lombards of Northern Italy, in the form "banco". It soon acquired the special sense of a moneylender's "bench" or table and found its way, together with the object it represents, into most of the countries of Europe. . . . In England the phrase *Bank of England* first appeared in 1694, describing a body of individuals associated for the purpose of lending money to the Government; and about thirty years later this still ... outstanding loan began to be known as the *National Debt*.' It is, therefore, all the more interesting to learn that both *bankruptcy* and *currency* arose in the earlier, *capitalistic* and *finance* (from *fines* or forfeitures of money at the end or *finis* of a far from perfect day) in the latter half of the eighteenth century. *Consols*, recorded first in 1770, are *consol*idated annuities, whereas *bonus* (1773), a bogus Latin word on Latin *bonum*, 'a good thing' (? for 'a good man', L. *bonus*), belongs to less solid finance: both words were originally Stock Exchange slang.

The second half of the eighteenth century was a period as full of significance as of liveliness, if one may be permitted to use the latter word in the sense of 'a certain liveliness on the Western Front', which, by the way, reminds us that *the late unpleasantness*, as applied to the wars of 1914–18 and 1939–45, was originally an American phrase, referring to the Civil War. *Civil War* was a phrase not unknown among Loyalists in America at the time of the American War of Independence (*independence* being a Puritan word, New England a Puritan province), a war to which we owe *the rights of man*, which owed something to Rousseau—as, indeed, the War of Independence also did. From the new United States of America, which sprang from Washington's cherry tree and grew even as the mustard tree, we turn to Rousseau's other revolution: to the French Revolution we owe *aristocrat* and *democrat* (both formed direct on the Greek originals), *revolutionize* and *terrorize*: to *terrorize* is the French Revolutionary adaptation of the Roman motto, 'Divide and rule'—divide body from soul, and rule the rest: this notion soon passed from Soviet Russia to Japan with her propagandist proverb, 'England never fights alone: isolate and destroy her'. To the French Revolution we are indebted also for *Liberty, Equality, Fraternity*, a political creed first expounded by a French pirate a generation before the French aristocrats went nonchalantly to the *guillotine*. The Revolution's thunder was stolen by the Napoleonic Wars; and to the Napoleonic era we owe *sectional*, France being divided into electoral sections under the Directory (1795–99), and *conscription*, the method by which Napoleon (with whom God at last grew bored) levied those troops who encouraged and enforced his megalomania. To the Boer War we owe *trek*; *kopje*, a Boer word of Dutch origin, the Dutch word meaning 'a little head'; and 'to *maffick*', from the rejoicing that ensued upon the Relief of Mafeking. To the war of 1914–18 we owe *camouflage*, from the French, and *get the wind up*; and it was that war which popularized *gadget*, originally a naval word, and *scrounge* ('to steal'), originally a dialect word, and *eyewash*, originally a musketry term, and *go west*, originally an underworld phrase.

But let us turn to peace. 'A list of new words like *anaesthetic, galvanometer, morse, railway* [American *railroad*], *telephone, turbine*, . . . which appeared in the 19th Century, would tell a full and fairly accurate story of its extraordinarily sudden mechanical and scientific development.' *Telephone*[1] belongs to the important *tele-*[2] group, of which the chief words, in chronological order, are *telescope, telegraph, telephone, telepathy*, and *television* with its derivatives *televisor, televise, teleview*. *Telescope*, from the Greek *tēlĕ*, 'afar' or 'far off' or 'at a distance', and the Greek *skŏpos*, 'far-seeing', arose in the earlier half of the seventeenth century; *telegraph*, from *tēlĕ* + *graphos*, 'writing' (adjective) or 'writer', came in the early 1790's, but was originally applied to some such signalling apparatus as the semaphore, the modern sense following as early as 1797, first as *electric* (or *electrical*) *telegraph*, and then in the 1840's as *magnetic* (or *electro-magnetic*) *telegraph*; *telephone*, literally 'a voice from afar', arrived in the 1830's as the name of a device for conveying sound to a distance, the 'electrical speaking telegraph' or modern telephone of Alexander Graham Bell (a Scottish-born American) being introduced in 1876; *telepathy*, Greek *tēlĕ* + *patheia*, 'feeling' or 'perception', was coined in the early 1880's for a communication made, or received, independently of the usual channels of sense; *television*, a hybrid (Greek *tēlĕ* + Latin *visio*, 'seeing' or 'thing seen'), arrived, in very imperfect state, in 1909; *televisor* (a back formation from *television*), not coined until 1926, is the instrument invented by J. L. Baird; *televise*, 'to transmit by television', is another back-formation from *television*, and it arrived in 1927; the horrible *teleview* ('to see by television') was mercifully spared us until 1934 or 1935 and is inexcusable, *view* being from the English noun *view*, itself from French *vue*; *televiewer* came in 1935 or 1936 and means 'one who televiews'. 'More interesting in many ways [than these technicalities] is the appearance of new metaphors and idioms, such as *to peter out, to pan out* (from mining), *to blow off* or *to get up steam* and *to go off the rails* from the steam engine, and many electrical metaphors such as' *live wire* and *tension*. 'For new ways of doing are bound up with new ways of knowing and thinking', and especially is this true of the period from about 1860.

[1] The dates and developments are taken from *The O.E.D.*
[2] In all these terms it is pronounced *tĕlĕ*; a permissible change from the pronunciation of the Greek word. But the pronunciations *tellyscope, tellyphone, tellygraph*, etc., are slovenly.

To go back for a minute or two, we may glance at the social as opposed to the political and scientific history of England: and here, words are no less illuminating, hence no less revelatory. 'To look up in *The Oxford Dictionary* such words as *blackguard* [1736], [a Christmas] *carol* [1502], *club* [1670], *morris* [*dance*, 1512], *teetotal* [1834], or a thousand others which seem to have no particular historical significance, and to read through the many illustrative quotations, is to take a wonderfully easy and intimate peep into the past, while the dates at which such words as *magazine* [a light periodical: 1731 when *The Gentleman's Magazine* was established], *news-letter* [1674], *newspaper* [1670], *novelist* [1728], [*the*] *press* [1797], or again, *callers* [1786], *small talk* [1751], *tea-party* [1778], *snob* [socially: 1848], *antimacassar* [1852] ... appeared, together with quotations showing the particular shades of meaning with which they have been used, are in themselves a little history of the English people. What could be more suggestive, for instance, than the fact that the adjective *improper* was first applied to human beings in the [eighteen-]fifties?'—when prudery was at its height.

Passing to broader issues, we may note, and get much fun from noting, that 'the characteristics of nations, as of races, are fairly accurately reflected linguistically in the metaphors and idioms they choose, in their tricks of grammar, in their various ways of forming new words'; for instance, the immense compounds affected by the Germans. In English and American, 'the number of words and expressions drawn from sport ... has already been touched on, and it is at any rate a question whether humour has not played a larger part in the creation of English and American words than in those of other languages', as, for example, in back-formation, though not all back-formations (e.g., *televise*) spring from humour. 'We realize the humorous intention when somebody invents from the noun *swashbuckler* a verb to *swashbuckle*, or *to buttle* and *cuttle* from *butler* and *cutler*, but it is not so well known that the same process (probably with the same humorous intent behind it) gave us such sober words as *burgle*, *sidle*, *edit*, *grovel*, *beg*, and *greed*. . . . The humorous device of understatement [*meiosis* is the grammarian's term] is responsible'—to choose one example from many—'for the modern meaning of *hit* and most of its synonyms. The notion of striking was once conveyed by the verb *to slay*; by Tudor times, however, *smite*, which in Old English meant "to smear" or "rub over", had become the commoner word. *Strike* itself in Old English meant "to stroke" or "rub gently", and *hit*, which is now universal in serious [spoken English], meant "to meet with" or "light upon"—"not

THE FUN OF WORD HISTORY   167

to miss", in fact. . . . *Blow* and *thrash* are both sly agricultural metaphors.' English, in brief, is—as its entire history has shown—a highly versatile language; and one phase of that versatility appears in 'the ease with which it has appropriated the linguistic products' of other nations. To quote the closing words of Owen Barfield's suggestive and illuminating historical sketch:

> Like Mr Shaw's Shakespeare, [the] genius [of English] seems to have lain not so much in originality [excepting always the unconscious originality of the mass of ordinary people] as in the snapping up of unconsidered trifles; and where it has excelled all the other languages of Europe, possibly of the world, is in the grace with which it has hitherto digested these particles of foreign matter and turned them into its own life's blood. Historically, the English language is a muddle; actually it is a beautiful, personal, and highly sensitive creature.

II. AN ASPECT[1] OF OCCIDENTAL CIVILIZATION, AS SEEN IN ENGLISH WORDS

The civilization of the western world can be considered from many aspects: but as this section is hardly a linguistic survey of that world, and as any one of several aspects will serve our purpose of showing where word history meets political and social history, we choose that aspect of occidental civilization which can, not too inaccurately, be labelled experiment.

'Astrology has changed to astronomy; alchemy to chemistry . . . At last . . . thought has shaken herself free.' From the Dark (but not incessantly dark) Ages, however, we have inherited such alchemic words as *alcohol*, *alembic* (a primitive form of chemical *retort*), *alkali*, *amalgam*, *tartar* (bitartrate of potash), and *alchemy* itself, which, all coming from Arabic, remind us that the medieval Arabs were the forerunners of modern chemistry. They were also philosophers, mathematicians, and astrologers: 'the appearance in English of such words as *azimuth* [any such arc of the heaven as stretches from zenith to horizon], *nadir* [that point of the heavens which is diametrically opposite the zenith], and *zenith* towards the end of the 14th Century suggests . . that the thinking of this Syrian race contributed in no small degree to the rise . . . of the new astronomy. These three Arabic words (two of them for the first time in English) are to be found in Chaucer's *Treatise on the Astrolabe*, written in 1391 . . . ; and this interesting docu-

---

[1] From Part ii, 'The Western Outlook', of Owen Barfield's *English History in Words*, where the other aspects or phases are Myth, Philosophy and Religion, Devotion, Personality and Reason, Mechanism, Imagination. This is a delightful and valuable book; it is a pleasure to be indebted to it.

ment contains many other words for which *The Oxford Dictionary* does not give any earlier quotation, such as *almanac* [Spanish-Arabic], *ecliptic* [Greek], *equinox* [Latin], *equator* [Latin: literally, "that which equalizes"], *horizon* [Greek], *latitude, longitude, meridian* [all three being from Latin], *minute* (meaning one-sixtieth of a degree [and also from Latin: *minutus*, made very small]), while *zodiac* [Greek] was used by Gower a few years before.'

It is probable that the use of the words noticed in the preceding paragraph brought into man's consciousness the ability to see himself as 'a solid object situated among solid objects'. It is also probable that 'those minds which were apparently the first to think of cutting up the sky without reference to the constellations, and which could, moreover, develop so fully the great and novel system of abstraction which they called *algebra*,[1] did their part in bringing about that extraordinary revolution in astronomical thought which is associated with the name of Copernicus'.

There was, too, a general revolution of physical outlook. 'As the discoveries of Kepler and Galileo slowly filtered through to the popular consciousness, first of all simple words like *atmosphere, down, earth, planet, sky, space, sphere, star, up* . . . underwent a profound yet subtle semantic change. And then, in the 18th Century, as Newton's discoveries became more widely known, further alterations took place. *Weight*, for instance, acquired a new significance, differing from *mass*, which also changed, having formerly meant simply a lump of matter. *Gravity*'—from Latin *gravitas*, heaviness—'took on its great new meaning, and the new words *gravitation* and *gravitate* were formed, the latter being soon adapted to metaphorical uses.'

The law of gravity takes us back to Francis Bacon, who was in some ways 'the moving spirit of that intellectual revolution which began to sweep over Europe in the 16th Century. . . . He was thoroughly dissatisfied with the whole *method*[2] of thought as he found it in his day': he introduced the inductive method, which was 'based on a systematic observation of Nature herself. . . . It was left to Bacon to . . . construct a prejudice-proof system of arranging and classifying the results. These *instances*, as they were called, were, on the one hand, to be manufactured by means of *experiment*,[3] and on the other to be arranged and weeded out

[1] Arabic *al-jebr*, literally 'the reunion of broken parts'; used in surgery before it was employed in mathematics.

[2] Greek *methodos*, pursuit of knowledge; specifically, mode of investigation.

[3] *Experiment* is probably adopted direct from Old French *experiment*, which represents Latin *experimentum*, a noun of action ('an active test or trying') from *experiri*, to try, to test.

according to their significance. The word *crucial* comes to us from Bacon's Latin phrase, "*instantia crucis*"[1]—the *crucial instance*—which, like a sign-post, decided between two rival hypotheses by proving one and disproving the other.' It was Bacon who introduced *dissection*, 'cutting up'; the increasing use of *dissection* caused *anatomy*, 'cutting up', to take as its predominant meaning, 'that which (by surgeons) is cut up', i.e. the human body. That he possessed the scientific attitude more than any of his predecessors and contemporaries is further indicated by his being the first to speak of *acid, hydraulic* and *suction*; by his employing *progressive* and *retrograde* in an historical sense that did not become general until well on into the eighteenth century; and by 'his equally innovating distinction between *ancient* and *modern*'. Not that he was alone in his desire for truth in the spheres of logic and science, for already in the sixteenth century there had occurred the semantic change of *observe* from 'to obey a rule' or 'to inspect auguries' into 'to examine (phenomena)', 'to perceive by scientific inspection', 'to pay attention to, in a scientific spirit'; there had occurred also the birth of the verbs *distinguish, analyse* (originally to dissect), and *investigate* (Latin *investigare*, to track).

'There are other influences . . . that must be taken into account. *Discovery* (it was a new word) was in the very air of 16th Century England. From the West came tidings of a new world; from the East news yet more marvellous of an old one; and the rebirth of science was, in its infancy, but a single aspect of that larger Renaissance which played such an important part in moulding the subsequent life and outlook of Europe. . . . By the time the Renaissance reached England it was already in full swing.' Little wonder, then, that the restless activity of this period considerably changed, developed variously, virtually modernized the English vocabulary. 'The genius of the language sprouted and burgeoned in the genial warmth of Elizabethan and Jacobean fancy, and—most effectually of all—it passed through the fire of Shakespeare's imagination' and came under the healthy influence of his detached, selfless realism. Quite apart from the very numerous words which he grafted upon the language—or, more accurately, planted in its very soil—and the magical new senses with which he endowed it, there are all those phrases and whole lines which are equally part of the English vocabulary. For instance, *give him his due, the glass of fashion, a good thing, too much of a good thing, pitched battle, play on words, more honoured in the breach than the observance,*

---

[1] Literally, an instance of the *crux* or cross serving as a sign-post at a cross-roads. Later in the 17th Century came *experimentum crucis*, a crucial experiment—one that decided the one way or the other. Hence, *crucial test.*

snapper-up of unconsidered trifles, well on your way. Of no one in the world's linguistic history is it so true as it is of Shakespeare to say that he came and saw and conquered, leaving a finer heritage than did Caesar.

Though too abstruse for adequate treatment here, the Platonic philosophy exercised a quiet, yet profound influence on English through Spenser and certain poets of the earlier half of the seventeenth century: to them we owe much of the richness of meaning now resident in *love* and *beauty*; it was they who did much to shape the modern sense of *idea*, which in Platonic philosophy meant 'a general or ideal form or type'.

These new senses were, in fact, due to a kind of philosophical experimentation; these words, these senses, possessed and still retain a beauty denied to or lacked by the modern words in *-ology* and *-ism*, the one a combining-form of *-logy* (Greek *-logia*, with which compare Greek *logos*, a discourse) and the other an anglicized form of the Greek *-ismos* (a noun suffix connoting action), via the Latin *-ismus* and, immediately, the French *-isme*. But, after all, there is beauty in truth; it may be defined as intellectual beauty: and it is largely through experiment that truth is revealed.

III. AMERICAN HISTORY IN AMERICAN AND ENGLISH WORDS[1]

There are certain American (or English and American) words that are inseparable from American history; and by *American* history is meant that of the United States of America. But here we shall deal with only a few words—a few whose linguistic, especially whose etymological and semantic development affords points of considerable interest and not inconsiderable entertainment. In the very roughly chronological order of their rise to importance in the U.S.A., they are: *Spanish Main; President, Congress, Yankee; bunkum, caucus, carpet-bagger, mugwump; O.K.; proposition; wild-cat* and *bucket shop; bootlegger; stunt; Doughboy; jazz; ballyhoo; haywire; Briticism.*

The Spanish Main[2] has, in the twentieth century, been applied mostly to 'the sea contiguous to [a certain region of America], or the route traversed by the Spanish[3] register ships'[3]: a usage

---

[1] See also ch. iii.—The dates and definitions are taken from *The O.E.D.* and *A Dictionary of American English.*

[2] Not specifically an American word; but its American associations render it a convenient transition.

[3] Ships 'having a registered licence authorizing [them] to trade with the Spanish possessions in America' (*O.E.D.*).

appearing first in print in 1839, when Longfellow wrote, 'Then
... spake an old Sailor, Had sailed the Spanish Main'. But
originally (1725) it meant 'the mainland of America adjacent to
the Caribbean sea, especially the coast stretching from the Isthmus
of Panama to the mouth of the Orinoco' (*O.E.D.*), which was
the sense predominant for over a century. In the original sense,
main is short for *mainland*; now archaic, this *main* was very
commonly used during the three hundred years beginning about
1550. *The main*, short for *the main sea*, 'the high sea, the open
ocean', did not arise until the 1570's, was in general use until
about 1850, and has since been mostly a poetic cliché or counter.

President as the head of a republic originated in the United
States; it travelled to South America; then to France. The
American title comes from the *President* (1774) of that congress
of separate provinces or States which sat during the War of
Independence. It had, in America, been earlier used both of the
chief magistrate of some of the North American colonies (1608)
and of the head of a university or a university college (Harvard;
1642), in imitation of English practice (1464). Another chiefly
American usage is: 'he who is at the head of a commercial company' (1781); where the English usage would be *chairman* or,
less frequently, *governor*. There are two important English usages
that considerably antedate the American ones: 'the head of an
advisory, especially if political council' (1530) and 'an appointed
governor or lieutenant of a province, a colony, or a city' (1375).
The origin of *president* is Latin *praesidens*, 'a president or governor', the agential noun corresponding to *praesidere*, literally 'to
sit over', hence 'to preside over' or 'to guard'.

With *President* goes *Congress*. The linguistic development of
the name for this legislative body is:

Latin *congredi*: to go together.
  ,,   *congressus*: a going or coming together; hence, a meeting.
English *congress*: a meeting: 1528.
  ,,   ,,   : a formal meeting of representatives or delegates: 1678.
American ,,   : an assembly of delegates: 1711; as a foreshadowing of a general American Congress: 1765.
    ,,   *Continental Congress*: 1774, 1775, 1776 (War of Independence).
    ,,   *Congress of the Confederation*: 1781–89.
    ,,   ,,   ,,   *United States*: March 4th, 1789 (first meeting).

Yankee did not become general until late in the eighteenth century. This term was at first applied to the inhabitants of the Dutch colonies in North America; for instance, to those who lived in New Amsterdam—i.e. New York. 'Now *Jan Kees* is a nickname still applied in Flanders to people from Holland proper. *Jan* of course is the common Dutch name corresponding to English John, and *Kees* may be either the usual pet-form of the name Cornelis, another Christian name typical of the Dutch, or else a dialectal variation of *kaas*, "cheese", in allusion to that typically Dutch product, or—what is more probable—a combination of both. *Jankees* . . . became *Yankees*, where the *s* was taken as the plural ending and eventually disappeared, and *Yankee* became the designation of any inhabitant of New England and even sometimes of the whole of the United States'[1]; the latter usage is loose, but it is at least preferable to calling any male inhabitant of the U.S.A. a *Yank*, which, by the way, is a back-formation.

Early in the nineteenth century arose a new name for claptrap. The modern spelling is nearly always *bunkum*, which, however, is recorded as early as 1827; the original spelling was *buncombe*, and it is this spelling which led to the discovery of its exact origin. Buncombe County, in North Carolina, was named in 1791 after a Colonel Edward Buncombe.[2] In due course, Felix Walker made in Congress a prosy and lengthy speech, so dull that many of the members left the hall. Noticing their departure, he told those who remained that, if they wished, they could go too, for, though he intended to continue speaking for some time, he was only *talking for Buncombe*, to please his constituents, as we are informed in John H. Wheeler's *Historical Sketches of N. Carolina*. A writer in 1827 says that *talking to Bunkum* (variants were *talking for* . . . , *speaking for Buncombe*, and so on) 'is an old and common saying at Washington, when a member of congress is making one of those hum-drum and unlistened-to "long talks" which are lately become so fashionable'; and twenty years later we find the word in its modern usage, thus: 'A great deal of "bunkum", sprinkled with a high seasoning of political jugglery'. 'But', as Jespersen[3] has shrewdly remarked, 'does anybody suppose that the name of Mr Walker's constituency would have been thus used if he had happened to hail from Annapolis or

---

[1] Jespersen, *Growth and Structure of the English Language*. McKnight records numerous guesses. *The O.E.D.* may be right in preferring origin in *Janke*, a Dutch diminutive of *Jan*; *A Dictionary of American English* says 'Of unknown origin'.

[2] R. H. Thornton, *An American Glossary*, 1912.   [3] *Language*, p. 409.

Philadelphia, or some other place with a name incapable of tickling the popular fancy in the same way as *Buncombe* does?' The short *u* occurs in an astonishingly large number of humorous words.

Caucus (originally a New England word) might have been mentioned earlier; but though it is recorded in 1760 and may have been used many years before, it did not become generally known until the year 1799 or 1800. Without going into a lot of political technicalities, we may accept Thornton's admirable definition: 'A meeting of politicians in order to settle their combined plan of action' for an electioneering campaign. The word came to England in 1878, by the agency of the ever-alert Disraeli, and has been misused, especially as an insulting, insinuating term. But then it has also been misused in America; even more so, indeed, for there it is often made synonymous with a 'meeting' of any kind. Its etymology is something of a mystery: certainly it has nothing to do with *caulkers*; possibly it is from the Algonquin dialect, for in New England, 'Indian names were commonly taken by clubs and secret associations', though 'there appears to be no direct evidence' (*O.E.D.*).

Mugwump certainly comes from a Red Indian word (*mugquomp*) meaning a 'chieftain'. It occurred in its Amerindian sense at least as early as 1832, but it is not until 1884 that it was applied politically. On June the 15th of that year, *The Sun* (New York) 'styled the Independent Republicans by this name', and Thornton records a politician as asserting in a speech made on September the 13th: 'I am an independent—a Mugwump. I beg to state that *mugwump* is the best of American. It belongs to the language of the Delaware Indians; it occurs many times in Eliot's Indian Bible; and it means a great man.' By 1888, as Bryce shows in his great history of the American Commonwealth, it had come to signify 'one who holds more or less aloof from party-politics, professing disinterested and superior views' (*O.E.D.*). The word soon travelled to England, where sometimes it bears the connotation of a political trimmer; and both in England and America, a famous president of an American university's witticism, 'A mugwump is one who sits on a fence, with his mug on one side and his wump on the other', has had much popularity and virtually determined the sense.

Another political term is *carpet-bagger*, literally 'one who travels with only a carpet-bag; that is, without much luggage or baggage'. In September 1857, *The Herald of Freedom* newspaper of Lawrence, Kansas, says that 'early in the spring several thousand excellent young men came to Kansas. This was jokingly called the carpet-bag emigration.' But after the American Civil War, as Thornton tells us (and Thornton is always worth listening to), it was applied to those 'immigrants from the North, who have thrown themselves into local politics; and through their influence the negroes obtained office' (*The Daily News*, London, September 18, 1868). And in 1904 an historian of old Virginia speaks of them as 'unprincipled adventurers who sought their fortunes in the South by plundering the disarmed and defenceless people'; but the term had reached the end of its tether twenty years earlier, and any later use is either merely historical or a transference, meaning 'anyone interfering with the politics of a locality with which he is thought to have no permanent or genuine connexion', a use that is fast dying out.

But we must abandon politics for a term of much wider popularity: *O.K.*: on which so much drivel has been written. The old story was that Andrew Jackson used it in 1790; and even that in the Presidential campaign of 1828 Andy Jackson, then a General, was publicly accused of being illiterate and particularly of spelling *all correct* as *oll* (or *orl*) *korrect* (or *k'rect*). But it was only in the 1840's that *O.K.!* become general in the U.S.A. for 'all correct!', 'right!', 'safe!', 'suitable!', 'what is required!'; only in the 1850's that it became widely used as an ordinary adjective, i.e. not necessarily in exclamations. It reached England about 1880 as slang; since the 1914–18 war it has ranked as a colloquialism. Early in the 1880's, Alfred Glanville Vance ('the great Vance') used to sing, on the London music-halls:

> 'The Stilton, sir, the cheese, the O.K. thing to do,
> On Sunday afternoon is to toddle to the Zoo.
> Week-days may do for Cads, but not for me and you:
> So dressed right down the road, we show them who is who.'

The chorus ran thus:

> 'The walking in the Zoo—
> Walking in the Zoo—
> The O.K. thing on Sunday is the walking in the Zoo.'

The much-disputed origin is certainly not *aux Cayes*, nor yet *och aye!* Thornton inclines to the view that *O.K.* was originally an error for *O.R.*, 'Order Recorded'; *The Oxford Dictionary*, that it stood phonetically and humorously for *all correct* and had nothing to do with Andrew Jackson. I own that until 1941 I believed that it represents the Choctaw Indian *oke*[1] (or *hoke*), 'it

---

[1] This etymology has been familiarized to the general public in England by the labels on *Mason's O.K. Sauce*.

is so'. In the July 1941 issue of *The Saturday Review of Literature*, Dr Allen Walker Read conclusively showed that *O.K.* was in 1840 the watchword of the O.K. Club, that Democratic club of New York City which took its name from *Old Kinderhook*, nickname of Martin Van Buren (1782–1862), born at Kinderhook in New York State and in 1836–40 the President of the United States. The verb is purely derivative; it arose not before the 1880's in America and reached England at the end of the century.

Proposition, oddly enough, is not listed in Thornton's dictionary of Americanisms: the omission indicates that, in 1911 (when *An American Glossary* went to press), the term was not yet 'of recognized standing or of special interest'; and *The O.E.D.*, in 1909, also omitted it. Yet in 1923 McKnight could remark, 'The disposition to' invest general terms 'with a concrete meaning appears in such equivalents of *thing* as *business* (in "the whole business"), *concern*, *affair*. In present-day American colloquial use the word *proposition* is paralleling in a striking way the earlier history of *thing*'; and three years later, Fowler (*Modern English Usage*) noted that it is misused for *proposal, task, problem, objective, job, undertaking, occupation, trade, possibility, prospect, area, field, sphere, method, experiment*, and even *opponent*, this last deriving from the *task* sense; and in 1935, Horwill (*Modern American Usage*) recorded that 'in America this word has lost its special'—and proper—'meaning of *something propounded*', Weekley in the same year gently murmuring that 'it is perhaps too optimistic to hope that the next generation will abstain from ... tending to substitute *proposition* for every other abstract noun in the language'. It is, however, only fair to remember that the *proposal* sense was used, in a specific official connexion, as early as the 1720's in England and that it may have been so used in America as early as 1870. The word arose in England in the fourteenth century as 'thing propounded'. It comes from the Latin *propositio*, 'a setting forth', 'a theme', from *ponere*, 'to place, set', hence 'to posit'.

The promoters of *wild-cat*[1] schemes doubtless submitted to their victims what they alleged to be 'sound propositions'. The term *wild-cat* was applied chiefly to *money* (e.g., *bills*) and *banks*, and it meant 'having a precarious value or existence'. In 1838, 'About four hundred Irishmen working on the Canal took offence at being paid in "Wild-Cat" money, instead of Illinois' (*The Jeffersonian*, April 14), and later in the year a correspondent to the same paper wrote, 'We shall have Orono bills, Exchange bills, and Lumbermen's bills, and Wild-cat bills, that nobody knows

[1] This paragraph is pure Thornton.

who the father or the maker is'; in 1840, Mrs. Kirkland, in *A New Home*, tells us that '[Many of the new banks] were without a local habitation, though they might boast the name, it may be, of some part of the deep woods, where the wild cat had hitherto been the most formidable foe. Hence the celebrated name "Wild Cat", justified fully by the course of these bloodsuckers.' This kind of bank had become rare by the 1880's, by which time, however, there had sprung up the *bucket-shops*, explained by the following quotation from an October 1881 issue of *The New York Evening Post*: 'A "bucket-shop" in New York is a low "gin-mill", or "distillery", where small quantities of spirits are dispensed in pitchers and pails (buckets). When the shops for dealing in one-share and five-share lots of stocks were opened, these dispensaries of smaller lots than could be got from regular dealers were at once named "bucket-shops".'

On top of the terrors of the bucket-shop were, in the latter part of the same decade, piled those caused by the bootleggers.[1] In *The Omaha Herald* of 1889, we learn that 'There is as much whiskey consumed in Iowa now as there was before, . . . "for medical purposes only", and on the boot-leg plan'; in the following year, somebody in *The* (New York) *Voice* shouted that 'The "bootlegger" is a grim spectre to the anti-Prohibitionist . . . He is a man who wears boots in whose tops are concealed a flask or two of liquor'; and in 1904, *The Topeka Daily Capital* deplored the fact that 'Bootlegging is a bad business'. It became a much worse, a highly organized business when, soon after the Great War, the United States were put into liquor-quarantine, as a wit once said; and in 1931, when the States were still in the throes of Prohibition, Godfrey Irwin could define bootlegger as 'one who sells contraband liquor, of whatever degree of excellence. Originally applied to those men who sold whiskey to the Indians . . . Now, usually [in the underworld] as *legger*.'

But now that, since 1934, Prohibition has been removed, bootlegging is not a particularly attractive 'proposition', for it is no longer a *stunt*. This word arose early in the 1890's, among college students, and it was originally applied to a feat or performance in athletics. In 1895 it was still only college slang, but by that time it was applied to almost any performance or act; for instance, *American Dialect Notes* for that year quotes: ' "He performed various stunts for the prof." (i.e., did things that would win him the professor's favor)'. Not until 1898 did the word get into general currency in the United States, where it soon came to have an extended application. About 1903 it began to be used as an adjec-

[1] The first three quotations are from *The O.E.D.*

tive; 'He might have made a successful actor, of the modern "stunt" sort', remarks a writer in 1904. By 1913 it had reached England, as we see by the fact that in that year Rupert Brooke wrote: 'Then I do my pet boyish-modesty stunt and go pink all over'. Among soldiers in the war that started in the following year, it meant an 'advance', 'attack', 'raid'; and among airmen it was employed as a verb as early as 1916, in reference to an aircraft feat—hence the phrase, 'a stunt flyer'. By 1919 it was ranked as a colloquialism; now, it is knocking at the door of respectable or Standard English. *The O.E.D.* lukewarmly supports derivation from German *Stunde*, 'an hour'; Weekley suggests, more probably, that it comes from Dutch *stond*, a lesson.

Many 'stunts' were performed by the *Doughboys* or soldiers of the United States Army. The name was popularized during and by the 1914–18 war, at which period it was preferred to *Teddies* (from Teddy Roosevelt) and before which it was scarcely known in England: it had arisen half a century earlier, in the Civil War. Thornton briefly and convincingly accounts for its genesis or development thus: 'Primarily [in the latter part of the seventeenth century] a dough-cake baked for sailors; then a brass button of similar shape, worn by the infantry: lastly, a foot soldier'; and he quotes from General Custer, who served in that war: 'Early in the civil war, the term was applied to the large globular brass buttons of the infantry uniform, from which it passed by natural transition to the infantrymen themselves'; this is the explanation accepted by *The O.E.D.* A more ingenious but less likely explanation is this, quoted by McKnight: 'Some infantrymen think they are called "doughboys" because they are always "kneaded" (needed), while other old-time infantrymen think they are so called because they are the flower (flour) of the army'.

And some of the infantrymen were very capable exponents of *jazz*, which, as a dance for the public, came to Europe from America towards the end of 1918, though the term *jazz band* occurs in England's theatrical periodical, *The Era*, as early as August the 20th, 1917. *Jazz* became an adjective ('showy', 'riotously coloured') in 1919, and the noun was soon applied, loosely, to any kind of syncopated dance music; as music it is, properly, that which accompanies *jazz*, a ragtime dance with three steps to four musical beats. 'Origin unknown: generally said to be Negro', remarks *The O.E.D.*; Irwin supports the Negro origin, and mentions that it was first played in low dance-halls as a stimulus to excitement; and Lafcadio Hearn notes the verb *to jazz* as being common among the Negroes of the South and as meaning 'to speed (things) up'—a sense that became general in the 1920's.

About jazz there has been much *ballyhoo* or 'blarney', 'eyewash', a sense that arose in 1925 or 1926; the now predominant sense, dating from the early 1920's, is that of 'advance publicity', 'concerted puffs'; but the original sense (1914 or earlier) is 'the free entertainment or "lecture" outside a sale or entertainment, to attract a crowd' (Irwin), a barker's speech, a cheapjack's discourse. Godfrey Irwin, in defining its underworld usage as 'loud talk; noisy conversation', may cause some of you to think of the word *hullabaloo*. Now, *hullabaloo* probably[1] sprang from *Ballyhooly*, an Irish village, at one time an exceptionally talkative one —even for Ireland. There is still less doubt that *ballyhoo* is a backformation from *Ballyhooly*, for the United States are—though less than they were—the happy hunting-ground of those Irish braves who do not migrate to England. Perhaps relevant are the facts that, many years before 1914, there was a music-hall catch-phrase *Ballyhooly truth*, 'the complete truth', often used ironically, and that in the 1880's there was a popular song entitled *Ballyhooly*.

Ballyhoo is often enlisted in the service of things that are *haywire* or 'ineffective' or 'inefficient' or 'broken down' or 'gone wrong'. The 'haywire mind' reached England in November 1933, according to *The Daily Express* of the 16th of that month.[2] It was originally a tramps' word 'from the West, where the poor rancher mends his broken implements and tools with the iron wire used to bale hay and . . . always to be found about a ranch when proper repair material is lacking', as Godfrey Irwin tells us, and one of Professor Weekley's correspondents has made the explanation clearer by reminding us that stiff wire, when cut, coils back on itself and that soon there is a horrible tangle of the wretched stuff. 'Then, when the radio industry first started, some of the earlier sets were known as a "bunch of haywire", because they were so crisscrossed and confused that nobody had any idea where the wires came from or went to. From that, there developed the use of the expression in connection with a person's mind. This is sometimes used as "going haywire", . . . to become mentally unbalanced.'

All these words are Americanisms: so, originally and still in the main, is *Briticism*. In 1868, an American philologist (R. G. White) said, 'This use [of a certain word] is a widespread Briticism', and fifteen years later an American newspaper spoke of 'a well arranged handbook of Briticisms, Americanisms,

---

[1] P. W. Joyce, *English as We Speak It in Ireland*.
[2] Weekley, *Something about Words*.

Colloquial Phrases, etc.'[1] With the variant *Britishism*, *Briticism* is moulded on the much earlier-coined *Gallicism*: and properly it means 'a phrase or idiom characteristic of Great Britain, but not used in the English of the United States or other countries',[2] especially the Dominions (*Africanderisms*, *Australianisms*). Even now, the term is much commoner in America than in Great Britain, but then Americans have always, since the 1840's, tended to say *British* and *Britisher* where an inhabitant of Great Britain would say, *English*, *Scotch*, *Welsh* or *Englishman*, *Scotchman*, *Welshman* or, generically, *English* or *Britons*; so, too, scholars in Great Britain usually speak of *an English word* (or term) or *English idiom* (or expression), or, if they are being specific, of an *Anglicism*, a *Scotticism*, a *Cymricism*. It is natural that scholars in Great Britain should not use *Briticism* of their own words and phrases, for to them they are the norm: but I was astounded when, late in 1937, a very capable American philologist, in writing to me, stated that the term *Briticism* appeared to enrage the learned men of Great Britain.

IV. WORD HISTORY RATHER THAN HISTORY IN WORDS

(Certain English and American Words with Interesting Etymologies)

There are many words with an etymology so entertaining that one could almost write stories and could certainly write short articles and essays about them. Indeed, there are three volumes of such essay-stories by Professor Ernest Weekley: *The Romance of Words*, *Words Ancient and Modern*, and *More Words Ancient and Modern*: without taking into account his books on names or such volumes as *Adjectives and Other Words* or *Something About Words*. Before passing on to some few etymologies of my own, I wish to make sure of your reading at least one of these delightful books of Professor Weekley's by repeating for your benefit two of his word histories; they are necessarily from among the shortest.

DICKER[3]

In a book published in 1917, Mrs Gertrude Atherton, the American novelist [who died in 1937], makes a character say that, as a result of the holocaust[4] of youth demanded by the War, 'husbands will be too scarce to dicker about', meaning that young women will have to take what they can get, without haggling. I first heard the word from a leather-merchant of philological tastes, who asked me why a bundle

---

[1] *O.E.D.*   [2] *O.E.D.*   [3] *Words Ancient and Modern.*
[4] Great sacrifice or slaughter; from the Greek, it means literally 'a complete destruction by fire' or 'something wholly consumed by fire'.

of ten skins was called a *dicker*.—This simple trade-word takes us back to the days of Imperial Rome, when skins and furs were one of the chief objects of barter between Roman and barbarian. Moreover, in some cases tribute was paid in the same form, e.g., by the Frisians ... The Latin name for a set of ten, *decuria*, from *decem*, ten, is used in the same sense of ten hides in a letter written by the Emperor Valerian, and, in various corrupted forms, it became the recognized unit of the trade in skins. As an everyday word wherever Roman and northerner came in contact, it passed into all the Teutonic languages (compare German *decher*, Danish *deger*). In Domesday Book it is used, in a barbarous Medieval Latin form, for ten bars of iron, but the general association in English, as in Dutch, German, and Scandinavian, is with hides, and in this sense it is still current among those who have to do with leather.—The sense of haggling, bartering, swopping, developed in the United States. In Fenimore Cooper's *Oak Openings* ... (1848) we read that 'the white men who penetrated into the semi-wilds were always ready to dicker and swap', and, as these men were mostly trappers and hunters in quest of pelts, it seems a reasonable inference that their use of the word reflected the fur-trade with the Indians. If so, it is a curious example of the continuity of word-history, that a term first used by the Roman in his mercantile dealings with the barbarian should, after twenty centuries, have started a new existence at the meeting-place of the settler and the savage in another hemisphere.

FOXGLOVE[1]

'Plant out sweet williams, foxgloves and canterbury bells. The foxgloves will do well in partial shade and will grow the taller there. The flame is really "folk's"—that is, fairy's—glove, from the shape of the flowers' (*The Daily News*, Gardening Note, March 29, 1927). This 'folk's-glove' is to be classed with the hardy perennials, or, better still, with the everlastings, for nothing seems able to kill it. It belongs to that age in word-study when everything had to be explained as a 'corruption' of something else, when *country-dance* was derived from French *contredanse* and the name Shakespeare was solemnly interpreted as coming from Jacques Pierre.—Most of the European races seem to have seen in the flower a resemblance to a thimble or finger-stall ... The flower is in some English dialects called *thimble*, a name also applied both to the sea-campion and the harebell. And the appropriateness of the name is evident. ... Early English folklore, however, usually associated the flower with the animal which is pre-eminent in legend and fable. A parallel to our *foxglove* is offered by Norwegian *revbjölla*, in which *rev* ... means fox. *The Oxford Dictionary* also quotes a Norwegian form *revbjelde*, literally fox-bell. But this parallel is not necessary, for the [Old English and Middle English] records are quite conclusive as to the original form and meaning of the compound. In the *Leechdoms* [about A.D. 1000] we find *foxes glofa*, the second word being

[1] *More Words Ancient and Modern.*

apparently plural (our word is often listed as *foxgloves* in early dictionaries). *Foxesglove* occurs twice in a vocabulary of plant-names written down [about] 1265, and in a botanical treatise of the 14th Century *foxglove* is glossed by *ceroteca vulpis*, the first word being for *chirotheca*, glove, from Greek *cheir*, hand, and *theke*, case, while *vulpis* is the genitive of Latin *vulpes*, fox. So if *fox* is here a 'corruption' of *folk*'s, it must have been corrupted at a very early age.

Let us now examine the group formed by the English *fellow*, *chap*, *merchant*, *customer*, *artist*, *cove*, *cully*, *bloke*, and by the American *good scout*, *guy*, *stiff*, *gink*, *bozo* and, simply as a curiosity, *palooka*. They all[1] mean 'a man': and some are familiar English, some colloquial, some slangy, some of the underworld; but whereas certain of these words have come down in the world, others have gone up. (The list is not quite complete, but I do not wish to labour the point to your exhaustion.)

Fellow,[2] which even now is familiar but good English rather than colloquial, comes from the Old Norse *felage* (from *felag*, partnership), and there it means, as it does in late Old English, 'one who lays down money in a joint undertaking with others' (*O.E.D.*). In the eleventh century it signifies a partner, a co-worker; as an associate, companion, comrade it arose late in the twelfth century; *good* or *jolly fellow*, a pleasant or a boon companion, arrived at the beginning of the fourteenth; as a member, later in the same century; as a familiar synonym for 'man' (male person) it came in the earlier half of the fifteenth, when the term commenced also its contemptuous sense, a person of no (or little) esteem or worth; these last two senses have sometimes been confused. Shakespeare has 'a paltry fellow' (1597) and 'a worthy fellow' (1607); Steele has 'I am an old fellow, and extremely troubled with the gout' and Pope can epigrammatically write, 'Worth makes the man, and want of it the fellow'; Fielding says, 'You don't know what a devil of a fellow he is', but he also says, at the same date of 1749, 'You ... have so disdainfully called him fellow'. And 'on that tragic occasion when [in *The Pickwick Papers*, 1837] Mr Pickwick and Mr Tupman nearly came to blows, the final exasperation of both was aroused by the epithet *fellow*. Even the genial Sam Weller became bellicose when "a indiwidual in company" called him a "feller" [the educated English pronunciation of the eighteenth century]. . . . The contemptuous use of *fellow* arose in the Middle Ages from the practice of addressing servants in this kindly fashion, just as Frenchmen of

---

[1] With the partial exception of *palooka*.
[2] The dates are taken from *The O.E.D.*

the old school use *mon ami* to their social inferiors. . . . It might almost be said that it became two words, one preserving the original sense, which survives in . . . *schoolfellow*, "hail fellow well met", the other used vaguely for "chap", with an undertone of condescension or contempt' (Weekley, *Words Ancient and Modern*, 1926); but that undertone is dying out (slowly enough), and *fellow*, like *chap*, is becoming a mere familiar synonym for 'man', 'male person'.

Chap is short for *chapman*, a merchant, trader, dealer; later, a purchaser or customer. *Chap*, a purchaser or customer, arose in the 1570's; in the nineteenth century it was dialect, as it is still, though it is now heard only rarely. Thence comes the sense, a male person: 1716, M. Davies, 'The names of these country-chaps'; 1824, Scott, 'The fishers are wild chaps'; 1862, Mrs Henry Wood, 'You might give a chap a civil answer'. In 1893, *The O.E.D.* remarked that, in 1818, Archdeacon Todd (who revised Johnson's *Dictionary*) said, 'it usually designates a person of whom a contemptuous opinion is entertained,' and added, 'but it is now merely familiar and non-dignified, being chiefly applied to a young man'; nowadays, however, we hear *an old chap* as often as *a young chap*, and in *old chap* as a term of address, *old* does not denote an advanced age but connotes affection. Ultimately, *chap* is 'cognate with *cheap*, *chaffer*, and German *kaufen*, to buy, and probably comes from Latin *caupo*, tavern-keeper' (Weekley, *The Romance of Names*).

Oddly enough, '*merchant* was used by the Elizabethans in the same way as our *chap*. Thus the Countess of Auvergne calls Talbot a "riddling merchant" (I *Henry VI*, ii, iii)', the term being in the late sixteenth to early seventeenth century a piece of Standard (though familiar) English that apparently lapsed until about 1880, when, especially among actors, it was revived as a colloquialism; it was common among English soldiers in 1914–18 (e.g., 'the machine-gun merchant')—which fact reminds us that, from a year or two before that war, soldiers have used *client* in precisely the same way. And Weekley reminds us that Scottish *callant*, lad, once bore the sense 'customer'; *callant* comes from the Dutch or the Flemish *kalant*, 'customer', from French *chaland*.

Customer itself is used in this way, especially in 'a rum customer'; Americans have shortened the term to *cuss*, which has been adopted in England; the former is colloquial, whereas the latter is slang. In its sense of 'buyer', 'purchaser' (mostly if regular), it sprang up in the 1470's; a sense earlier by a generation was 'custom-house officer'. As 'a person that one meets', hence any 'male person', it began its career towards the end of the sixteenth century, and in the nineteenth and twentieth century it occurs most in the phrases *ugly customer* (Scott, 1818), *awkward customer*, *queer* or *rum customer*. The word is formed from *custom* (a habit or a usual practice), itself from Latin via Old French.[1]

But it is not only merchants and retail-dealers or their customers whose precise designations have been changed to the vague sense, 'male person'; even the *artist* has been thus misused. This piece of slang hardly antedates the twentieth century, and already it is used rather less than in 1914-18; the word that, since ca. 1918, has been displacing it, especially in combination, is not *customer* but *merchant* ('the speed merchant').

And now we come to three terms that not only have untraced etymologies but began their existences in the underworld: *cove*, *cully*, *bloke*. *Cove* seems to have come to England with the gypsies early in the sixteenth century and is almost certainly connected with a word in Romany, the language of the English gypsies: *cova* or *covo*, that man. On the other hand it may be cognate with the Scottish *cofe*, a hawker, and therefore—compare the German *kaufen*, to buy—with *chap*; but the former suggestion is the likelier. Until about 1810, it was cant; from then until about 1880, low slang ('Do you see that old cove at the bookstall?', Dickens in *Oliver Twist*); from 1880 or so, just ordinary slang, now rather less common than it was before the War of 1939-45.

Cully is probably a diminutive of *cull*: in the seventeenth century (second half) both were used of a dupe, a fool, and also of any man whatsoever. In the seventeenth to eighteenth century, *cully* was an underworld term; in the nineteenth to twentieth century it has been low slang, and, from about 1840, mostly a Cockney endearment, roughly equivalent to *chum*. The origin is obscure: possibly the word is a derivative of the obsolete Standard English *cullion*, a vile and low fellow; or it may derive from the Continental-gypsy radical signifying 'a man'.

Bloke, which antedates 1839, was an underworld term until about 1860, after which date it is low slang, though in the present century it is often used humorously, as in 'her bloke' (fiancé). It means simply 'man', 'fellow', 'chap', as in 'The old blokes know more than us young fellows, but we young blokes can do more work than they can'. The origin is a puzzler: Weekley thinks that it comes from Shelta (the secret language of the Irish tinkers); Hotten that it comes from Hindustani *loke*, a man—the various gypsy dialects being based on some forerunner of Hindustani;

[1] This paragraph is based on the entry in *The O.E.D.*

Barrère and Leland, in their dictionary, refute the Hindustani origin and propose the Dutch *blok*, a block, hence a fool; but *bloke* does not signify a fool, and the eighteenth to early nineteenth-century form—or perhaps we should say predecessor—of *bloke* is *gloke* or, more usually, *gloak*[1]; I myself incline to the *loke* origin and believe that the *b-* was caused by the initial letter of a word too low for mention here.

From England to America. A fairly recent Americanism is *good scout*, as in 'Smith is a good scout' or as an exclamation 'good scout!'; thus it is synonymous with the English *good fellow*. The phrase was anglicized very soon after 1918, probably owing to the influence of the American soldiers. It originated in the days —or in memory of the days—when a good scout was constantly in demand in new country possibly infested with dangerous animals and especially Red Indians,[2] despite the fact that it seems not to have arisen before the twentieth century: but the colloquialisms, like slang, often had a spoken long before they had a written existence.

Slightly older is *guy* for a man, 'chap', 'fellow'; it occurs in 1896, in an early work of that master humorist, George Ade: 'You guys must think I'm a quitter' (*O.E.D.*). It seems to have reached England about 1910, but not until 1918 did it become at all general. Mencken says that this American sense 'seems to be derived from the *guy-rope* of a circus tent, and first appeared in the complimentary form of *head-guy*': 'seems' is the right word, for this explanation is as far-fetched as it is unnecessary, there being no reasonable doubt that *guy*, 'an amiable synonym for *fellow*' (Mencken) derives directly from the English sense, 'a person of grotesque appearance' (1836), which sense in turn derives no less directly from *guy*, 'an effigy of Guy Fawkes' (1806), which obviously comes from *Guy* (*Fawkes*).[3] The derivation cautiously mentioned by Mencken affords an excellent example of 'too clever by far'.

First printed in 1896, like *guy*, is *stiff*; and in the same author: 'There I sat like a big stiff for five hours', George Ade (*O.E.D.*). Apparently the word was anglicized about 1912, and Australianized several years earlier, chiefly in jocular contempt, as 'you stiff!', 'the big stiff!'; even in the United States, it has never been

---

[1] Precisely as *bloak* was once a common spelling of *bloke*.

[2] This seems more probable than Professor G. P. Krapp's suggestion that *good scout* may have been influenced by the Dutch *schout* (a kind of mayor-sheriff-attorney), for there has, in America, been little Dutch influence since the 18th Century.

[3] The dates and development are from *The O.E.D.*

a particularly flattering term, Webster defining it as 'one who is unsocial or lacking in liveliness' and *The O.E.D.* conveying the English usage in the definition, 'a hopeless or incorrigible person'. Its origin is the American slang *stiff*, a corpse. The term shows an unmistakable tendency to become exactly synonymous with *chap* and *guy*, as we see both from the English and Australian phrases quoted above and from the fact that in the speech of the American tramp, it is 'a generic term for the worker, such as a "lumber stiff", a woodcutter; a "bindle stiff", [a worker carrying] a bundle' (Irwin[1]).

Gink did not arise until the present century, the first printed record so far adduced being: 1912, Edna Ferber, *Dawn O'Hara*, 'I'm th'gink you killed off two or three years back' (*O.E.D.*). It appeared in English print at least as early as 1920 (P. G. Wodehouse), but it cannot be said to have been naturalized until 1930; that is, until after 'the talkies' had been at work in England for a few months. In England it is always contemptuous, as it still is, mildly, in America: 'A generic term for a man, rather slighting in its use, and when applied to a tramp especially so. The word ... is possibly derived from "gink", a trick, whence "ginkie" a term of reproach applied to a woman in Scottish dialect' (Irwin), an origin that seems much more probable than a derivation from *Ginx's Baby: his Birth and other Misfortunes*,[2] an extremely sentimental English novel of the early 1870's. *The O.E.D.*, certainly with some wisdom, permits itself only an 'of obscure origin'.

More recent is *bozo*, which is mentioned in the fourth edition (1936) of Mencken's vastly informative and interesting work, *The American Language*, as having possibly been a piece of vaudeville slang ('I gotta ... make comical for the bozos'); it seems hardly to antedate the year 1927; the 1934 edition of *Webster's International Dictionary* defines it as 'a fellow' and classifies it as slang and, what is more, suggests an origin by comparing *bozo* with Spanish *bozal*, which means 'fool', 'simpleton', 'novice', and also 'boss' (but may not this sense have been grafted on to Spanish *bozal* in order to provide an equivalent for U.S. *boss*?). Diffidently I propose an origin either in *boss* + Anglo-Irish *boyo* (a lad) or in *boyo* + *boysie* (though this is perhaps less probable), and advance the possibility that the short *o* of *boss* (or *boysie*) and *boyo* has been displaced by the long *o*'s of *calabozo*. The

---

[1] The Irwin quotations are from *American Tramp and Underworld Slang*, by Godfrey Irwin, a leading authority on American cant.

[2] The baby is unwanted. First issued in 1870, the book reached its 29th edition in 1873. The author was ostensibly John Ginx, actually J. E. Jenkins.

origin in Spanish *bozal* is rendered slightly the more tenable in that *bozal* is itself a derivative of Spanish *bozo*, a horse's muzzle.

Even less known in England is *palooka*,[1] which does not mean 'fellow', 'guy', but 'third-rater'; there are, however, signs that it may come to be used in much the same way as *gink*. In Harry Charles Witwer's amusing novel, *The Classics in Slang*, 1927, one boxer addresses another as 'you great palooka' or some such phrase. The word is supposed to have been coined by Jack Conway, who (peace to his humorous ashes!) died in 1928: in other words, it is an artificial or manufactured term, though it may possibly be from *pal*, with a fanciful suffix, or constitute a blend of *pal* and something else.

Still more interesting, etymologically, is the following sextette, ultimately selected from a much longer list of words that had been soul-searchingly gathered for your delectation: *Tarot* of the Tarot pack of cards; *queer* and *rum*, both in the sense of 'odd', 'strange'; *tanner*; and *shenaneckin* (or *shenanigan*) and *attaboy*![2]

Of the 78 cards in a *Tarot* pack, only 26 are essential Tarot. Some of these 26 represent powers friendly to man, but most of them represent powers unfriendly or even actively hostile. *The Oxford English Dictionary* relates the word to the Italian *tarocchi* (with presumed singular *tarocco*), which becomes *Tarock* in German; and implies that it derives immediately from the French *tarot*, which in Old French is *tarau* or *tarault*; and gives the now obsolete form *taroc* (or *tarock* or *tarok*), which would seem to have come from the Italian, a supposition supported by an entry in the Italian-English dictionary (1611) of Florio: '*Tarocchi*, a kind of playing cards called Tarocks or Terestrial Triumphs'. The *O.E.D.* and Weekley dismiss *Tarot* with: 'Of unknown origin'; Skeat judiciously omits the word from his etymological dictionary. It is irrelevant—though interesting—that these playing cards were, in Europe, used first in Italy in the fourteenth century: it is relevant—and important—that these cards have, for centuries, been used in fortune-telling, originally and still mainly by gypsies. The connexion with gypsies reminds one of Egypt; true, the gypsies came from India but they passed through—may long have lived in—Egypt, as their old name, *Egyptians*, suggests. With this link in mind, I happened to look into Wallis Budge's *Egyptian Dictionary*, and there, sure enough, I found *Tar*, the name of a certain mythological fiend, and *taru*, 'fiends, demons,

---

[1] Mencken, *The American Language*, 4th edition. Not in *The O.E.D.* nor even in *Webster*. Perhaps a Red Indian word.

[2] These six words are more fully treated in *A Covey of Partridge*, in the essay entitled 'Neither Cricket nor Philology'.

devils, enemies', and many other words connected with *taru*. There seems to be little need to go further back than that or to elaborate on that significant probability.

Rum and *queer*, as adjectives, have also bothered the philologists. In the nineteenth to twentieth century, both words have meant 'odd' or 'disreputable' and are slang; but in the sixteenth to eighteenth century they were underworld terms and were opposites, *queer* being 'bad', 'inferior', 'ugly', 'of the underworld', and *rum* being 'good', 'superior', 'beautiful', 'of the overworld'. The latter acquired an unpleasant sense because of its association with underworld activities in such phrases as *rum bit* (or *bite*), a very good trick, i.e. a swindle; *rum-padder*, a 'high-class' highwayman; and *rum cove*, a great rogue—admired by the underworld but detested by the upper classes. *Queer* occurs earliest in Scottish literature, in the senses 'odd', 'eccentric', 'of questionable character': and there is little (or no) doubt that this *queer* originates in the German *quer*, 'across', 'athwart', hence 'crooked'. But in the sixteenth century the cant form is *quire* (or *quier* or *quyer*), and the earliest cant phrase is *quire-bird* (i.e., choir-bird), a man 'only recently let out of gaol, but already returned to crime': compare the cant *canary bird*, a gaol-bird, of the approximate period 1670–1840. Probably, however, the origin of the cant word is the same as that of the sixteenth-century Scottish word; the underworld, as is its way, may have corrupted *queer* to *quire* and then brightly 'thought up' the pun, *quire* (choir) *bird*. Now, *rum* does not mean 'bad' or 'inferior' until late in the eighteenth century, the term having always, until then, connoted the warmest approval. Skeat derives the word from Romany *rom*, a man, especially a male gypsy, presumably on the grounds that the gypsies considered anything gypsy to be excellent; *The O.E.D.* and Weekley are unenthusiastic supporters of this not very convincing theory. But I believe that *rum*, which in the sixteenth century was frequently spelt *rome*, comes from the Latin or the Italian *Roma*, as John Camden Hotten suggested, or from an adjective formed therefrom: compare the Turkish *rûm*, 'Roman' (adj.), and the Persian *rumi*, 'Byzantine', from Greek *Romaios*, 'a Roman'. The gypsies were in Rome in 1422–23 and of course, later: it may have been they who brought *rome* or *rum*, 'splendid', 'fine', 'beautiful', 'excellent', to England. I cannot prove that they did: but it is not improbable that the poverty-stricken, wandering gypsies were much impressed with the comparative glory and splendour of fifteenth-century Rome.

The slang *tanner* (a sixpence) has caused almost as much trouble as *rum*. The proposed origin in Romany *tarno* or *tauno* hardly bears consideration, for *tauno* means 'young', not 'little'; the proposed origin in Latin *tener* is improbable. The origin I shall suggest may seem a very odd one: but then, the origin of many slang words is, at first sight, fantastic. In the late seventeenth to mid-nineteenth century, there was another slang word for a sixpence, and that word was *simon* or *Simon*. In the Bible, St Peter 'lodged with one Simon, a tanner': a passage that led to the old joke about St Peter's lodging a tanner with Simon. Not the pun, which is much later than the earliest record (1797) of *tanner*, but the Biblical passage itself may, to an ingenious mind, have suggested *tanner* as a new term for a sixpence. The improbability grows mercifully less if you examine the following equation, based on 'St Peter lodged with one Simon, a tanner':

'one Simon, a tanner';
1 Simon = a tanner;
i.e., 1 sixpence = a tanner;
therefore, 1 tanner = a sixpence,
or, a tanner = sixpence.

Originally an English dialect word, *shenanigan* (or *shenannigan*) or *shenan(n)ecken* or *shenan(n)ecking* appeared in America in the late 1860's and was reintroduced into England, as slang (now a colloquialism), about 1890. Meaning 'chaff', 'nonsense', or—predominantly in the twentieth century—'trickery', ' "funny" business', its use is exemplified in 'If I were to pay them they might think there was some shenanigan about it' (Robert Barr, the English novelist, 1902). Webster says that it is probably from Erse *sionnach-uighim*, I play tricks or act the fox (Erse *sionnach*, a fox). In support of this are the two facts that *sionnach* is pronounced, approximately, *shinnuck*, and that Anglo-Irish has *foxing*, hiding or malingering. Note, however, that English dialect has *nannicking*, playing the fool (East Anglian *nannick*, to play the fool, to idle away one's time); and *nannick* is not impossibly connected with *nanny*, a she-goat: compare the colloquial phrase, 'to play the goat'. What then of the *she-* in *shenanigan*? It may be an American intensive addition, of the same order as *ker-* in *kerwallop*.

No less humorous is *attaboy!*, a cry of encouragement—originally to a participant in a sport, contest (e.g., rowing), or game, but very soon to anyone whatsoever; since 1930 or 1931, it has often been used as a mere exclamation of approval. Arising in the United States about 1910, it reached England, via 'the Doughboys', in 1918. Both *The O.E.D.* and Collinson (*Contemporary English*, 1927) derive it from *that's the boy!*; a possibility. Not impossibly it represents *at her, boy!*, where *her* is sexless (as in *she* applied to a ship). My own view is that *attaboy* is a corruption of the *staboy!* recorded by Thornton for 1774 as 'an exclamation addressed to hounds'; Dow, junior, *Patent Sermons*, 1854, has 'Let slip the dogs of war, and I for one will hallo, "sta! boy", till the heavens turn green'. Compare *hist-a-boy!*, an American exclamation 'used to incite or urge on': the *boy* is the vocative *boy*, often used to a dog; *hist* is an inciting cry or hiss; and *a* is added for euphony, or it represents *there* (hist there, boy!).

In words, then, there is much to interest and to amuse us; in grammar, much to test and exercise our intelligence; in language as a means of communication, much that deserves careful consideration; in the English and American language, much to surprise us—but much that we can admire. And if the author has been able to provide a jumping-off ground for word trips to various regions of Linguistica, or a basis for detailed study, he is richly rewarded for his attempt to survey the entire field.[1]

---

[1] With several minor exceptions, which he has duly indicated.

APPENDIX: PHONETIC SYMBOLS

The following symbols for the English speech-sounds are international—understandable by everybody. Although phonetics can properly be learnt only orally, yet these phonetic symbols can easily be memorized without lessons in phonetics.

ɑ = *a* as in 'r*a*ther'
a = i (or ɪ) sound in 'fl*y*', or 's*igh*' or 'b*ite*'
æ = *a* as in 'c*a*b', or 't*a*b'
e = *e* ,, ,, 'n*e*t',
ei = the vowel in 'th*ey*' or 'b*ay*'
ɛ ,, ,, 'f*ai*r'
ə: ,, ,, 'b*ir*d'
ə ,, ,, '*a*bove', 'Chin*a*'
i: ,, ,, 's*ee*' or 'b*e*'
i ,, ,, '*i*t' or '(to) l*i*ve'
o ,, ,, 'sch*o*lar',
ou ,, ,, 'g*o*',
ɔ: ,, ,, 's*aw*' or 'r*aw*'
ɔ ,, ,, 'g*o*t' or 'n*o*t',
ʌ ,, ,, '*u*p' or 's*u*p',
u: ,, ,, 'r*u*le' or 'f*oo*d'
u ,, ,, 'g*oo*d' or 'w*oo*d',
[ju = the sound in 't*une*' or 'n*ew*']

b = *b* as in '*b*oy'
[dʒ] = *j* in '*j*am' or '*j*et'; *g* in '*g*em', '*g*iant']
d = *d* as in '*d*ance'
f = *f* ,, ,, '*f*air' or '*f*oot'
g = *g* ,, ,, '*g*o' or '*g*ood'
h = *h* ,, ,, '*h*ay', or '*h*ard'
j = the consonant in '*y*es', or German '*ja*'
k = ,, ,, '*k*angaroo' or '*c*old'
l = ,, ,, '*l*ive' or '*c*oo*l*'
m = ,, ,, '*m*ad'
n = ,, ,, '*n*o'
ŋ = *ng* as in 'lo*ng*',
p = *p* ,, ,, '*p*art' or 'ca*p*'
r = *r* ,, ,, '*r*eady',
s = *s* ,, ,, '*s*oon', or '*s*un'
ʃ = *sh* ,, ,, '*sh*ow',
ʒ = ,, ,, 'trea*s*ure',
z = *z* ,, ,, '*z*eal'
t = *t* ,, ,, '*t*in'
[tʃ = the *ch* of '*ch*ain', the *tch* of 'wa*tch*']
θ = *th* as in '*th*in',
ð = *th* ,, ,, '*th*en',
v = *v* ,, ,, '*v*ery' or '*v*ain',
w = *w* ,, ,, '*w*ater' or '*w*ine'
The letter *q* (r *qu*) is pronounced k in 'con*q*uer';
kw in '*qu*een'.

Note.—The best books on the subject of English and American speech-sounds are perhaps Daniel Jones's *An Outline of English Phonetics*, and the same author's *An English Pronouncing Dictionary*; and 'A Guide to Pronunciation' in *Webster's New International Dictionary*.

INDEX

I. AUTHORS, AUTHORITIES AND SUBJECTS

accidence, 132, 137–40
Ade, George, 184
adjectives, 138
adverbs, 138
African native languages, diagram I; 5, 6
Albanian, 4; diagram II
alchemy, 167
algebra, 168
alliteration, 18, 94
American language: influence on English, 43–5; historical sketch, 46–58; Standard, 110–12; American words, 170–80
Amerindian, diagram I; 6
analogy, 76
Ancillon, 41
Ancrene Riwle, 25
Angles, 14
Anglo-Irish 57
Anglo-Saxon, *see* Old English
Apabhramsas, diagram II
Arabic, diagram I; 4, 167
Aramaic, 4
architecture, 40, 60, 167
Armenian, diagram II
Armorican, 6; diagram II
Aryan. *See* Indo-European; 4, the name
Assyrian, diagram I; 4
astrology, astronomy, 168–9
Atherton, Gertrude, 179
athletics, 161
Australian, 109
Australian Aborigine, diagram I; 5
Ayer, A. J., 136

back-formation, 39, 166

Bacon, Francis, 168–9
Baird, J. L., 165
Baltic, diagram II
Balto-Slavonic, diagram II; 4
Bantu, diagram I; 5
Barfield, Owen, 145, 156, 167, 168
Barrie, Sir James, 89
Basque, diagram I; 5, 67
Battle of Maldon, The, 18
B.B.C., the, 142
Bede, 14, 93
Bell, Alexander Graham, 165
Bengali, diagrams I, II; 4
Beowulf, 5, 17
Berber, diagram I; 4
Bible, the, 40
Bihari, diagram II
bird names, 52
Black Death, the, 78
blends or portmanteau-words, 149–50
Boer terms, 164
bowls, 161
Bow-Wow Theory, 60, 62
Bradley, Henry, 114, 115
Bréal, 154
Bredsdorff, J. H., 76, 77
Breton, diagrams I, II
Bright, John, 31–2
Brophy, John, 44–5
Browne, C. F., 43
Budge, Wallis, 186
Bulgarian, diagram II
Bunyan, 31
Burmese, diagram I; 5
Bushmen, 5
business terms, 44

191

Cabell, J. Branch, 57
Cade, Jack, 78
Cambridge University, 101
Camden, William, 11–12
Campbell, Roy, 109
Canada, 109
cant, 116–17
Carew, Richard, 11–12
Carlylese, 97
Carnap, Rudolf, 75, 136
case, 135
categories in grammar, 135–6
Caucasian Group, diagram I
Celts; Celtic, diagrams I, II; 4, 14–15, 157–8
Central African Group, diagram I; 6
Central American languages, diagram I; 6
Centum Group, diagram II
change, 76–84 (languages), 84–8 (words)
Chaucer, 2–4, 101, 102, 167
chemistry, 167
chess, 161
Chinese, diagram I; 5
Christianity, 15–16
Church, the. *See* Christianity; *also* 22 (ecclesiastical terms)
cinema, influence of, 44, 58
Circassian, diagram I; 5
Civil War, American, 56, 177
Classics, the; their influence. *See* Greek; Latin
classification of languages, 1–6 (especially diagram I)
cock-fighting, 161
Cockney. *See* London speech
cognate words, 98
Collinson, W. E., 44
colloquialism(s), 111, 113–14
comparison, 134
compounds, 16
concord, 122
conflicts in grammar, 123–4
conjugation, 135, 140, 142
conjunctions, 138, 139
connotation; denotation, 91

consonant-shift, 76–8
Conway, Jack, 186
cooking, 23
Cooper, Fenimore, 43
Cornish, diagram II
Court, the, 21, 102–3
crafts, 111
cricket, 161–2
Custer, General, 177
Cymric, diagram II
Czech, diagram II

Danes, 18–19
Danish, diagram II; 19–20
Darwin, Charles, 10, 31
death of words. *See* life . . .
declensions in Old English, 79–80, 140–1
Defoe, 31
degeneration of words, 89–99
denotation. *See* connotation
derivation, derivatives, 148; *see* etymology
dialect, 110, 112–13
Dickens, 181
dictionary indications, 102
Dictionary of American English, A, ix, 170
diminutives. *See* endearments
Ding-Dong Theory, 61, 62
Dodgson, C. L., 95, 149–50
Dominions, Standard English in the, 109
Dos Passos, John, 96
Dow, Jr., 189
Dravidian, diagram I; 5
Dutch, diagram II; 13, 50 (influence on American), 162

ease, principle of, 78, 80
East Midland dialect, 101–3
echoism, 74–5, 145–8
education, 101
Edward I and II, 101
Egyptian, Ancient, diagram I
Eighteenth Century, the, 96, 102, 164
ejaculations, 138, 139

INDEX

elevation of words, 91–2, 99–100
Elizabethans, 94, 102, 169
emotion, 146
emphasis, 147
endearments, 7
English history in words, 156–67
English language, an historical sketch, 7–45; characteristics, 7–12; expansion, 41–3; Standard, 101–12; unconventional, 113–17
Erse, diagram II; 313
Eskimo, 167
Ethiopic, 4
Etruscan, 5
etymology, 145–189
etymons, 148
euphemism, 40–1
euphony, 82
Euphuism, 94

familiar English (and American), 111
families of languages, 1–6
fashion in words, 89–100
fashions, 24
Faulkner, Wm., 96
fencing, 161
Feudalism, 21–8, *passim*, 158–9
Fielding, 181
Finnish, diagram I; 5
Finno-Hungarian, 5
Firth, Professor R. W., 6
fixed groups (of words), 125–8
Flemish, diagram II
flexions, 65, 140
Florio, 41, 186
folk etymology, 150–3
food terms, 23
form. *See* morphology
formulas. *See* fixed groups
Fowlers, the, 112, 115, 123, 124
France. *See* French
Franconian (or Frankish), Low, diagram II
Franklin, Benjamin, 56
Franklyn, Julian, 152
Freeman, 15

free expressions, 125–8
French, diagram II; 12, 20–8 (in U.S.A.), 49, 65
Frisian, diagram II; 13, 14
function, 131, 137

Gaelic, diagram II
Galileo, 168
Gardiner (historian), 15
gender, 135–6, 141
genitive. *See* possessive.
Georgian languages, diagram I; 5
German, 4; diagram II; 10, 36, 50 (influence in U.S.A.), 72, 75, 77, 97, 100, 136, 137, 141, 148, 154, 155, 158, 166, 177, 180, 182, 183, 186, 187
Germanic invasions, 13–14
Germanic languages, diagram II
Gödel, K., 136
Goldsmith, 32
golf, 162
Gothic, diagram II; 13; and *see:*
Gothonic, diagram II; 13–14, 68, 76–7
Gower, 102
grammar, 119–43
grammar, history of, 140–3
grammatical elements, 121
Great Russian, diagram II
Greek, 4; diagrams I, II; 13, 28–36, 94, 159–61, 170
Green, J. R., 18
Greenough and Kittredge, 29 and *passim*
Grimm's Law, 76–8
Grose, Francis 152
group genitive, 131
Gypsy, diagram I; 4, 187

Hamitic, diagram I; 4
Harris, Joel Chandler, 43
Harte, Bret, 43
Haussa, diagram I; 4
Hawaian, 7
hawking, 161
Hawthorne, Nathaniel, 43

Hebrew, diagram I; 4
Hemingway, Ernest, 95
High German, diagrams I, II
Hindi, 4; diagram II
Hindustani, diagram II; 183
Holland, 36
Horwill (*Modern American Usage*) 175
Hotten, J. C., 305, 311
Hottentot, 5
Humboldt, W. von, 1
humour, 43
Hungary, its influence, 36
Huxley, T. H., 31
hybridism, 27, 30
hypercorrectness, 83–4

Icelandic, diagram II; 13
ideographs, 70
idiom, 111–12
India, 36
individualism, 96
Indo-Ayran, diagram II
Indo-European, 4; diagram II; 62, 158
Indo-Germanic, 4
Indo-Iranian, diagram II
infixes, 9
inflicted, forms. *See* flexions
interjections. *See* ejaculations
Iranian, diagram II
Irish, 109
Irving, Washington, 43
Irwin, Godfrey, 185
Italian, diagram II; 12, 36

Jackson, Andrew, 174
Japanese, diagram I; 5
jargon, 117–18
Jespersen, Otto, ix and *passim*
John of Salisbury, 24
Johnsonese, 32, 35
Johnston, C., 152
Jolas, 95
Jones, Daniel, 315
Joyce, James, 94–5
Joyce, P. W., 53, 84, 94–5
Jutes, 14

Keats, 31
Kelts, Keltic. *See* Celts
Kentish dialect, 172
Kepler, 168
Kittredge. *See* Greenough
Kluge, 149
Korean, 5
Krapp, George Philip, 47

Langenfelt, Gösta, 21, 25
Latin, diagrams I, II; 4, 13, 28–36, 64–5, 94, 159–60
law, the, 19, 22, 101, 159–60
laws, phonetic. *See* Grimm's, and Verner's. *Also* at 148, 149
laziness, 76, 78
Le Clerc, 41
Leechdoms, 180
Lettish, diagram II
Lewis Carroll. *See* Dodgson
Libyan, diagram I; 4
life and death of words, 89–100
linguistic lunacy, 33, 149
Linguistica, 189
linguistics, 2, 130
literary-linguistic trends in English (and American), 57, 104–9
Literary Standard, 104, 110
Lithuanian, diagram II
Little Russian, diagram II
living grammar, 124–9
Logical Positivists, the, 75, 136
logical syntax, 75
London speech, 101, 102
Low German, diagram II
low language, 114–15
Lowell, James Russell, 43
lucidity, 95, 96
Lydgate, 102

Magyar, diagram I; 5, 72
Malay-Polynesian Group, 5
Malayan, diagram I; 5, 36
Manchu, diagram I; 5
Manx, diagram II
Maori, 5
Marathi, diagram II

INDEX

Mark Twain, 43
McKnight, G. H., ix and *passim*
meaning, significance, signification, 82
meiosis, 166
Melanesian, diagram I; 5
memory, 76
Mencken, H. L., 44, 47
Menner, R. J., 84
Mercian, 14
metaphor, 96, 165
metathesis, 82
method, 280-1
Mexico; Mexican terms, 36
Middle English, 7
military terms, 19, 22
Milton, 97
mining, 43
misapplication, 76
mishearing, misunderstanding, 76
Modern English, 7
Modified Standard, 104-12
Mohicans, 67
Mongol, Mongols, diagram I; 5, 6
Monsyllabic Group, diagram I; 5
monosyllabism, 5, 8
mood, 135
Morley, Christopher, 57
morphology, 8, 131-3
Mulcaster, Richard, 41
Murray, Sir James, 111
Murray, Lindley, 123
mutation, 79

Napoleon Bonaparte, 164
natural grammar, 75, 136
nautical and naval terms, 19, 22
Negrito, diagram I; 5
neologism, 127
Newton, 168
Nineteenth Century, 93
Normans, Norman influence, 14, 20-28, 101, 158-9
Norse. *See* Norwegian
Northern dialect, 101-3
Norwegian, diagram II; 19-20
nouns, 137-9
number, 130, 134

objective and subjective, 87-8
Occleve, 102
Oehlenschlager, 68
Old English, 7, 12-20, 79-80
Old Prussian, diagram II
O'Neil, Eugene, 96
onomatopoeia. *See* echoic words
origin of language, 59-75
Oxford, 101
Oxford English Dictionary, The, 111, 115, 166, 170

P Celtic, diagram II
Pali, diagram II
Papuan, diagram I; 5
parts of speech, 135-40
pedantry, 96, 105
Persian, 4; diagram II; 36
person, 135
philosophy, 28, 122, 139
Phoenician, diagram I; 4
phonetics, phonology, 63-7, 82-4, 130-1, 148
physics, 165, 168
pioneering spirit, 151-3
Pisaca, diagram II
pitch-accent. *See* tone-accent
plant names, 51-2
Platonism, 170
Poe, 32
Polish, diagram II
political terms, politics, 54-5 (American); 163
Polynesian, diagram I; 5, 36
polysyllabism, 63-7
Pooh-Pooh Theory, 61, 62
portmanteau-words. *See* blends
Portugal and Portuguese, diagram II; 36
possessive, 134
Pound, Louise, 47
Pound, Roscoe, 108
Prakrit, diagram II; 13, 62
Prayer Book, the, 40
prefixes, 39
prepositions, 138
President's English, 48
Primary Prakrit, diagram II

primitive speech. *See* savages
Prohibition, 176
pronouns, 138, 141
Provincial English, 104, 112
Proto-Aryan(s), 75, 149
psychology, 121, 125
Public School English, 104
Punjabi, diagram II
pure English. *See* Standard English
purism, 96, 108–9
Puritans, 40–1, 95–6
Putnam, Samuel, 112

Q Celtic, diagram II

radiation (of senses), 86–7
radicals (roots, stems), 148
Raffald, Elizabeth, 152
railroad (railway) terms, 54–5
Rask, Rasmus, 76
Read, Allen Walker, 290
Received Standard, 104–12
Red Indian influence, 36, 43, 48–9, 163, 174
Red Indians and their dialects, diagram I; 6
Reformation, the, 160
Regional dialect, 104
remnants (linguistic) in Europe, diagrams I, II
Renaissance, the, 14, 28–35, 160–1
Restoration, the, 95
Robert of Gloucester, 25
Romance (Romanic) languages, diagram II; 63
Romans, the, 12–14
Romanticism, 96
roots. *See* radicals
Rousseau, 164
Rumanian, diagram II
Russell, Bertrand, 74
Russian, 4; diagram II; 36, 42
Ruthenian, diagram II

Samoyed, diagram I; 5
Sanscrit (or Sanskrit), diagrams I, II; 4, 13

Satem Group, diagram II
savages, speech of, 60–75 *passim*
Saxons, 13–14
Scandinavian, diagram II; 13, 14, 18–20, 158
Schlick, M., 136
science, 34, 35, 165, 168–9
Scotch, diagram II
Scythian Group, diagram I; 5
Selden, 32
semantics (or semasiology or sematology), 153–6
Semitic, diagram I; 4
Serbian, diagram II
Seventeenth Century, the, 31, 163
Shakespeare, 34, 41, 169–70
Shaw, George Bernard, 81, 167
shopping terms, 55
Shorter Oxford Dictionary, The, 4, 54, 64
Siamese, diagram I; 5
signification. *See* meaning
slang, 44–5 (American), 115–16, 117
Slavonic, diagram II
Slovene, diagram II
Smith, Logan Pearsall, 106–8
Société de Linguistique, 59
Sorb, diagram II
soul of grammar, 121–3
sound in English, 17–19
sound-combinations, 130–3
sound-elements, 130–3
sound-laws. *See* phonetics
sound-shift. *See* Grimm's Law
sound-symbolism, 145–8
South African, (primitive) 63, 163, 164
South-American Indian, diagram I; 6
South-Eastern Asiatic, diagram I; 5
South-Indian Group, diagram I; 5
Southern dialect, 101–3
Spain and Spanish, diagram II; 12, 49 (in U.S.A.), 162–3
specialization in sense, 142, 143–8, 153
speech-habits, 97

INDEX

speech-sounds. *See* phonetics
spelling, 58 (American), 102 (English)
Spencer, 31, 32
Spenser, 96
Spooner, Spoonerisms, 94
sport, 93, 161–2
Sprachgefühl, 97
Standard American, 110–12
Standard English, 101–9
standardization, 104–9, 143
statistics, 25 (French imports into English), 42 (European-language speakers)
Stein, Gertrude, 95
Steinbeck, John, 96
Stolt, Jonas, 69
stress, 77 (stress-shift), 80 (value)
Sturtevant, E. H., 84
subjective. *See* objective
suffixes, 39, 127
Swahili, diagram I; 4, 5
swearing, 40–1
Swedish, diagram II; 22
Swinburne, 34
symbols, phonetic, 190
synonyms, 33, 93
syntax, 105, 128, 133–7
Syrian, diagram I; 4
systematic, 129–31

tabou (tabu), 68
Tatar, 5
technicalities. *See* jargon
tense(s), 119, 134–7, 142
Teutonic, diagram II; *also see* German, Germanic
Thornton (*An American Glossary*), 52, 174
Tibetan, diagram I; 5
Turanian, diagram I; 5
Turkish, 5, 36
Tyler, Wat, 78

Ulysses, 95
underworld. *See* cant
universal grammar, 136
Ural-Altaic Group, diagram I; 5

Vance, A. G. ('the Great'), 174
variable formations. *See* free expressions
Veneroni, 41–2
verbs, 138
Verner's Law, 77
Vienna Circle, the, 75
vocabulary, 32–3 (Classical influence); 36–9 (various sources of the English)
voice (in grammar), 135
Vossler, Karl, 75
vulgarisms, 114–15

Walloon, diagram II
War of 1914–18, 44, 93, 96, 164–5
War of 1939–45, x, 93
Washington, George, 164
Webster, Noah, 56
Weekley, Ernest, ix and *passim*
Welsh, diagram II; 13
Wends, diagram II
Wessex dialect, 14
West Germanic, diagram II
White Russian, diagram I
Whitman, Walt, 56
Whitney, 2, 5, 59
Wilkins, John, 75, 136, 147
Wittgenstein, Ludwig, 74, 133, 136
Witwer, Harry, 186
Woolf, Virginia, 95
word-classes. *See* parts of speech
word-elements, 131–2
word-formation, 131–3, 140
word-history (general principles), 145–56; (particular examples) 156–89
Wulfstan, 17
Wycliffe, 101
Wyld, H. C. K., 101–4 *passim*

Yiddish, 4
Yo (-He)-Ho Theory, 61, 62

Zeitgeist, 97
Zend, diagram II; 63
Zulus, 67

WORDS AND PHRASES
Only those treated in some detail are included.

abominable, 153
acorn, 151
adulterate, 91
alchemy, 167
alligator, 162
allure, 161
alter, 91
American dialect, *English*, 46
analyse, 169
anatomy, 169
antlers, 155
aristocrat, 164
artist, 183
aschet, 161
ash, 148
assize, 22, 163
asylum, 91
attaboy!, 188–9
avon, 158

ballyhoo, 178
bank, 163
Bank of England, 163–4
bankruptcy, 164
bats, 194
bead, 85
beauty, 170
bench, 163
Bible, 154
bloke, 183–4
Bombay duck, 152
bonus, 164
book, 154
boon, 85
boor, 98
bootlegger, 176
bozo, 185–6
brass, 196
breeze, 162
Briticism, 178–9
bucket shop 175–6
buckwheat, 151
bunkum, 172–3
buttery, 151
buzzard, 151

cabal, 163
cad, caddie, caddy, 162
calculation, 154
cannibal, 162
capital, 163
carpet-bagger, 173–4
cattle, 163
caucus, 173
cellar, 152
centum, diagram II, footnote 1
chaffer, 182
chamberlain, 99
chap (fellow), 182
cheap, 100
chess, 161
Chester, 158
childish, childlike, 100
church, 15, 159
churl, 97
clove, 155
cockatoo, 163
coconut, 163
cold-slaw, 151
comet, 150
common, 90
Congress, congressional, 170–1
corn, 85–6
costly, 100
court, 98–9
cove, 183
Creole, 49
crow, 147
crucial; crucial instance, 168
cubit, 154
cully, 183
culprit, 160
cunning (American), 85
customer, 182–3
cutlet, 151

danger, 28
deer, 85
degraded, 90
demagogue, 163
dicker, 179–80

INDEX

discovery, 169
dog, 75
donkey, 153
doubtful, 88
Doughboy, 177–8
doughty, 97

Easter, 16
esquire, 99
experiment, 168
eyewash, 165

fain, 85
fair, adj., 85
feast, 23
feeble, 161
fellow, 181–2
foot, 154
forlorn hope, 162
foxglove, 180–1
frill, 100
furlong, 154

gadget, 164
gerrymander, 54
gink, 184
glad, 85
gloak (*gloke*), 184
good scout, 184
Gothic, 99
grandiloquent, 90
grandiose, 90
gravity (physics), 168
grog, groggy, grogram, 156
grumble, 146
guts (courage), 100
guy (a fellow), 184

hansom, 72
hard, 85
haywire, 178
heathen, 16
heaven, 158
hit, v., 166
Hobson-Jobson, 150
holocaust, 299
homely, 90
honour (*honor*), 88

horizon, 168
hullabaloo, 178
humdrum, 146
husky, 147

idea, 170
independence, 164
Indian, 162
-ing, 141–2
insane, 89
investigate, 169
-ise, 31
-ish, 37
island, 25, 153
-ism, 170
-ize, 31

jazz, 177–8
jingle, 146
juggins, 146

kangaroo, 163
keel, 162
kemp, 113
ker-, 188
kerwallop, 188
kick off, 162
knave, 98
knight, 99
kopje, 164

landau, 81
late unpleasantness, the, 164
Liberty, Equality, Fraternity, 164
live wire, 165
-logy, 170

maffick, 164
main (ocean, sea), 170–1
marshal, 99
mate, 161
meat, 85
mental, 33
merchant, 182, 183
method, 168
Methodist, 99
minute, 168
mocassin or *moccasin*, 163

mugwump, 99, 173
musk-rat, 151

nail, 155
nanny, 188
not, 142
nut, 149

obligation, 159
odd, 88
odium, 88
O.K., 174–5
Old Contemptibles, the, 99
-ology, 170
opinion, 87–8
ordinary, 90

palooka, 181, 186
pantaloon, 72
pantry, 151
paper, 154
Parleyvoo, 146
peasant, 98
pedant, pedantry, 98
peep, peepers, 155–6
petticoat-tails, 162
piccaninny, 147
pigeon, 147
pips, 155
pitiful, 88
play on words, 169
pluck, 100
port, 158
power, 86–7
precious, 100
President, 171
pretty, 85
proposition, 174
proud, 90
prove, 88
prude, 90
puerile, 100
puny, 22

Quaker, 99
queer, 187

radiation, 86

rarebit. See *Welsh rabbit*
rash, 100
rattle, 146
reindeer, 151–2
rhyme, 153
riband, 151
rich, 25
rifle, 81
rime, 153
rind, 99–100
rub, n., 161
rum, adj., 187
ruse, 161
rustic, 98
rustle, 145

sanctimonious, 90
satem, diagram II, footnote 1
semantics, 154
send to Coventry, 163
session, sessions, 163
shame, shameful, 88
shenaneckin, shenanigan, 188
silly, 90
Simon (sixpence), 188
simple, 90
Slav, slave, slavish, 98
soon, 185
sovereign, 151
Spanish Main, the, 170–1
sparrow-grass, 151
specious, 90
sphere, 168
sponge cake, 152–3
steward, 99
stiff (a fellow), 184–5
stout, 100
strike, v., 166
Stuart, 99
stump, v., 161
stunt, 176–7
sturdy, 100
susurration, 145
sward, 100

taboo, 36
tanner (sixpence), 187–8
tarot, 186–7

Teddies, 177
tele-words, 165
terminological inexactitude, 147
thrash, 167
trek, 164
Tripos, 86

usk, 158

vile, 91
villain, 91, 98
vulgar, 90

Welsh comb, W. fiddle, W. rabbit, 152
wench, 98
whippoorwill, 146
wild-cat (bills), 175–6
window, 19
worthy, 90

Yank, 172
Yankee, 99, 172
young, youthful, 100